About the Author

Ramon Lemos received his B.A. in 1951 from the University of Alabama, where he was elected to Phi Beta Kappa, and did his graduate work in philosophy at Duke University, from which he received the M.A. degree in 1953 and the Ph.D. in 1955. During the 1955–56 academic year he was a postdoctoral Fulbright scholar in philosophy at the University of London. Since 1956 he has been a member of the faculty at the University of Miami, where he is now professor of philosophy. From 1971 to 1984 he was chairman of the department. He is the author of *Experience, Mind and Value: Philosophical Essays* (1969), *Rousseau's Political Philosophy: An Exposition and Interpretation* (1977), *Hobbes and Locke: Power and Consent* (1978), *Rights, Goods, and Democracy* (1986), and several dozen essays and reviews.

Metaphysical Investigations

Metaphysical Investigations

RAMON M. LEMOS

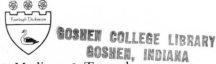

Rutherford • Madison • Teaneck
Fairleigh Dickinson University Press
London and Toronto: Associated University Presses

Associated University Presses
440 Forsgate Drive
Cranbury, NJ 08512

Associated University Presses
25 Sicilian Avenue
London WC1A 2QH, England

Associated University Presses
2133 Royal Windsor Drive
Unit 1
Mississauga, Ontario
Canada L5J 1K5

The paper used in this publication meets the requirements
of the American National Standard for Permanence of Paper
for Printed Library Materials Z39.48-1984.

Library of Congress Cataloging-in-Publication Data

Lemos, Ramon M., 1927–
    Metaphysical investigations.

    Bibliography: p.
    Includes index.
    1. Metaphysics.   I. Title.
BD111.L43   1988   110   86-46324
ISBN 0-8386-3307-2 (alk. paper)

Printed in the United States of America

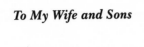

To My Wife and Sons

Without doubt, metaphysics has to do with everything that exists. However, the totality of what exists, including what has existed and will exist, is infinitely small in comparison with the totality of Objects of knowledge.

—Meinong

Contents

CONTENTS

Preface

THE work that this section prefaces ranges over such a wide area that I have been unable to think of a better title for it than the rather nondescript name it bears. Because it contains discussions of so many different topics, it might be helpful if I present here a brief summary of its course.

In the opening chapter I present an account of the nature of philosophy intended to be both sufficiently broad to apply to all activities that historically have been regarded as philosophical and sufficiently narrow to distinguish philosophy from other areas of activity such as science. This is followed by a brief account of the development, since the seventeenth century, of subjectivism in philosophy and a plea for an objective, realistic, rationalistic metaphysics. A demonstration of the possibility of such metaphysics begins in the second chapter with an attempt to establish that there are synthetic necessities and impossibilities that hold for all conceivable worlds and that such necessities and impossibilities can be apprehended by the human intellect.

Attention is given next to language and meaning. In chapter 3 an account is presented of the distinction between tokens and types and their ontological status, and the late medieval scholastic doctrine of the supposition of terms is employed to develop a generous view of the meaningfulness of terms and sentences. Distinctions are then drawn in the fourth chapter between sentences, statements, judgments, beliefs, propositions, states of affairs, and facts. It is argued that none of these categories, with the exception of facts, is reducible to any of the others, taken either singly or in combination. Four different senses of 'fact' are distinguished, according to which facts are either existent entities, states of affairs that obtain, the obtaining of states of affairs, or true propositions.

The discussion of facts is followed by a treatment in chapter 5 of intentionality and reality. Anything of which anyone thinks is an intentional object, and as such it has intentional or objective being or reality.

From this, however, it does not follow that it is also a formal reality, since to be a formal reality is to have being independently of being an intentional object for anyone. Formal realities are divisible into those that are and those that are not existent entities. Existent entities have being in time, whereas those formal realities that are not existent entities do not. These issues lead to a discussion of the nature and significance of the *cogito* and of the structure of intentions of intentions.

Chapter 6 contains a discussion of the ontological status of possibilities and impossibilities, the nature of kinds, the structure and constituents of states of affairs, the distinction between intentional and nonintentional states of affairs, and the question of whether propositions are formal realities. This is followed in the seventh chapter by a discussion of essences and properties, the distinction between essential and transcendental properties, the various forms of being and the concept of nothing, and the connection between formal realities and their properties.

The problem of universals and the nature of predication and predicables are then discussed. In chapter 8 it is argued that nominalism and conceptualism are unacceptable and that universals are formal realities, although not existent entities, regardless of whether they are exemplified. It is also argued, however, that the properties possessed by particulars, as distinct from the universals they exemplify, are neither particulars nor universals but singular cases of universals. This leads to a discussion in the ninth chapter of unacceptable views of predication, the distinction between quidditative and qualitative predication, and the ontological status of predicables.

The book concludes with a treatment of the constitution of particulars and their relation to the universals they exemplify and the singular cases of universals they possess. This involves a discussion of wholes and parts. Parts of particulars, to use Husserl's language, are either pieces or moments. Pieces are themselves particulars, whereas moments are singular cases of universals. The distinction between determinables and their determinations is discussed, as is also the question of whether the moments of particulars are absolutely determinate. A discussion of sensible appearances or appearings of material objects is also presented, and it is argued that they have a peculiar ontological status, being neither mere intentional objects nor full-fledged formal realities.

Various of the ideas presented in the pages that follow have developed gradually over the years in courses and seminars I have taught, in discussions with colleagues, and through reflection on the writings of others. For the help of my students and colleagues I am most grateful. I am indebted also to many who have written on the topics treated in the pages that follow even though I have made very few explicit references to and have limited severely my discussion of the work of others. The present work is long enough as it is, if indeed it is not already too long, and extended discussion of the work of others would have made it even longer. Those familiar with the writings of others that deal with the topics treated in the present work will have some idea not only of the degree to which I disagree with but perhaps also, at least to some extent, of the degree to which I am indebted to the work of others far too numerous to mention here.

My gratitude extends also to the Sabbatical Leave Committee of the University of Miami for granting me a leave for the first six months of 1980. This leave enabled me to pursue in detail the ideas that had been developing gradually over the years and to complete the first draft of the present work by August of 1980. The entire second draft was read and commented on by Professors Panayot Butchvarov of the University of Iowa and John Knox of Drew University, and the second draft of the second, third, and fourth chapters was also read and commented on by Professor Eddy Zemach of the Hebrew University of Jerusalem. I have benefited enormously from and am deeply grateful to them for their conscientious, detailed, and insightful comments, suggestions, and criticisms. The many flaws that doubtless remain are my responsibility alone, especially since I have been recalcitrant, quite probably in many instances wrongly so, concerning various points they have criticized. I wish also to express my continuing gratitude to my wife for her unfailing cheerfulness and encouragement and constant maintenance of absolutely ideal conditions under which to work.

1
Science, Philosophy, and Metaphysics

I should like at the outset to attempt to indicate my view of what metaphysics is. It is, of course, a branch of philosophy. How it differs from other areas of philosophy we shall consider presently. But first I should like to discuss the nature of philosophy and how it differs from science. Since metaphysics is a branch of philosophy, this discussion will serve to indicate my view as to how metaphysics differs from science. We shall then be in a position to specify what metaphysics is and how it differs from the other branches of philosophy.

1. Philosophy and Science

In attempting to specify the nature of philosophy and how it differs from science, one might be endeavoring to do either of two things. One might be trying to specify what it is in virtue of which those activities that historically have been regarded as philosophical or as scientific have been so regarded. One who seeks to give such an account may be said to be attempting to present a historical account. In endeavoring to present such an account there are two opposite dangers to guard against. One is that the conception of philosophy one formulates is too broad and fails to discriminate between what has historically been regarded as philosophy and what has generally been regarded as science. The other is that the conception one formulates is too narrow and fails to apply to all forms of activity that have generally been regarded as philosophical. This means that any historical definition of philosophy is adequate only if it is sufficiently catholic in scope to embrace all the various activities that historically have been regarded as philosophical and also sufficiently narrow to distinguish such activities from those of scientists. This is to say, in short, that such a definition, if it is to be acceptable, must apply to all and only those activities generally regarded as philosophical and not to those generally regarded as scientific.

On the other hand, one who attempts to specify the nature of philosophy might also be trying to delineate the sorts of activities philosophers, as such, ought to engage in. One who tries to give this kind of definition may be said to be seeking to give a persuasive definition. Usually those who endeavor to specify the nature of philosophy are attempting to give both sorts of definition. This is especially true of those who are content that philosophers have generally engaged in the kinds of activities they ought as philosophers to engage in. Since I number myself among those who are thus content, I shall be attempting to present both sorts of definition. But there have also been people who are not content with the sorts of activities, or at least with certain kinds of activities, they believe philosophers historically have engaged in. In defining the nature of philosophy these individuals might therefore be inclined to give persuasive rather than historical definitions. It will, however, be obvious that even they must have some idea, regardless of how imperfect it might be, and regardless of whether they attempt to formulate it precisely, of the types of activities philosophers historically have engaged in. Otherwise they could not be unhappy with the kinds of things they take philosophers as having attempted to do.

One who gives only a persuasive definition and does not claim to be giving a historical definition in any sense at all cannot legitimately be criticized on the ground that his definition includes either more or less than has historically been recognized as philosophy, for he is saying nothing at all about what has or has not been recognized historically as philosophy. Usually, however, such persuasive definitions presuppose some view of what philosophers historically have done, and the definitions of this type presented by various logical empiricists and ordinary-language philosophers presuppose also some notion of what science has been historically. Both logical empiricists and linguistic philosophers frequently assume that all factual questions about the nature of man and the world fall within the province of science and can be answered properly only by using the methods of the sciences. Should certain philosophers happen to hit upon the answers to certain of these questions, they could do so only by chance. But it is not the task of the philosopher to answer such questions. Instead, his task is said to be logical, conceptual, or linguistic analysis and clarification. Logical empiricists and linguistic philosophers may therefore be said to be scientistic, in the sense that they contend that it is the business of science alone, and not of philosophy, to seek to answer factual questions about man and the world.

There are, however, two senses of 'science', a broader and a narrower. In the broadest sense of the term, 'science' refers to any systematic search for truth contributing to or resulting in a more or less organized body of knowledge or belief. In this sense of the term philosophy is a science. So also are theology, logic, and mathematics. But there is also a narrow sense of 'science' according to which the term is equivalent in meaning to 'empirical science'. This use of the word has become so firmly established in the English language that when one speaks of 'science' without the qualifying adjective 'empirical' one is understood to be referring simply to the empirical sciences. In this narrow sense of the word philosophy is not a science, since it is not an empirical science. For the sake of simplicity, however, I shall continue to use the word "science" when it is clear from the context that I am referring to the empirical sciences.

Both philosophy and science have their origin ultimately in man's effort to understand himself and the world in which he lives. Initially no distinction was drawn between those questions that are philosophical and those that are scientific. The same individuals who endeavored to solve philosophical problems also frequently sought to solve scientific problems, without always distinguishing between the two. From the beginnings of ancient Greek philosophy on down through the seventeenth century and even into the twentieth we sometimes find the same thinker dealing with both sorts of problems in the same work without distinguishing clearly between them. Thus even after distinctions come to be drawn between philosophy and science we sometimes find the same thinker functioning both as a philosopher and as a scientist. But as knowledge accumulates it becomes increasingly difficult for one person to master all fields of knowledge, much less to make significant original contributions to all. Specialization thus becomes increasingly necessary as knowledge continues to accumulate.

This, however, does not mean that there was no specialization at all among ancient thinkers, nor does it mean, as is sometimes supposed, that as knowledge accumulated the various empirical sciences gradually broke away from philosophy. Although there is some truth in the latter supposition, it is not entirely true, since there was specialization among ancient thinkers. Archimedes, for example, is remembered today primarily as a physicist, not as a philosopher, Euclid as a mathematician, Ptolemy as an astronomer, and Herodotus as a historian. There were also thinkers, such as Socrates, who specialized as philosophers rather than as what today we would call scientists and others, such as Aristotle, who were both philosophers and scientists. Although, then, there would be more truth in saying that the various empirical sciences gradually separated from philosophy than in claiming the reverse, the truth of the matter seems to be that specialization both in philosophy and in the sciences began at about the same time among the ancient Greeks. This has been obscured by various factors, among which the following may be mentioned.

One is that ancient and medieval science failed to achieve a level of sophistication relative to that of modern science comparable to the level of sophistication of ancient Greek and late medieval scholastic philosophy relative to that of modern philosophy. There are two major explanations of this. One is that ancient and medieval scientists did not employ sufficiently the methods that must be employed if advances in science comparable to those achieved by modern science are to be widespread, whereas Plato, Aristotle, and the scholastics did employ sufficiently the methods of philosophy. (What these respective methods are I shall attempt to specify presently.) The other explanation is that, beginning with the patristic period and the rise and spread of Christianity, thinkers came to be dominated by religious interests that were not wholly congenial to the development of the kind of interest in nature necessary for the development of the natural sciences. It was only with the development of this kind of interest during the Renaissance that the rise of modern science in the sixteenth and seventeenth centuries became possible.

This leads to the second factor that tends to obscure the fact that specialization in philosophy among the ancient Greeks arose at about the same time as did specialization in certain sciences. It seems sometimes to be supposed that since the level of sophistication in the sciences rose markedly in the sixteenth and seventeenth centuries, it did so through these sciences separating off from philosophy. This supposition, however, ignores the fact that during the Renaissance philosophy became almost, although not quite, as sterile and decadent as science had been throughout the medieval period. Throughout the Renaissance and on into the seventeenth century until the middle of that century, when Cartesianism began making inroads into various universities, the type of philosophy that dominated universities was essentially a version of late medieval scholasticism. Yet with the possible exception of Francisco Suarez (1548–1617), during this period no scholastic philosopher appeared who could reasonably be ranked with such great scholastics of the thirteenth and fourteenth centuries as St. Thomas Aquinas, John Duns Scotus, and William of Ockham. Instead, during this period university philosophy consisted mainly of studying and commenting on, with little advance over, the work of late medieval scholasticism, and outside the universities nothing comparable to the achievements of the late medieval scholastics appeared. What got significant original work in philosophy going again on the part of such thinkers as Descartes, Hobbes, Spinoza, Locke, and Leibniz was the rise of modern science as a consequence of the work of men such as Copernicus, Kepler, and Galileo. Rather, then, than modern science developing through separating off from philosophy, it was the rise of modern science that initially stimulated the rise of modern philosophy. Thus, in this case at least, those who maintain that science develops out of philosophy have things backward.

A third factor that tends to obscure the fact that specialization in philosophy and in science began at about the same time among the ancient Greeks is the development of specialists in various human or social sciences within the last two hundred years. Economics began to develop as a separate science during the latter part of the eighteenth century, and in the nineteenth, anthropology, sociology, psychology, and political science began to develop as separate sciences studied by specialists. The fact that various disciplines have developed as separate sciences in the modern age has contributed to an acceptance among certain thinkers of what may be referred to as a kind of Comtean scientism, somewhat akin to the kind of positivism espoused by Auguste Comte. This is the view that philosophy will eventually disappear as separate empirical sciences continue to develop, since eventually, when all the different areas of inquiry are parceled out among the various sciences, there will be nothing left for philosophers to investigate.

This kind of scientism differs from that of the logical empiricists and ordinary-language philosophers. The scientism of the latter two groups consists, as we have seen, in their maintaining that only the empirical sciences, as contrasted with philosophy, afford us any factual knowledge of man and the world. Both logical empiricists and linguistic philosophers concede that there will be work for philosophers to do so long as there are conceptual or linguistic problems arising from either logic, mathematics, science, or moral, religious, aesthetic, or political discourse. Since, they would argue, there is no reason to believe that such problems will cease to arise, there is no reason to believe that eventually there will no longer be any work for philosophers to do. Logical empiricists and linguistic philosophers would doubtless also claim that what I have referred to as Comtean scientism has a mistaken view of the task of philosophy. This is so because Comtean scientism, in supposing that the work of philosophy will eventually be parceled out completely among the separate empirical sciences, is assuming that philosophy, like the empirical sciences, is concerned to supply us factual knowledge of man and the world, when in fact this is not its proper function.

There is some truth in logical empiricism and linguistic philosophy on the one hand and Comtean scientism on the other. The former are correct in recognizing that there are conceptual or linguistic problems that are philosophical and not empirical. They are also right in maintaining that such problems will continue to arise so long as logic, mathematics, and science continue to be studied and so long as people continue to think and talk about morality, religion, art, and politics. They are right also in pointing out that Comtean scientism, in claiming that philosophy will eventually disappear through the parceling out of all its problems to the various empirical sciences, is mistakenly assuming that philosophical problems are factual in the same sense in which the problems of the empirical sciences are. But Comtean scientism is at least correct in recognizing that some philosophical problems are factual and logical empiricists and linguistic philosophers mistaken in denying that any are. But, it may reasonably be asked, if some philosophical problems are factual, what distinguishes them from scientific problems?

2. Science

This question may be answered summarily as follows. Science is concerned to answer questions about either man or the world that can be answered properly only by using the methods of observation or experimentation, whereas philosophy is concerned to answer questions about man and the world (and also about values and God) that can be answered only by means of critical reflection on the experience and knowledge the philosopher typically has already acquired by the time he raises these questions. This statement is quite rough as it stands and requires considerable explication and refinement if its meaning is to be made clear.

The word 'science' is being used here to refer to any empirical science, whether it be a natural science or a human or social science. Both natural sciences and human sciences have nomological, taxonomic, and historical aspects. A science is nomological insofar as it seeks to discover laws, taxonomic insofar as it seeks to classify the phenomena it studies in terms of certain principles of classification, and historical insofar as it seeks to discover, describe, and/or explain what exists or occurs at various times and places. The nomological and taxonomic aspects presuppose the historical. This is obvious in the case of the taxonomic aspect, since the scientist would have nothing to classify unless observations were made of what exists or occurs at various times and places. Similarly, the scientist must observe what happens at certain times and places when certain conditions obtain or when certain other events occur if he is to establish empirical laws inductively. This is not to say that such laws are established by means of a process of induction by simple enumeration. On the contrary, they are usually established only through performing experiments or making observations in order to test some hypothesis. This, however, does not mean that empirical laws are not inductively established. A few experiments or observations might suffice to test some hypothesis and establish a law. But such experiments or observations serve to establish laws only if some version of the principle of the uniformity of nature is assumed—only if, that is, it is assumed that when an event of a certain kind occurs under such and such conditions at a certain time and place, then similar events will occur under similar conditions at other times and places. The particular experiment performed or the particular observation made to test some hypothesis would have no general significance at all unless this inductive assumption were made and the appropriate inductive generalization drawn. Without this assumption, all that could be said is that an event of a certain kind occurred under such and such conditions at a certain time and place, and this would be to make merely a historical statement, not an inductive generalization, and thus would not amount to the assertion of an empirical law. It is with the establishment of such laws that a science, so far as it is nomological, is concerned. Nonetheless, the fulfillment of the nomological function of a science still has an indispensable historical aspect, in the absence of which there would be no guarantee that the laws of that science apply to the world. This is the case even though the historical aspect is only subsidiary to the fulfillment of the nomological function of the science, as it is insofar as the interest of the scientist is exclusively or primarily nomological.

This last, however, does not mean that an area of investigation is scientific only if, or only to the extent that, it is nomological. One can, if one chooses, use the word 'science' so narrowly that only those areas of investigation that are nomological are to count as scientific. But this would be to use the word in a persuasive rather than a historical sense, for the word historically has been used in such a way that taxonomic and historical interests count as scientific fully as much as do nomological interests. Those who use the word in such a narrow persuasive sense sometimes do so because they take physics and chemistry as the ideal types of science, after which other sciences are to be modeled in such a way that they count as sciences only to the extent that they approach the nomological ideal of these two sciences. To use the word in such a narrow sense, however, is to ignore the fact that natural history has long been counted as a science and that biology, geology, and astronomy, so far as they are concerned with natural history, are irreducibly historical in character. This is to say that an interest in natural history is as legitimately scientific as is any nomological interest—that an interest in discovering, describing, and/or explaining what exists or occurs at certain times and places and how some object or species has developed is as legitimately scientific as is an interest in the discovery of laws.

Another narrow persuasive use of 'science' is its use in such a way that an area of investigation is to count as scientific only if, or only insofar as, it is experimental. Here too physics and chemistry, perhaps along with biology, are taken as the ideal types of science. Whether, however, a science can be experimental and, if so, the extent to which it can be, depends upon its subject matter. In general, the subject matter of the human or social sciences is such as to inhibit their development as experimental to the degree to which the natural sciences are. Although psychology constitutes something of an exception to this, it is nevertheless obvious that the subject matter of cultural anthropology, sociology, political science, and economics is such as to preclude their development as experimental sciences to the extent to which physics, chemistry, and biology are. Such sciences, because of their subject matter, must remain primarily observational rather than experimental, especially insofar as their subject matter is such that it does not lend itself to the kind of experimental treatment that can be achieved only in the setting of a laboratory. Even certain natural sciences have an aspect that must remain primarily observational. Astronomy, for example, so far as it is concerned with the historical question of the distribution of planets and stars in the heavens, must remain primarily observational. The fact, however, that certain sciences must remain primarily observational does not mean that they have no nomological or taxonomic aspects. On the contrary, the establishment of empirical laws and the classification of phenomena, especially in the human sciences, require only that observations be made, not that experiments be performed.

But regardless of whether a science be experimental or observational, hypotheses can be tested and laws established only by making some observation or by performing some experiment. This does not mean that every scientist must make observations or perform experiments. On the contrary, one person might function exclusively as a theorist who suggests hypotheses for experimental or observational testing, whereas another functions exclusively as an experimenter or observer who tests the hypotheses proposed by the theorist. Usually, however, the scientist, at least to some extent, is at once both theorist and experimenter or observer. The theorist on the one hand and the experimenter or observer on the other are both necessary. Moreover, if a hypothesis is to be worthy of sufficiently serious scientific consideration to justify an experimental or observational test of it, usually it must be formulated on the basis of a knowledge of the achievements and contemporary status of the science in question and not be concocted in ignorance of which theories within that science have met the test of experiment or observation and which have not. Given, however, the satisfaction of this condition, the ultimate test of the truth of the hypothesis comes through making some observation or through performing some experiment that has not yet been made or performed in order to test it. It is only in this way that science advances.

3. Philosophy

The situation is somewhat similar, but also somewhat different, in philosophy. Taking 'philosophy' in its most comprehensive or generous sense, what philosophers historically have endeavored to do is to understand God, man, the world, and values and their relationship to one another so far as such understanding is attainable by means of critical reflection on the experience available to the philosopher. The experience in question is not merely the personal experience of the philosopher but includes also the experience of the human race so far as it is accessible to him. Philosophical reflection cannot appear suddenly out of nowhere, but presupposes experience and belief of some sort as a given or datum out of which problems arise. To some extent the experience and belief the philosopher reflects on will be common (or nearly so) to mankind, to some extent it will be peculiar to the philosopher's own age and culture, and to some extent it might also be what may be referred to as special experience and knowledge. Something must be said about each of these.

First, I do not think it open to serious doubt that there is something that may properly be referred to as the common experience and belief of mankind. All human beings, regardless of where or when they have lived, have had sensations, perceptions, ideas, beliefs, feelings, emotions, desires, and aversions. They have all made both factual judgments and moral judgments and have all acted and been acted upon. They have all lived in human societies of one sort or another, and all have shared a language in common with certain other human beings. They have all very probably shared certain simple yet fundamental beliefs of the sort listed by G. E. Moore in "A Defence of Common Sense," such as that material objects exist, that other persons exist, and that time is real, in the sense that some events are contemporaneous and others successive. This common experience and belief has been given as a datum for reflection to all philosophers, from the earliest of the ancient Greeks down to the present day. In reflecting upon this common experience and belief and in attempting to solve the philosophical problems that arise out of it, the philosopher need not attempt to acquire further experience of the sort the scientist seeks to obtain by making observations or by performing experiments to test some hypothesis. On the contrary, the common experience and belief of mankind out of which philosophical reflection grows and which the philosopher seeks to understand have been the common possession of mankind since recorded human history began, so that in order to answer his questions he need not go out into the world to acquire new data not yet in, as the scientist must do.

In addition to data of the sort just described, which are accessible to every philosopher regardless of where or when he lives, there are also data which vary with time and place, with the age and the culture in which the philosopher lives. Thus the accumulated historical and cultural experience presented for philosophical reflection to the contemporary philosopher is considerably different from that presented to ancient Greek philosophers. To the extent that this historical and cultural experience varies from age to age and from culture to culture, the philosophical problems that arise will correspondingly vary. Such changes in historical and cultural experience are the result of developments in the various aspects of culture—in art, religion, science, technology, economics, politics, and also in philosophy itself. I have already mentioned the fact that the rise of modern science in the sixteenth and seventeenth centuries presented data for philosophical reflection that had not previously been presented, and stimulated the rise of modern philosophy in the seventeenth century. Indeed, even philosophical reflection on the common experience and belief of mankind is the child of its time. Philosophers who investigate this common experience and belief invariably stand upon the shoulders of their philosophical predecessors and have the benefit of prior philosophical reflection. Should any philosopher ignore completely this previous reflection and attempt to begin again from the ground as if there were no history of previous philosophical reflection, it is quite unlikely that he would advance much beyond the level of sophistication and refinement attained by the pre-Socratics.

Future developments within the various aspects of culture cannot be predicted with a perfect precision of detail. Indeed, the artist, the philosopher, and the scientist cannot even predict the final fully determinate character of the finished work he is setting out to produce. He initiates the production of his work with only a relatively abstract, general, indeterminate, schematic, or amorphous idea of the determinate character of the finished work he is seeking to produce, and it is only in the process of endeavoring to produce it that his idea of it increasingly acquires form or content and grows increasingly concrete, specific, or determinate.[1] But if this be so, it is also impossible to predict in detail the determinate character of works of art to be produced only in the future by future artists and the knowledge to be acquired only in the future by future scientists and philosophers. A brief formal proof of the latter can easily be presented. If one could have in the present the knowledge that is going to be had only in the future, then one would know in the present what is going to be known only in the future. This, however, would involve a contradiction and is therefore impossible. Therefore, as Professor Popper has argued,[2] one cannot predict in detail the determinate character of future technological, economic, social, and political developments insofar as such developments are influenced by or depend upon increases in the acquisition of knowledge, especially scientific knowledge. Since the cultural and historical experience presented to the philosopher for reflection thus varies from age to age and culture to culture, there can be no final system of philosophy completely adequate to future cultural and historical developments, especially insofar as such developments are essentially unpredictable. Thus to some extent every system of philosophy is of necessity the child of its own age, subject to various of the limitations and illusions that afflict its epoch, and subject to refinement, correction, and supplementation in the light of future cultural and historical developments. This is at least part of the truth expressed by Hegel's dictum that "the owl of Minerva spreads its wings only with the falling of the dusk."[3]

The preceding considerations, however, do not constitute or require an acceptance of historicism or relativism, if these terms be used to refer to the view that the beliefs, values, and practices of one age or culture are no better or worse than those of any other. Such relativism or historicism does not follow from the fact that to some extent philosophical reflection and its products are conditioned and limited by the age and the culture in which it occurs. On the contrary, this fact is quite compatible with the view that various of the beliefs, values, and practices of one culture are better than those of some other culture. It is also compatible with the view that within the same society or civilization real development and decay occur from age to age within the various components of its culture and in its beliefs, values, and practices. Rather than constituting or requiring an acceptance of such historicism or relativism, the considerations in question in fact require their rejection, since they imply that cultural and philosophical development from age to age does in fact occur.

In addition to the data afforded for philosophical reflection by the common experience and belief of mankind and by the cultural and historical experience accumulated up to the philosopher's own age and culture, there is also what I have referred to as special experience or knowledge. This is the experience or knowledge the philosopher must acquire if he is to do competent comprehensive work in certain special fields of philosophy. Thus if a philosopher is interested in doing such work in the philosophy of science, mathematics, religion, art, history, law, or political philosophy, he ought to know something about the corresponding nonphilosophical areas. He might make particular contributions to the solution of various problems occurring in certain of these areas by applying to them certain results he has obtained through working in logic, epistemology, metaphysics, or moral philosophy. But if he is to specialize in or do comprehensive work in any of these fields, then some special knowledge of the corresponding nonphilosophical area is certainly helpful, if not in fact essential. Moreover, the results of philosophical work in any of these special fields are subject to refinement, revision, and supplementation as developments occur in the corresponding nonphilosophical areas. The absolutely final word cannot be said in any of these special fields any more than it can be said in areas such as logic, epistemology, metaphysics, or moral philosophy. Indeed, there is perhaps even less chance of its being said in these special fields than in the latter areas. This is the case because the latter are more closely connected with the common experience and belief of mankind, whereas the special fields in question are concentrations upon different aspects of the changing cultural and historical experience of mankind. This is to say that the specialized knowledge of the corresponding non-philosophical area presupposed by each of these special fields is merely knowledge of one aspect of the total changing cultural and historical experience of mankind presented as a datum for philosophical reflection to any philosopher, regardless of whether he does specialized work in any of these special fields.

But although the accumulated cultural and historical experience of mankind, and developments within special areas of this experience, out of which philosophical problems emerge varies from age to age and from culture to culture, the philosophical problems that arise from this experience, like those that emerge from the common experience and belief of mankind, are not scientific and therefore cannot be solved by using the methods of science. It is true, as we have seen, that the data afforded for philosophical reflection by the common experience and belief of mankind were much the same for ancient as they are for contemporary philosophers, whereas the accumulated cultural and historical experience of mankind, and of special areas within it, of one age and culture differs, sometimes considerably, from that of another. The data provided by the common experience and belief of mankind are therefore all in, whereas the data afforded by cultural and historical developments are not, since new data will be presented in the future as a result of future developments. This, however, does not mean that the philosophical problems that arise out of these developments can be solved through forming hypotheses that can be tested only by performing experiments or by making observations. Instead, it means only that the philosopher can reflect only upon the data already in as a consequence of the cultural and historical developments that have occurred up to the age in which he lives. This in turn means that philosophy, unlike the empirical sciences, is essentially a retrospective and reflective rather than a predictive enterprise. It is the business of the scientist, not of the philosopher, to make predictions and to test them by appropriate experiments or observations. It is the business of the philosopher only to attempt to solve the philosophical problems that issue from data already in, while recognizing that his solutions must be presented tentatively, as subject to possible revision, refinement, and supplementation as data for reflection are presented by future developments.

If the preceding considerations are acceptable, then philosophy, like the empirical sciences, is essentially an existential or factual discipline, as contrasted with a nonexistential or nonfactual discipline such as pure mathematics. It is true that the philosopher, working as a pure phenomenologist, might concern himself only with the nature of various essences and their relationships to one another and have no interest whatever in questions of existence. But phenomenology is only one branch of, or approach to, philosophy and is not identical with the whole of philosophy. It is true also, as we have seen, that it is not the business of the philosopher, as it is of the empirical scientist, to attempt, by performing experiments or making observations, to discover empirical facts not yet discovered. Instead, his task is to endeavor to solve the philosophical problems that arise from the knowledge of empirical facts he already has by the time he becomes cognizant of and undertakes to solve these problems. Thus although philosophy is not existential or factual in precisely the same way in which the empirical sciences are, it is nonetheless, like them, interested in understanding various aspects of the actual world. It is interested in understanding actual human beings and their relationships to one another and to the actual world and perhaps also to God. Insofar as it is interested in various ideals or criteria of excellence, goodness, or rightness, it is interested in them primarily, indeed perhaps only, insofar as they have some relation to actual human beings and the actual world. Even the pure phenomenologist is usually interested in examining essences and their relationships to one another only insofar as such an examination contributes to an understanding of the actual experience, consciousness, knowledge, and action of existing human beings. Philosophy therefore differs from a hypothetical or nonexistential science such as pure mathematics, since the pure mathematician, as such, has no interest in the question of whether the concepts and relationships he investigates have any application to actual entities or to the actual world. Whereas the pure mathematician may be said to be interested only in possibilities and impossibilities, the philosopher, like the empirical scientist, is interested in actualities as well as in possibilities and impossibilities.

Thus far I have written as though the lines separating philosophy from science could be simply and sharply drawn. I have, however, been oversimplifying in a way that can be misleading unless a caution is entered here. The lines marking philosophy off from science are not always sharp and clear and easily definable. Instead, the relation of philosophy to science is somewhat analogous to the relationship of the colors of the spectrum to one another. Just as certain colors shade off into others in such a way that one can say that a certain determinate shade of color is either orange or yellow or even both, so also certain activities or problems one might classify as philosophical might also with as much justice be classified as scientific. I have in mind here such things as attempts by both philosophers and scientists to justify the acceptance of one scientific theory over another on the ground that one in some sense is simpler than the other, even though each has as much explanatory or predictive power as the other. In such cases there might be unanimous agreement that the competing theories are scientific, yet disagreement as to whether such attempts to justify the acceptance of one theory and the rejection of the other are philosophical or scientific. Thus one person might argue that such attempts are scientific on the ground that the competing theories are, whereas another might argue that such attempts are philosophical on the ground that the acceptance of neither theory in preference to the other can be justified by appealing to any empirical facts explained or predicted by one but not the other.

There is, however, another aspect of the analogy with the color spectrum that ought not to be overlooked. Although it is true that certain determinate shades of color may properly be said to be either yellow or orange or both, it is also true that certain other determinate shades can easily be seen to be orange and not yellow or yellow and not orange. So also certain problems can easily be seen to be philosophical rather than scientific or scientific rather than philosophical. Although, then, the considerations I have presented in attempting to distinguish between philosophical and scientific problems are not always sufficient to enable us to classify certain problems as unquestionably philosophical and others as scientific, they do nevertheless, I believe, help us to do so in certain other cases.

4. Metaphysics

The analogy with the color spectrum applies also to attempts to distinguish between metaphysics and the other branches of philosophy. With this caution in mind, let us nonetheless endeavor to draw the distinction. We shall begin by attempting to specify what metaphysics is not, then attempt to specify what it is. The first task is considerably easier than the second; it is much easier to distinguish metaphysics from science and the other branches of philosophy than it is to specify in positive terms just what metaphysics is.

Since metaphysics is a branch of philosophy, the considerations adduced above, especially when conjoined with the caution recently entered, suffice to distinguish metaphysics from the empirical sciences if they suffice to distinguish philosophy from such sciences. Second, metaphysics differs from each of the special fields of philosophy mentioned above, such as the philosophy of mathematics, science, language, art, history, law, and political philosophy, in that each of these special fields is an attempt to understand philosophically the corresponding non-philosophical area, whereas metaphysics is not. Although, as was indicated above, the philosopher working in any of these special fields may use and apply to them considerations taken from metaphysics, logic, epistemology, or moral philosophy, this does not mean that any of the special fields is identical with any of the latter areas. Third, metaphysics may be distinguished from these latter areas by specifying very briefly and generally what the concern of each of the latter is. Taken in its most generous or comprehensive sense, logic is an attempt to distinguish between good and bad forms of reasoning and to determine what makes the good forms good and the bad forms bad, whereas metaphysics is not. Epistemology, taken in its most generous sense, is an attempt to understand the nature and kinds of knowledge and its sources, conditions, and limits, whereas metaphysics is not. And moral philosophy, taken in its most comprehensive sense, is an attempt to understand such concepts as good and evil, right and wrong, and duty or obligation, whereas metaphysics is not. Metaphysics is connected in various ways with each of these three areas, and in his work the logician, epistemologist, and moral philosopher may use considerations taken from metaphysics. This, however, does not mean that metaphysics is identical with any of these areas. Finally, metaphysics differs from phenomenology, or at least from pure phenomenology, by virtue of the fact that the latter, in concerning itself only with essences and their relationships to one another, prescinds from all questions of existence, whereas metaphysics does not.

With the possible exception of the contention that metaphysics, unlike phenomenology, does not prescind from all questions of existence, the preceding, taken as a characterization of metaphysics, is wholly negative. It tells us only what metaphysics is not, not what it is, so that the question of what it is still remains. One possible answer to this question is that metaphysics is that branch of philosophy that deals with what remains after the concerns of all the other branches of philosophy are specified. This answer, however, while true so far as it goes, will not do, since it too is negative and fails to tell us what remains. Our question therefore becomes: what remains as the subject matter of metaphysics after the special concerns of the other branches of philosophy are parceled out among them?

By way of an answer, I think we can do no better than begin with the traditional Aristotelian view that metaphysics is the discipline that deals with being as being (or being as such). This answer, however, is at best only the beginning of an answer, since the question of what it means immediately arises. I suggest that its meaning may be rendered as follows. Metaphysics is the discipline that attempts to answer questions of the following sorts. (1) What is being in the most comprehensive sense of the term? (2) Are there different forms of being or senses of 'being', and, if so, what are they, and how are they related to one another? (3) What kind of constitution must something have if it is to have being, be a being, or *be* in one of these senses of 'being'? (4) What kind of structure must something have if it is to be a possible world? (5) What is the constitution or structure of the actual world and of the major forms of being contained in the actual world or required by its existence? Since each of these is a metaphysical question, any philosopher who attempts to answer any of them is to that degree a metaphysician. And since each is a philosophical question, each can be answered by the metaphysician only by means of critical reflection upon the data accessible to him as a philosopher.

The metaphysician, like the philosopher working in any of the other branches of philosophy, is subject to various of the limitations and illusions afflicting his own age and culture. Thus his conclusions, like those of any other philosopher, must be presented tentatively, as subject to correction, refinement, and supplementation in the light of future metaphysical reflection on data presented for reflection to future metaphysicians. This does not mean that in metaphysics and the other branches of philosophy nothing is evident or can be known with certainty. Instead, it means only that, given that various of the views of past metaphysicians and philosophers have required revision, refinement, and supplementation because of later cultural and philosophical developments, it is unlikely that *none* of the views of contemporary metaphysicians and philosophers will require such correction, refinement, and supplementation in the light of future developments. From the fact, however, that it is unlikely that *no* views will require revision it does not follow that it is likely that *all* will require such correction, nor does it follow that nothing in metaphysics or the other branches of philosophy is evident or can be known with certainty.

The preceding considerations therefore do not constitute an argument for the kind of historicism or relativism mentioned earlier. Nor do they constitute an argument for skepticism. At most they would constitute an argument for a very attenuated form of Peircean fallibilism. Even this, however, might be doubtful, since they are compatible with the claim that there are various facts, truths, or propositions that are evident and that can be known with certainty. But even if we admit (as I think we ought) that there are various things that are evident and that can be known with certainty, there seems to be little if any point, in metaphysical or philosophical discussion or exposition, in basing an argument or contention on the claim that a certain fact, truth, or proposition is evident or known with certainty. Even if I do in fact see that something is evident, I cannot get another to see that it is, simply by claiming that I see that it is. It is true that by making such a claim I might succeed in convincing him that it is evident, but this is only to get him to believe that it is evident, not to see that it is. Similarly, even if I do in fact know something with certainty, I cannot enable another also to know it with certainty simply by claiming that I do, but at most can only succeed in convincing him that I do in fact so know it. Nor can I succeed in seeing that something is evident or in knowing something with certainty simply by claiming that I do, since I must first see that something is evident or know something with certainty if my claim that I do is to be true. Since, then, such claims do not by themselves succeed in enabling either the person who makes them or those to whom they are made to see that something is evident or to know something with certainty, there seems to be little if any philosophical point in making them.

Sometimes the making of such claims seems only to be a way of claiming, on the part of the person who makes them, that he has no doubt of the truth of the proposition he claims to be evident or to know with certainty. And sometimes having no doubt of the truth of a given proposition does seem reasonable, especially when the evidence in its favor appears greater than that in favor of any contrary proposition and we have no reason to doubt its truth. But even here the claim that I have no doubt of the truth of a given proposition does not suffice to establish its truth, although it might suffice to convince those to whom it is made also to have no doubt of the truth of the proposition in question. And even when we have no reason to doubt the truth of a given proposition, it does not follow that the proposition is in fact true or that there is no reason, unknown to us, for doubting it. It would therefore seem better, rather than claiming simply that I have no doubt of the truth of a given proposition, to claim instead that I have no particular reason to doubt it and that on the basis of an assessment of the evidence available to me I have more reason to accept it than to doubt it, while admitting that future evidence might make it more reasonable to reject it. Although those unwilling to accept even so attenuated a form of fallibilism as this might thereby escape what they find to be various of the discomforts of doubt, they do not thereby succeed in establishing a single truth that cannot also be established by those who do accept such a modest fallibilistic attitude.

The acceptance of such an attenuated form of fallibilism is compatible with what may be referred to as an objective as opposed to a subjective approach to metaphysics. As might already be apparent from the set of questions presented above as being questions of the sort metaphysics is concerned to answer, and as will become increasingly apparent as we proceed, I conceive metaphysics as an objective rather than a subjective discipline. This means that I accept essentially the same approach to metaphysics that was taken by most metaphysicians until Kant, who, more than any other thinker, is responsible for initiating a subjective approach that has been prevalent if not indeed dominant for the past two hundred years. Put simply, an objective approach treats the thinking subject as merely one of the kinds of being among various kinds of being the nature of which the metaphysician seeks to understand, whereas the subjective approach treats the thinking subject as central. Those who take an objective approach do, of course, admit that without thinking subjects there would be no metaphysics. This, however, means neither (1) that the being of beings of all other types depends upon the experience or activity of thinking subjects nor (2) that it is impossible for thinking subjects to know at least to some extent the nature of beings of other sorts as they are in themselves. To accept either (1) or (2) is to take a subjective approach to metaphysics; to deny them both is to take an objective approach.

To some it might seem that the real progenitor of the subjective approach to metaphysics in modern philosophy was not Kant but rather Descartes. If so, such a belief would doubtless be based upon what seems to some to be the central role of the *cogito* in Cartesianism. Descartes, however, accepted neither of the contentions mentioned above, and he attempts to guarantee the truth of various beliefs about matters other than his own existence by an appeal not to the *cogito* but to the goodness of God, whose existence he attempts to demonstrate in the Third and Fifth Meditations by means of arguments that in no way depend upon an acceptance of the *cogito*, even though he presents them as if they do. The major modern philosopher who came closest to anticipating Kant was Locke, in that he, like Kant, made a sustained attempt to determine the extent and the limits of human knowledge and in the process gave epistemology precedence over metaphysics.

Locke's achievement was appreciated more fully in the eighteenth century than it seems to be today. In recent times the merits of Hume's work have been widely praised while those of Locke's have by comparison tended to be somewhat ignored. Yet Locke has the great merit of having been the first philosopher in the entire history of the subject to attempt in detail to substantiate the ancient empiricist claim that all ideas and knowledge come ultimately from experience by making a sustained effort to show how ideas and knowledge of all kinds can in fact ultimately be derived from and traced back to simple ideas of sensation and reflection. The achievement of his successors Berkeley and Hume consists mainly of two major accomplishments, one intentional, the other inadvertent. The intentional achievement consist in their carrying out more fully and consistently Locke's empiricist program than he had succeeded in doing by eliminating certain common-sense and rationalistic elements in Locke's thought that are inconsistent with his empiricist premises. This intentional achievement, however, had the inadvertent consequence, as philosophers such as Reid, Kant, and T. H. Green attempt to show, of demonstrating the bankruptcy of the empiricist program accepted by the three great empiricists, since if we develop consistently and fully the implications of their empiricist premises we see that if these premises are true we cannot have ideas and knowledge of certain kinds that we nonetheless do in fact have. If, for example, we take literally Hume's initial assumptions that all perceptions are either impressions or ideas and that all ideas are copies of impressions, and if these assumptions are true, then none of us can have the idea of material objects existing independently of being perceived, since none of us can have an impression of their so existing. But in fact we do have such an idea.

In contrast to Locke's "historical plain method," Kant's attempt to determine the extent and limits of human knowledge consists of an attempt to specify the a priori conditions of human experience and knowledge. The result he reaches is that synthetic a priori judgments are possible in mathematics and natural science but not in metaphysics, since the a priori forms of intuition and concepts and judgments of the understanding apply only to the manifold of intuition and to phenomena and not to noumena or things in themselves. This means that rationalistic metaphysics is impossible, since it attempts to transcend the a priori limits of human experience and knowledge. It means also that if any form of metaphysics at all is possible it can only be what Green terms "the metaphysics of experience or knowledge" and "the metaphysics of moral action."[4] This in turn means that what I have referred to as objective as opposed to subjective metaphysics is also impossible.

Kant's attempt to determine a priori the extent and the limits of human knowledge was met shortly thereafter by Hegels' rejoinder that "to seek to know before we know is as absurd as the wise resolution of Scholasticus, not to venture into the water until he had learned to swim."[5] Hegel's point is that the extent and the limits of human knowledge of reality cannot be known in advance or a priori but instead can only come to be known through actually conducting investigations in various sciences, including metaphysics, which gradually reveal the nature of reality. Accordingly, in *The Phenomenology of Spirit* he presents a dialectical treatment of various forms of human consciousness culminating in what he regards as absolute or philosophical knowledge of reality as it is in itself and in *The Science of Logic* presents a metaphysical logic designed to develop dialectically a series of categories definitive of the conceptual structure of reality as it is in itself. Not even Hegel, however, succeeded in overcoming fully the influence of Kant, since the system he develops is essentially idealist and therefore contains elements of a subjective as opposed to an objective approach to metaphysics. This is the case because although the object of absolute or philosophical knowledge is reality as it is in itself and not merely the phenomenal world, it is also reality as it is for itself, and reality as it is in and for itself turns out to be identical with absolute or philosophical knowledge or knowing.

Despite Hegel, Kant's strictures against the possibility of synthetic a priori judgments in metaphysics, and thus against the possibility of rationalistic metaphysics and an objective approach to metaphysics, continued as one of the dominating influences in philosophy throughout the nineteenth century and on into the twentieth. This influence manifested itself in a variety of ways. One was the idealism of such thinkers as Fichte in Germany, Green in England, and Royce in the United States. Another was the voluntarism of Schopenhauer and what I think may with some justice be referred to as a certain despair of reason on the part of such thinkers as Kierkegaard and Nietzsche. Still another, of great importance for the development of American philosophy, was pragmatism. Thus Peirce, despite his acceptance of what he calls critical commonsensism and Scotistic realism, writes (perhaps in this instance as much under the influence of Hegel as of Kant) of truth and reality in this way: "The opinion which is fated to be ultimately agreed to by all who investigate, is what we mean by the truth, and the object represented in this opinion is the real."[6] With just a slight variation this leads to Dewey's animadversions (also perhaps as much under the influence of Hegel as of Kant) on a reality antecedent to inquiry to which the latter must conform itself if it is to lead to truth and knowledge. This in turn with only a slight variation yields the conceptual pragmatism of C. I. Lewis's *Mind and the World-order* (a direct descendant of Kant through Peirce and Dewey, but not by way of Hegel), the title of which, if not indicative of what I have termed a subjective approach to metaphysics, at least is indicative of an approach that gives epistemology precedence over metaphysics. In this work Lewis, by arguing that we are free to conceptualize and organize the given data of experience in terms of whatever concepts we think best enable us to achieve whatever purposes we might have, questions not only the possibility of our discovering an objectively necessary conceptual framework that reflects the necessary objective constitution or structure of reality as it is in itself but also the a priori fixity or necessity of Kant's scheme of a priori concepts and judgments. Although published in 1929, this work anticipates certain of the central contentions of such successors of Lewis as Professor Quine and others, whose work in certain respects consists of variations on major themes sounded what seems now rather long ago by Lewis.

Perhaps the outstanding recent example of the Kantian influence on philosophy and of what I have termed a subjective approach to metaphysics is Professor Strawson's *Individuals: An Essay in Descriptive Metaphysics*. Strawson contrasts descriptive metaphysics with what he calls revisionary metaphysics. The difference between them he states as follows: "Descriptive metaphysics is content to describe the actual structure of our thought about the world, revisionary metaphysics is concerned to produce a better structure."[7] This contrast between descriptive and revisionary metaphysics is presented as though it were exhaustive—as though, that is, all metaphysics were either descriptive or revisionary— and Strawson never mentions any other kind of metaphysics. And since Strawson conceives both forms of metaphysics as being concerned only with "the actual structure of our thought about the world," one to describe it and the other to improve upon it, it would seem that he conceives metaphysics, regardless of which of the two forms it takes, to be concerned not with the structure of the world but rather with the structure of our thought about the world. His conception of metaphysics, whether it be descriptive or revisionary, is therefore subjective and fails entirely to take into account the possibility of an objective approach to metaphysics that seeks to uncover, not simply the structure of our thought about the world, but also the structure of the world as it is in itself as contrasted with our thought about it. In addition, the distinction between descriptive and revisionary metaphysics seems to presuppose the possibility of an objective approach to metaphysics. This is the case because one of the reasons, if not indeed the main or the only reason, revisionary metaphysicians have been concerned to produce a better structure than that of our actual thought about the world is that they think the latter in some way is inadequate to the actual structure of the world, not to the actual structure of our thought about the world. The actual structure of our thought about the world can be neither adequate nor inadequate to itself; instead, it can be adequate or inadequate only to the actual structure of the world. Thus the revisionary metaphysician, in attempting to improve upon the actual structure of our thought about the world, is presupposing that some access to the actual structure of the world is possible and thus that an objective approach to metaphysics is possible.

Not only does Strawson seem to fail to see that the possibility of revisionary metaphysics presupposes the possibility of an objective approach to metaphysics, he also seems to fail to understand adequately what those he terms "revisionary metaphysicians" are endeavoring to do, as the following considerations indicate. The concept of a basic particular plays a central role in Strawson's book. Stated simply, a particular of type *a* is ontologically prior to or more fundamental or basic than a particular of type *b* if and only if a particular of type *a* can be identified without first identifying a particular of type *b* but a particular of type *b* cannot be identified without first identifying a particular of type *a*.[8] In Strawson's view material objects and persons are the ultimately basic particulars, since they can be identified without first identifying particulars of other types whereas particulars of other types cannot be identified without first identifying some material object or person. He then goes on to argue that entities such as Leibnizian monads cannot be basic particulars.[9] In doing so, however, he seems to fail to recognize that metaphysicians such as Leibniz and Whitehead, who argue for the existence of such entities as monads and actual entities, would not dream of maintaining that such entities are basic particulars in Strawson's sense. Neither Leibniz nor Whitehead, that is, would dream of contending that a monad or actual entity can be identified by us without our first identifying some particular of some other type, such as a material object or a person, but that no particular of some other type, again such as a material object or a person, can be identified without first identifying some monad or actual entity. For Leibniz and Whitehead monads and actual entities are not basic particulars in Strawson's sense but instead are ontologically prior to or more fundamental or basic than particulars of other types in the sense that their existence or occurrence does not depend upon the existence of particulars of other types whereas the existence of particulars of other types does depend upon their existence or occurrence. They therefore could readily agree with Strawson that material objects and persons, not monads and actual entities, are basic particulars in Strawson's sense and yet consistently maintain that monads or actual entities are ontologically prior to material objects and persons in the sense just indicated. What Strawson has done is to confuse priority of identification or epistemological priority with ontological priority. From the fact that material objects and persons are epistemologically prior to entities such as Leibnizian monads and Whiteheadian actual entities it does not follow that they are also ontologically prior.

These animadversions on Strawson's distinction between descriptive and revisionary metaphysics are intended to indicate that his distinction is inadequate and confused and are not intended as a justification of revisionary metaphysics. His account of the two types of metaphysics simply fails to apply to the type of metaphysics with which we shall be concerned in this work, which is neither descriptive nor revisionary but rather objective. We shall be concerned, that is, neither "to describe the actual structure of our thought about the world" nor "to produce a better structure" but, instead, to answer questions such as the five questions listed above concerning the nature and types of being. Whatever results we reach are to be tested not by comparing them with "the actual structure of our thought about the world," whatever that might be, but rather by comparing them with what seems to be the case after careful critical reflection upon the data accessible to us as philosophers, while remembering throughout that our results are subject to correction, refinement, and supplementation in the light of future data and future critical reflection.

Notes

1. See my "Art and the Embodiment of Ideas," *Experience, Mind, and Value: Philosophical Essays* (Leiden: E. J. Brill, 1969).

2. Karl R. Popper, *The Poverty of Historicism* (London: Routledge & Kegan Paul, 1957), pp. v–vii.

3. *Hegel's Philosophy of Right*, trans. with notes by T. M. Knox (Oxford: The Clarendon Press, 1952), p. 13.

4. Thomas Hill Green, *Prolegomena to Ethics*, ed. A. C. Bradley with an introd. by Ramon M. Lemos (New York: Thomas Y. Crowell, 1969), sec. 85, p. 90.

5. *The Logic of Hegel*, trans. from *The Encyclopaedia of the Philosophical Sciences* by William Wallace, 2d ed., rev. and augmented (Oxford University Press, 1892), p. 17.

6. "How to Make our Ideas Clear," in *The Philosophy of Peirce: Selected Writings*, ed. Justus Buchler (London: Routledge & Kegan Paul, 1940), p. 38.

7. P. F. Strawson, *Individuals: An Essay in Descriptive Metaphysics* (London: Methuen & Co., 1959), p. 9.

8. Ibid., p. 17.

9. Ibid., chap. 4.

2
Objective and Conventional Necessity

IN the last chapter mention was made of the fact that Kant argues against the possibility of rationalistic metaphysics on the ground that although synthetic a priori judgments are possible in mathematics and natural science, they are not possible in metaphysics. Some philosophers have gone even further and denied that such judgments are possible in any area, whether it be mathematics, natural science, metaphysics, or any other area. Instead, they maintain, all necessary truths are analytic. They disagree, however, as to the nature of analytic truth. Some, such as Friedrich Waismann, contend that all analytic truths are conventional, whereas others, such as C. I. Lewis, admit what I shall term objective as well as conventional analytic truths. I shall argue that Kant is correct in maintaining that there are synthetic a priori as well as analytic truths but deficient in his account of the nature of analyticity and of the synthetic a priori. Lewis, I shall argue, is correct in recognizing that there are objective as well as conventional analytic truths but mistaken in denying that there are any synthetic a priori truths. And Waismann, I shall argue, is correct in recognizing that there are conventional necessary truths but mistaken in maintaining that all necessary truths are conventional and thus in denying that there are any objective necessities. This in effect means that I shall argue that there are two major kinds of necessary truths—those that are objective and those that are conventional. It also means that I shall argue that although all conventional truths are analytic, not all objective necessary truths are, since although some are analytic others are synthetic. I shall therefore be contending that there are two kinds of objective necessary truths—those that are synthetic and those that are analytic—and that there are two kinds of analytic truths—those that are objective and those that are conventional.

1. Analytic and Synthetic Propositions

It will be important first to distinguish between sentences and propositions. To some this distinction is so obvious and elementary that there is no point in mentioning it, much less in emphasizing it. Yet a failure to keep this elementary distinction in mind has, I believe, been at least partly responsible for the claim of certain philosophers that all necessary truths are conventional. In making this distinction I do not intend to assert the existence of propositions as a distinct irreducible ontological category. Whether propositions do in fact constitute such a category is a question we shall consider later. But we do need some term to refer to assertable contents or to ideas, thoughts, or judgments that are either true or false, as distinct from the sentences used to express them, and for this purpose in this chapter I shall use the term *proposition*. What I am interested in doing is to call to attention what seem to me to be undeniable facts—the fact that the same sentence can be used to assert a variety of assertable contents, ideas, thoughts, or judgments (propositions) and the fact that the same assertable content, idea, thought, or judgment (proposition) can be asserted by a variety of sentences. More specifically, I am interested in emphasizing that certain sentences can be used to assert either analytic or synthetic propositions. They can be used on one occasion to assert an analytic proposition, on another to assert a synthetic proposition; and they can be used by a speaker to assert an analytic proposition, yet be understood by the hearer as asserting a synthetic proposition, and vice versa.

This distinction can be easily overlooked. Lewis, for example, both makes it and also implicitly denies it, since he says that a proposition is a term of a certain type having intension and extension yet also states that a proposition is an assertable content.[1] Moreover, failure to keep this distinction in mind might easily lead one to suppose that the ability to show that a sentence expresses a conventional truth is sufficient to show that it cannot also be used to express a synthetic a priori truth. Waismann, for example, makes this mistake when he writes that "whoever will maintain that a particular proposition is a synthetic a priori judgment has to demonstrate in a precise way that it cannot be deduced from mere conventions as to the use of language."[2] This ignores what was said above—that the same sentence can be used to express both an analytic and a synthetic proposition. It also ignores the fact that the synthetic proposition the sentence expresses need not be necessary or a priori but might instead be contingent or empirical. If so, then what Waismann says about those who maintain that a given proposition is synthetic a priori also applies to those who maintain that a given proposition is empirical, so that whoever will maintain that a given proposition is an empirical judgment "has to demonstrate in a precise way that it cannot be deduced from mere conventions as to the use of language." Waismann obviously would not want to say this, for he, no more than anyone else, doubts that there are empirical propositions or judgments but instead doubts only that there are any synthetic a priori propositions. Yet the fact remains that the words composing certain sentences used to express empirical propositions can also be interpreted in such a way that the sentence also expresses an analytic proposition. As we shall see, "All bodies have weight" may be interpreted as expressing either an analytic or an empirical proposition, depending upon how "body" is used or understood.

If, then, a necessary condition of showing that a sentence can be used to express a synthetic a priori proposition be that one "demonstrate in a precise way" that it cannot also be used to express an analytic proposition, then it is no more possible to show that certain sentences express empirical propositions than it is to show that certain sentences express synthetic a priori propositions. It will, in short, be impossible to show that these sentences express either an empirical or a synthetic a priori proposition, since it is impossible to demonstrate that they cannot also be used to express an analytic proposition. If this consideration does not lead one to deny that certain sentences can be used to express empirical propositions, then neither ought it lead to a denial that certain other sentences can be used to express synthetic a priori propositions. It ought, however, to lead to neither denial, for these sentences can be used to express analytic propositions if they can be used to express either empirical or synthetic a priori propositions, so that the question of whether they can be used to express propositions of the latter two types cannot be answered merely by answering the question of whether they can be used to express analytic propositions. As has been said, no one doubts that sentences can be used to express empirical propositions. It is partly because of this that Waismann's position reduces to a reductio ad absurdum. But that there are synthetic a priori propositions is not a proposition universally accepted, so that, even though Waismann's argument shows neither that there are none nor that we cannot know that there are any, a question still remains as to whether there are any.

Before this question is discussed it will be helpful to discuss first the distinction between the analytic and the synthetic. Kant draws this distinction by saying that analytic propositions are those in which the subject contains the predicate, synthetic those in which the subject does not contain the predicate. He also says that the contradictory of an analytic proposition is self-contradictory, whereas the contradictory of a synthetic proposition is not. There are at least four deficiencies in Kant's way of making this distinction.

The first deficiency is that the distinction, as he presents it, applies only to judgments of the subject-predicate form. This means that the distinction, as he presents it, applies only to simple judgments and not to compound judgments such as those having the following forms: If p, then p; p if and only if p; It is false that p is true and p is false; Either p is true or p is false; If p, then either p or q; and so on. This, however, is only a minor deficiency, especially if we interpret Kant as intending, as he doubtless did, his way of drawing the distinction to apply only to judgments of the subject-predicate form. In addition, for the purposes of this chapter we need consider only judgments having this form. This is the case because one of the major aims of this chapter is to establish that there are objective analytic necessities and synthetic necessities as well as conventional necessities, and this aim will be accomplished if I succeed in showing that some subject-predicate judgments do in fact express objective analytic necessities and others synthetic necessities. I shall therefore, following Kant, limit my discussion of the analytic/ synthetic distinction to a consideration of judgments of the subject-predicate form.

The second deficiency in Kant's account is that it, if interpreted strictly, includes as analytic only those propositions in which the predicate is contained in the subject and excludes those propositions in which the subject and the predicate are identical, such as "All bodies are bodies." In these propositions there is an identity of subject and predicate if the subject and predicate terms are used in the same sense, not an inclusion of the predicate in the subject. Such propositions may be referred to as identical propositions, since if the subject and predicate terms are used in the same sense the sentences expressing these propositions can be reduced immediately to formal expressions of the law of identity simply through substituting some variable such as "A" for the subject and predicate terms. I shall argue later that the law of identity and the law of contradiction are objective rather than conventional necessities. Since the sentences expressing identical propositions can be reduced immediately to formal expressions of the law of identity, such propositions are also objective rather than conventional necessities, and their contradictories are objective rather than conventional impossibilities.

This brings us to the third deficiency in Kant's account of the distinction between the analytic and the synthetic. It is that his way of drawing the distinction does not get to the heart of the matter, since it fails even to raise, and thus even more to answer, the question of what the source is of the containment of the predicate of a nonidentical analytic proposition in its subject. To use his examples, why is the predicate of "All bodies are extended" included in the subject, whereas the predicate of "All bodies have weight" is not? The conventionalist, I believe, has supplied us with the correct answer. The predicate of the first proposition is included in the subject, whereas that of the second is not, because of the definition of the term *body*. If we define 'body' as referring by definition to all and only extended things and do not define it as referring by definition to all and only things that have weight, then the predicate of

"All bodies are extended" is included by definition in the subject, so that this proposition is true by definition, whereas the predicate of "All bodies have weight" is not included by definition in the subject, so that this proposition is not true by definition. The first proposition is therefore analytic because it is true by definition. Its predicate is included in its subject because of the definition of its subject term, and its contradictory is self-inconsistent also because of the definition of its subject term. The second proposition is synthetic because it is not true by definition. The definition of its subject term does not entail the inclusion of its predicate in its subject, nor does it entail the self-inconsistency of its contradictory. Thus if we define the word 'body' simply as having the same meaning as the expression 'extended thing', so that the expressions 'body' and 'extended thing' are used synonymously, the sentence "All bodies are extended things" is translatable into the sentence "All extended things are extended things." Substituting the variable "A" for "extended things," we obtain a formal expression of the law of identity. If we make the same substitution in the contradictory, "Some extended things are not extended things," we obtain a formal expression, "Some A are not A," that violates the law of contradiction. In this way we can maintain that the principles of analyticity are the law of identity and the law of contradiction. But the conventionalist point, which I believe to be unassailable, is that the source of our ability to reduce a sentence expressing a nonidentical proposition to a formal expression of the law of identity and its contradictory to a formal expression that violates the law of contradiction, by substituting some variable for the subject and predicate terms, is the definition we assign the subject term.

This can also be seen by entertaining a consideration that will also serve to support the contention that the same sentence can be used to express either an analytic or a synthetic proposition, depending upon how we interpret the subject term of the sentence. We have just been reminded of the conventionalist point that "All bodies have weight" expresses a synthetic proposition if we do not define "body" in such a way that it refers by definition to all and only things that have weight. But part of the conventionalist point is that it can also be used in such a way that it does refer by definition to all and only things that have weight. If we use it in this way, then "All bodies have weight" expresses an analytic proposition, and its contradictory, "Some bodies do not have weight," is self-inconsistent. Thus whether a nonidentical sentence expresses an analytic or a synthetic proposition can be ascertained only by determining how the subject term is being used. If the subject term is used in one way the sentence expresses an analytic proposition, but if it is used in another way the sentence expresses a synthetic proposition.

The preceding, however, does not mean that the subject and predicate terms must be used synonymously if a sentence is to express an analytic proposition. In at least some of their uses 'body' and 'extended thing' are not synonymous. Lines, surfaces, colors, and shadows are all extended, but none of them are bodies. Instead, 'body' is commonly used in such a way that a necessary but not a sufficient condition of something's being a body is that it be extended, since it is commonly used in such a way that if something is to be a body it must be extended in three dimensions in public or physical space, have some degree of solidity or impenetrability, and so on. Hence "All bodies are extended" cannot be reduced to a formal expression of the law of identity by substituting some variable for the subject and predicate terms if such a substitution means that these terms are synonymous, for they are not synonymous.

Such a substitution, however, need not be interpreted in this way. Instead, if we use 'body' as referring, say, to anything that has the properties ABCD, and if we use 'extended thing' to refer to anything that has the property A, which is the property of being extended, we can interpret "All A are A," taken as a formal expression of "All bodies are extended," as an abbreviated form of the expression "All ABCD are A." This latter expression can be taken as a formal expression of "All bodies are extended," provided that we use 'body' to refer to anything that has the properties ABCD and that we use 'extended thing' to refer to anything that has the property A. If we use 'body' and 'extended thing' in these ways, then "All ABCD are A" can be taken as a literal formal expression only of "All bodies are extended things," and "All A are A" can be taken as a literal formal expression only of "All extended things are extended things." On the other hand, if we use 'body' and 'extended thing' in these ways, then being extended is included in being a body, since having the property A is included in having the properties ABCD. Thus the expression "All ABCD are A" is a more felicitous formal expression of Kant's conception of the logical form of an analytic proposition than is the expression "All A are A," since it shows by its form that in an analytic proposition the subject may include its predicate and need not be identical with it, whereas the expression "All A are A," taken as a formal expression of the logical form of an analytic proposition, might, by its form, mislead one into supposing that the subject of such a proposition must be identical with its predicate and may not merely include it.

So long, however, as one understands that "All A are A," in this context, is to be interpreted only as an abbreviation for "All ABCD are A," i.e., as a formal expression of the inclusion of the predicate of a proposition in its subject, and not as an expression of an identity between the subject and the predicate, there is no harm in taking it as a formal expression of the logical form of both identical and nonidentical analytic propositions, and therefore in regarding the law of identity as one of the two principles of analyticity. Nor is there any harm in regarding the law of contradiction as the other principle, since "Some ABCD are not A" is as much a formal expression that violates the law of contradiction as is "Some A are not A." But the conventionalist point is still sound—whether any nonidentical sentence is such that it can legitimately be reduced to a formal expression of the law of identity and its contradictory to a self-inconsistent formal expression that violates the law of contradiction depends ultimately upon the meaning assigned the subject term of the sentence. If one meaning be assigned it the sentence might express an analytic proposition, but if another be assigned it the sentence might instead express a synthetic proposition.

The fourth deficiency in Kant's account of the distinction between the analytic and the synthetic is that he makes the distinction in such a way that all analytic propositions are necessarily true. Kant is not alone in drawing the distinction in such a way that this consequence follows. Thus Lewis, for example, along with many other philosophers, makes the distinction by saying that analytic sentences are those that are true by virtue of their meaning alone, whereas synthetic sentences are not, so that an analytic sentence can be known to be true merely through an analysis of the meanings of its terms, whereas the truth of a synthetic sentence cannot come to be known in this way.[3] But if all analytic propositions are necessarily true, then their contradictories must be synthetic. If "All bodies are extended" is analytic and therefore necessarily true, then its contradictory, "Some bodies are not extended," which is self-inconsistent and hence necessarily false, must be synthetic. The question then arises of whether it is a priori or empirical. It obviously is not empirical and therefore must be a priori. But if it is a priori and also synthetic, then there will be a host of synthetic a priori propositions, namely the contradictories of all analytic propositions.

The mere fact that there will then be a host of synthetic a priori propositions occasions no difficulty for Kant, for he freely admits, and indeed is concerned to show, that there are such propositions. The difficulty for him issues instead from the fact that he maintains that all propositions are either analytic or synthetic, so that if the contradictories of analytic propositions are not analytic, since their predicates are not included in their subjects, then they must be synthetic. But it is hard to see how the contradictory of an analytic proposition can be synthetic. Lewis, on the other hand, along with many other philosophers, denies that there are any synthetic a priori propositions and maintains instead that all propositions are either analytic or empirical. He therefore contradicts himself. This contradiction, however, is not serious, in the sense that it is the result, I think, more of a slip on his part than of anything else and could easily be avoided simply through amending the distinction he draws between analytic and synthetic sentences. All one need do is maintain that analytic sentences are true, if true, or else false, if false, by virtue of their meaning alone, whereas synthetic sentences are not. Thus "All bodies are extended" is analytic by virtue of the meaning of 'body,' and "Some bodies are not extended," though self-inconsistent and hence necessarily false, is also analytic by virtue of the meaning of 'body'. The difficulty in Kant's position is also, I think, more the result of a slip than anything else, which one could avoid simply by amending his account of analyticity so that the contradictories of analytic propositions are also analytic. This one could do by distinguishing between three kinds of analytic proposition—identical propositions, propositions whose subjects contain their predicates, and self-inconsistent propositions.

To some the view that self-inconsistent propositions are analytic will doubtless seem strange. There are, however, two considerations that might serve to dissipate somewhat this strangeness. One is that if all propositions are either analytic or synthetic, then so are self-inconsistent propositions, and regarding them an analytic seems less strange than regarding them as synthetic. The other is that the notion of a proposition's being analytically false is not at all strange, and to say that self-inconsistent propositions are analytic and necessarily false may be taken as a way of saying that they are analytically false. From this point on, however, we shall concentrate on true analytic propositions, which are either identical or nonidentical. I have shown (or at least argued) that the latter and their contradictories are conventionally necessary and have maintained but not shown that the former and their contradictories are objectively necessary. I turn now to show that this is in fact the case.

As has been seen, identical sentences such as "All bodies are bodies," in which the subject and predicate terms are identical and have the same sense, can be reduced immediately to formal expressions of the law of identity and their contradictories to formal expressions that violate the law of contradiction simply by substituting some variable such as 'A' for the subject and predicate terms. To make such a substitution and to obtain such formal sentences one need only know that the subject and predicate terms are being used in the same sense and need not know what that sense is. Provided that the subject and predicate terms have the same meaning, every identical sentence can be reduced to such formal expressions, regardless of the meaning of its subject and predicate terms, so that their meaning is irrelevant to its reducibility to these formal expressions. Regardless of how the subject and predicate terms of an identical sentence might be defined, so long as they are used in the same sense the sentence is reducible immediately to a formal expression of the law of identity and its contradictory to a formal expression that violates the law of contradiction. Nor is the necessary truth of "All A are A" and the necessary falsity of "Some A are not A" dependent upon what term is substituted for "A" or upon how that term is defined. Instead, "All A are A" is to be understood as asserting that everything is identical with itself, and "Some A are not A" as asserting that something is not identical with itself. The necessary truth of the first and the necessary falsity of the second are necessary conditions of our thinking consistently about anything, regardless of what it is we think about. One might choose to think inconsistently, in violation of the laws of identity and contradiction. But if one did succeed in doing so his beliefs would not apply to anything. And that anyone could succeed fully in doing so, and even, indeed, that it makes sense to suppose that one could succeed fully in so doing, may well be doubted.

Lewis, then, I believe, is correct in maintaining that there are objective as well as conventional necessities. But, as we have seen, he contends that all objective necessities, like all conventional necessities, are analytic and denies that there are any synthetic objective necessities—that there are any synthetic a priori propositions. The question therefore arises of whether there are any compelling reasons for denying that any objective necessities are synthetic. One reason that might be given does not seem to me to be compelling. It issues from a certain deference to Kant's terminology and position. Kant appropriated the expression "synthetic *a priori*" to refer to judgments he believed to be grounded ultimately upon what he took to be the a priori constitution of the human sensibility and understanding. This being so, one might argue, it is better, to avoid an initial commitment to a Kantian view of the nature and ground of objective necessities, to refer to all such necessities as analytic than to refer to some as analytic and to others as synthetic. To this there are at least two replies. One is that one need not accept a Kantian position if one refers to certain objective necessities as synthetic, nor need there be any danger that others will believe that one is taking a Kantian position if sufficient care is taken to make it clear that such a position is not being assumed. The other reply is that if we refer to all objective necessities as analytic we are confronted with the task of distinguishing between, on the one hand, those objective necessities whose necessity issues from their reducibility to the laws of identity and contradiction and, on the other, those whose necessity is not reducible to these laws. Since the necessity of the latter is not thus reducible, why refer to them as analytic? If, then, one is to show that all objective necessities are analytic, he must also show that they are all reducible to these laws. But this coin has another side, which is that if one is to show that some necessities are synthetic he must show that they are not reducible to these laws.

Before, however, turning to this task it is necessary to clarify somewhat further the notion of objective necessity. The conventionalist, as we know, denies that there are any objective necessities at all and maintains instead that all necessities are conventional. He thus holds that all analytic propositions are conventional. Thus for him the question of whether there are any objective necessities is identical with the question of whether there are any synthetic a priori propositions. And since he denies that there are any synthetic a priori propositions he is also thereby denying that there are any objective necessities. He also tends to treat all synthetic propositions as factual, so that the question of whether there are any synthetic a priori propositions becomes the question of whether there are any factually necessary propositions. He assumes, that is, that if the truth of an a priori proposition does not issue from linguistic conventions, then that proposition must be a factual proposition, and then identifies this alleged necessarily true factual proposition as a synthetic a priori proposition. Both this assumption and this identification are made by Waismann when he equates the question of whether any factual propositions are necessarily true with the question of whether any synthetic propositions are a priori.[4] But Waismann's assumption is mistaken. There is no more reason for regarding objective necessities, regardless of whether they be analytic or synthetic, as factual than there is for regarding conventional necessities such as "all mermaids are female" as factual.

There is, of course, a sense in which every true proposition is factual, regardless of whether it be hypothetical or categorical, analytic or synthetic, a priori or empirical, conventionally a priori or objectively a priori. This is the sense in which we can always substitute "it is a fact that p" for "it is true that p" and "it is a fact that if p is true then q is true" for "it is true that if p is true then q is true." But this is not the sense of 'factuality' Waismann has in mind when he raises the question of whether any factual propositions are necessarily true. For, obviously, if all true propositions are factual in this sense, then one cannot distinguish between those that are factual and those that are not. Instead, the distinction he has in mind is that between existential propositions on the one hand and nonexistential or hypothetical propositions on the other— between those propositions which, in asserting, we assert, at least implicitly, that the subject term of the sentence used to assert them denotes something existent and, on the other hand, those propositions which, in asserting, we do not assert this. But, again, there is no reason whatever to suppose that all objective necessities, whether they be analytic or synthetic, are factual in this, the existential, sense. Instead, as we shall see, one may easily argue that at least some, and perhaps even all, objective necessities, whether they be analytic or synthetic, are nonexistential or hypothetical. Thus the question of whether there are any objectively necessary propositions is not the question of whether there are any factually necessary propositions. Instead, it is the question of whether there are any propositions whose truth or falsity is independent both of what exists or occurs in time and also of any linguistic decisions or conventions. Three comments need to be made in explication of this.

The first is that implicit in the above formulation is a distinction between the truth or falsity of a proposition on the one hand and the apprehension of its truth or falsity on the other. The latter is obviously an event that does occur in time and usually, if not indeed always, depends upon the apprehension of other events that also occur in time.

The second comment is connected with the first. It has to do with Kant's conception of the nature and the ground of the synthetic a priori and its relation to the characterization of objectively necessary propositions as propositions whose truth or falsity is independent of anything that exists or occurs in time. A critic might object that this characterization of objective necessity is question-begging against Kant, since it, by definition, rules out as a priori any proposition he would regard as synthetic a priori. This is so because he grounds the synthetic a priori, at least insofar as it is constitutive of the phenomenal world, upon a priori forms of human sensibility and understanding. But, the critic continues, the fact that the human sensibility and understanding have this a priori structure is an empirical or temporal fact, as is indeed the existence of any human beings at all. Given the existence of human beings and the a priori structure of their sensibility and understanding as Kant conceives it, certain a priori propositions follow as constitutive of or applicable to the phenomenal world. But both the existence of human beings and also the structure of their sensibility and understanding are empirical or contingent rather than necessary facts; it is certainly conceivable that no human beings at all should exist, and, given that they do exist, it is also conceivable that their sensibility and understanding should not have precisely the a priori structure Kant thinks they have. Therefore Kant grounds the synthetic a priori on certain empirical or contingent facts, so that on his view synthetic a priori propositions are not completely independent of what exists or occurs in time.

To this there are two replies. The first is that I do not intend the claim that the truth or falsity of objectively necessary propositions is independent of time as a criticism of Kant's conception of the synthetic a priori. The second is that, given the existence of human beings and what Kant takes to be the a priori structure of their sensibility and understanding, then, so long as they continue to have this a priori structure, we can know, independently of any further appeals to experience, that certain propositions are synthetic a priori and perhaps even constitutive of or at least applicable to the phenomenal world. This is to say that, given the continued existence of human beings and their continued possession of a sensibility and understanding with a certain a priori structure, the truth of certain synthetic a priori propositions is assured regardless of whatever else might exist or occur in time. This does not mean that I believe that Kant's conception of the synthetic a priori is satisfactory. I do not believe that it is. It means only that I do not intend my characterization of objective necessity as a rejection of Kant's position and certainly not as a question-begging rejection of it.

The third comment I wish to make on the claim that the truth or falsity of objectively necessary propositions is independent of anything that happens in time is connected with the first two. It is that there is a sense in which conventional as opposed to objective necessities are contingent upon the occurrence of certain temporal events. This is the case because the necessity of a conventional necessity issues from certain linguistic decisions or conventions, and the latter occur or exist in time. Thus the necessary truth of the conventionally a priori proposition "All bodies are extended" is dependent upon the decision to use the term 'body' in such a way that anything it refers to must, by definition, be extended. The proposition expressed by this sentence is conventionally a priori only so long as the decision to use 'body' in this way is adhered to. But the fact that conventionally a priori propositions are thus dependent for their truth upon the occurrence of certain temporal events does not mean that they are empirical rather than a priori propositions. So long as the decision to use 'body' in the way specified is adhered to, nothing that happens in time is relevant to the determination of the truth or falsity of "All bodies are extended," so that appeals to experience either to confirm or to falsify this proposition are pointless; instead, its truth can be known prior to all further experience. All that further experience could do is to provide us a reason for modifying or abandoning the convention we have adopted, either through revealing that it is not sufficiently precise or sufficiently useful as it stands or else through showing that our definition no longer applies to anything actual or, if it does, to anything of continued importance.

Objectively a priori propositions, on the other hand, do not depend in any way upon the occurrence of any temporal events whatever, and especially not upon the linguistic decisions from which the necessity of conventional necessities issues. They would still be necessarily true or necessarily false regardless of whether any temporal events of any kind ever occurred, so that their truth or falsity is not contingent in any way upon the existence of a world of temporal events. The apprehension of their truth or falsity by human beings does, of course, depend upon the occurrence of temporal events and is indeed itself temporal; but their truth or falsity itself is atemporal, timeless, or eternal. One who admits the existence or subsistence of objective necessities is thereby committing himself to at least a modest form of Platonism. An aversion on the part of some to even such a modest form of Platonism as this has doubtless operated as a powerful motive generating a strong disinclination to admit the reality of the objective a priori.

2. Arithmetic Necessities

With the preceding as prolegomena, we are now in a position to address ourselves to the question of whether there are in fact any synthetic a priori propositions. We shall deal first with the question of whether there are any such propositions in mathematics, especially arithmetic and geometry. To do so it will be helpful to begin with a few words about formal deductive systems. Such systems consist of various components, among which are primitive or undefined terms, definitions, undemonstrated propositions (which are either axioms or postulates), theorems or demonstrated propositions, and rules of procedure. In an uninterpreted system all undemonstrated propositions may be treated as definitions, and this I shall do, for the sake of simplicity, in the elementary uninterpreted systems I shall deal with. Also, again for the sake of simplicity, I shall not state the rules of procedure I shall follow. What they are will, I believe, be obvious enough from how I proceed, and for our purposes it is not necessary that they be stated. Nor shall I derive any theorems from the primitive terms and definitions of the simple systems I shall deal with, since it is not necessary for our purposes to do so. Moreover, I shall use the same primitives in each of these simple systems. These are '1', '+', and '='. It will be obvious that I am operating with '+' and '=' in the way in which these symbols are operated with in ordinary elementary arithmetic, with the exception, if indeed it is an exception, that I shall also use '=' as a substitute symbol for 'means', which I shall use as a symbol indicating definition. Thus "'a' means 'b'" means that 'a' is defined in terms of 'b' in such a way that 'a' may be substituted *salva veritate* for 'b' and 'b' for 'a' in any expression in the system in which they are used and not mentioned. Obviously 'b' cannot be substituted for 'a' in an expression such as "'a' means 'b'" in which they are mentioned and not used, for if such a substitution were made we should obtain "'b' means 'b'," which, obviously, is a significantly different expression from "'a' means 'b'."

Given, then, '1', '+', and '=' as primitives, we may define other terms in terms of them. The other terms of the simple systems I shall consider are '2', '3', '4', and '5'. These terms will occur in each system, but their definitions will differ. Thus in one system, which I shall label "system A,"

'2' has the same meaning as '1 + 1', '3' the same meaning as '1 + 2', '4' the same as '1 + 3', and '5' the same as '1 + 4'. As has been said, in this context to say that one expression has the same meaning as another is to say that each can be substituted for the other in any expression in which they are used but not mentioned without changing the truth-value of the expression. Using '=' as a symbol expressing, in this context, the substitutivity of one expression for another, we can express the definitions listed above as follows: '2 = 1 + 1', '3 = 1 + 2', '4 = 1 + 3', and '5 = 1 + 4'. Since the definitions of an uninterpreted system can be treated as unproved propositions, or at least as expressing unproved propositions, each of the expressions, '2 = 1 + 1', '3 = 1 + 2', '4 = 1 + 3', and '5 = 1 + 4', can be treated as expressing a proposition that, in system A, is true by definition, and therefore as conventionally analytic in system A. We turn now to another system, system B. In this system '2' has the same meaning as '1 + 3', '3' the same meaning as '1 + 4', '4' the same as '1 + 1', and '5' the same as '1 + 2'. In order, however, to introduce each of these terms into the system in such a way that each, upon its introduction, is defined either in terms only of the primitives of the system or else in terms of the primitives and terms that have already been defined, we should have to introduce them in the following order: '4' means '1 + 1', '3' means '1 + 4', '2' means '1 + 3', and '5' means '1 + 2'. Given these definitions, '4 = 1 + 1', '3 = 1 + 4', '2 = 1 + 3', and '5 = 1 + 2' are all true in system B, and thus each expresses a proposition that is conventionally analytic in system B.

Thus far everything that has been said is compatible with the conventionalist thesis. The propositions of an uninterpreted system are conventionally analytic within the system of which they are parts. In system A but not in system B '2 = 1 + 1' is analytic, and in system B but not in system A '4 = 1 + 1' is analytic. The analyticity of '2 = 1 + 1' in system A derives from the definition of '2' in system A, and the analyticity of '4 = 1 + 1' in system B issues from the definition of '4' in system B. We may therefore agree with the conventionalist that the propositions of uninterpreted formal systems of mathematics are conventionally analytic, one set of propositions being analytic in one system because derivable from the definitions of that system, another set being analytic in another system because deducible from the definitions of that system. If, then, we interpret the question of whether the propositions of mathematics are analytic as identical with the question of whether the propositions of uninterpreted formal systems of mathematics are analytic, we must agree with the conventionalist that they are. But this is not the end of the matter, for there is another interpretation that may be placed upon this question. On this second interpretation, the question is whether all the propositions of *interpreted* as well as those of uninterpreted systems of mathematics are analytic. Thus the question of whether all the propositions of mathematics are analytic is not sufficiently precise. This simple question masks two distinct questions. One is the question of whether all the propositions of *uninterpreted* systems of mathematics are analytic. To this question the conventionalist gives the correct answer—they are analytic. The other is the question of whether all the propositions of *interpreted* systems of mathematics are analytic. From the fact that the answer to the first question is yes it does not follow that this is also the correct answer to the second. To this second question we now turn.

One of the essential differences between an uninterpreted and an interpreted system is that the terms of an uninterpreted system have only what may be labeled 'linguistic' or 'syntactical' meaning as opposed to what may be termed 'denotative' or 'semantic' meaning, whereas the terms of an interpreted system, with the exception of those that are purely syntactical or syncategorematic, have both sorts of meaning. The meaning of the terms of an uninterpreted system consists only of the terms that may be substituted for them and of the relations in which they stand to the various component parts of the system. They have no denotative or semantic meaning, since they do not denote or refer to anything outside the system. Thus the meaning of '2' in system A is '1 + 1', in system B the expression '1 + 3'. In neither system does '2' denote or refer to anything nonlinguistic outside the system; it could be given such denotative or semantic meaning only by placing some interpretation on it. If an interpretation is placed on it in either system, the latter is thereby transformed to that extent from an uninterpreted into an interpreted system. A system is 'completely' interpreted if an interpretation is placed on every term in it with the exception of those that are purely syntactical or syncategorematic, 'incompletely' interpreted if some terms within it other than those that are purely syntactical or syncategorematic are given no interpretation.

The interpretation we place on the terms of a system is arbitrary or a matter of convention. On some interpretations, however, the interpreted terms will denote something actual outside the system, whereas on others they will not; and on some interpretations the sentences of the system will apply to actual and not merely possible states of affairs and thus be empirically true and perhaps practically useful, whereas on others they will not. But the question of whether there are any synthetic a priori propositions expressed by interpreted sentences is the question of whether there are any interpretations that render the sentences as interpreted either necessarily true or necessarily false. If there is at least one interpretation of one nonidentical sentence that renders it, as interpreted, either necessarily true or necessarily false, then there is at least one synthetic a priori proposition; if there is not, then there is no interpretation of any sentence that enables it to express a synthetic a priori proposition. It must be kept in mind, however, that the question of whether the sentences of a system can be interpreted in such a way as to render them, as interpreted, either empirically true or false or else necessarily true or false is independent of the question of whether these sentences are conventionally analytic. As we have seen, the question of whether a sentence expresses a conventionally analytic proposition can be answered only by discovering whether it is true by definition. Whether there is also some interpretation of it that enables it to express, as interpreted, either an empirical or a synthetic a priori proposition is irrelevant to the question of whether, as uninterpreted, it expresses a conventionally analytic proposition. Failure to keep this in mind might lead one to suppose that the ability to show that a sentence expresses a proposition that is true by definition is sufficient to show that it cannot also express a proposition that is synthetic a priori. As we have seen, this is one of the mistakes Waismann makes. We still, however, have not answered the question of whether in fact there are any interpretations that, when placed on sentences expressing conventional necessities, enable these sentences also to express synthetic a priori propositions.

To deal with this question I shall place interpretations on the symbols '1', '2', '3', '4', '5' occurring in systems A and B. The first interpretation I shall place on them is the standard or ordinary one. In placing interpretations on them I shall use asterisks as what Peirce would perhaps call iconic symbols. Each asterisk is to be understood as standing for a single discriminable entity. Since I am using *entity* here to refer to anything conceivable, regardless of what it might be, each asterisk is to be understood as standing for anything conceivable as a discriminable entity. One asterisk is to be understood as standing for one entity, two asterisks as standing for two entities, three as standing for three, four for four, and five for five. In the preceding sentence I am, of course, placing the ordinary interpretation on 'one', 'two', 'three', 'four', and 'five'. I shall also use parentheses to enclose groups of asterisks. The number of asterisks enclosed within a pair of parentheses is to be understood as standing for a group of entities containing the same number of entities as there are asterisks enclosed within the parentheses. Finally, when the symbol '=' is placed between two asterisks or two groups of asterisks, it is to be interpreted as asserting that there is the same number of asterisks immediately to its left or preceding it as there is immediately to its right or following it.

Placing, then, the standard interpretation upon the symbols '1', '2', '3', '4', '5' occurring in systems A and B, '1' is to be interpreted as standing for * entity, '2' as standing for ** entities, '3' for *** entities, '4' for **** entities, and '5' for ***** entities. Placing these interpretations on the symbols expressing the definitions or propositions in system A, we obtain the following results: for '2 = 1 + 1' we obtain (**) = ((*)(*)), for '3 = 1 + 2' (***) = ((*)(**)), for '4 = 1 + 3' (****) = ((*)(***)), and for '5 = 1 + 4' (*****) = ((*)(****)). The expressions containing asterisks are to be read as follows, in order beginning with the first: "Whenever (or if) two discriminable entities exist or are thought or conceived of, then, so long as these entities exist or are thought of and remain self-identical, i.e., do not lose their self-identity either through dividing to form two or more entities or through merging with another entity or group of entities to form with it a single entity, the same number of entities exist or are thought of as when one entity and one entity exist or are thought of," and so on. This expression, and each of the corresponding succeeding expressions, expresses a synthetic a priori proposition. Each expresses a proposition that is necessarily true regardless of any linguistic conventions adopted by anyone at any time. Moreover, each expresses a proposition that is necessarily true in the sense that no conceivable world or state of affairs could ever falsify it, whether this be a Kantian phenomenal world or a noumenal world of things-in-themselves. Therefore each expresses a proposition necessarily true of, or necessarily applicable to, any conceivable phenomenal or noumenal world containing the number of entities it refers to. At the same time, though, each expresses only a nonexistential or hypothetical proposition, since none of them asserts the existence of any entities at all. In this sense, then, it is not necessary that a proposition be factual or existential to be synthetic a priori.

Let us now turn to see what happens when we place the same interpretations on the symbols '1', '2', '3', '4', '5' as they occur in the expressions expressing the definitions or propositions of system B. For '4 = 1 + 1' we obtain (****) = ((*)(*)), for '3 = 1 + 4' (***) = ((*)(****)), for '2 = 1 + 3' (**) = ((*)(***)), and for '5 = 1 + 2' (*****) = ((*)(**)). The expressions containing asterisks are to be read in the same way, with, of course, the necessary changes, as those occurring in the preceding paragraph. Each of these expressions also expresses a synthetic a priori proposition. But in this case each of these propositions is false. Each expression may therefore be said to express a synthetic impossibility. Each expresses a proposition that is necessarily false regardless of the linguistic conventions anyone at any time might happen to adopt. Each of these propositions is necessarily false in the sense that no conceivable phenomenal or noumenal world or state of affairs could possibly exemplify it. We therefore see that, just as it is not necessary that a proposition be factual or existential to be synthetic a priori, so also it is not necessary that it be true.

But, someone might object, it has not yet been shown that any of these propositions is synthetic a priori, since it has not yet been shown that their truth or falsity are in fact independent of linguistic conventions. As a means of replying, let us see what happens when we place different interpretations on '1', '2', '3', '4', '5'. I shall therefore interpret '1' as standing for *** entities, '2' as standing for ***** entities, '3' for ** entities, '4' for * entity, and '5' for **** entities. Placing these interpretations on the symbols expressing the propositions of system A, we obtain the following results: for '2 = 1 + 1' we obtain (*****) = ((***)(***)), for '3 = 1 + 2' (**) = ((***)(*****)), for '4 = 1 + 3' (*) = ((***)(**)), and for '5 = 1 + 4' (****) = ((***)(*)). On these interpretations the first three sentences, as interpreted, turn out false, whereas the fourth, as interpreted, turns out true. Let us now place these interpretations on the symbols expressing the propositions of system B. This gives the following results: for '4 = 1 + 1' we obtain (*) = ((***)(***)), for '3 = 1 + 4' (**) = ((***)(*)), for '2 = 1 + 3' (*****) = ((***)(**)), and for '5 = 1 + 2' (****) = ((***)(*****)). On these interpretations the third sentence, as interpreted, turns out true, whereas the others, as interpreted, turn out false.

What makes the fourth sentence of system A and the third of system B turn out true, as interpreted, and the rest false, as interpreted, is the interpretation placed on them. Each sentence, as uninterpreted, is conventionally true within the system in which it occurs, so that the question of whether each, as interpreted, is true cannot be answered by determining whether they are conventionally true. Instead, it can be determined only by discovering, once an interpretation is given the sentence, whether there are the same number of asterisks immediately to the left of the symbol '=' as there are immediately to the right. Given the ordinary standard interpretation of '2 = 1 + 1', our iconic symbolization is (**) = ((*)(*)). So long as '(**)' is the iconic symbol immediately to the left of '=' and '((*)(*))' the iconic symbol immediately to the right, we necessarily have the same number of asterisks immediately to the left of '=' as we do to the right. The fact that we have the same number of asterisks in the iconic symbol '(**)' as we do in the iconic symbol '((*)(*))' is not a fact that issues merely from our definition of '2' as a symbol for which the symbol '1 + 1' may be substituted. The necessity that the first iconic symbol have the same number of asterisks as the second does not issue from any linguistic conventions we might adopt but derives instead from the nature of the iconic symbols themselves. This, I believe, might be at least part of what Peirce had in mind when he spoke of mathematicians discovering necessary truths through the construction and examination of diagrams, which for Peirce were iconic in nature.[5] This is also, I think, part of what Kant had in mind when he spoke of counting on one's fingers to confirm or to have the intuition that $7 + 5 = 12$. Kant, I believe, had in mind only interpreted systems of arithmetic when he maintained that the propositions of arithmetic are synthetic a priori. Indeed, so far as I know, to him the distinction between an interpreted and an uninterpreted system was entirely foreign. This, however, is a historical surmise that might or might not be true. The important point is that sense can be made of Kant's contention that the propositions of arithmetic are synthetic a priori only if we suppose that he was speaking only of the sentences of arithmetic as interpreted and, moreover, as interpreted in the standard or ordinary way.

Additional support for and clarification of the preceding are supplied by the following considerations. I have maintained that each of the following iconic symbols, understood in the way I have suggested, expresses a true synthetic a priori proposition: '(**) = ((*)(*))', '(***) = ((*)(**))', '(****) = ((*)(***))', '(*****) = ((*)(****))', Each of these propositions is synthetic a priori regardless of the notation and the linguistic conventions adopted to express them. Each is necessarily true because, in the iconic symbolism, there are in each case the same number of asterisks immediately to the left of the symbol '=' as there are to the right, regardless of what notation or linguistic convention we employ to express this equality. As has been seen, the sentences of system A, when given their ordinary or standard interpretation, also express these equalities. This might easily mislead one into supposing that the source of the equalities is therefore the ordinary or standard interpretation placed on the sentences of system A. It is true, as we have seen, that the interpretations thus far placed on the sentences of system B do not enable them to express these equalities, nor does the unusual interpretation that has been placed on the sentences of system A enable them to do so. It is nevertheless possible to discover an interpretation for the sentences of system B that would enable them to do so. All that is necessary is that we interpret '1' as standing for * entity, '4' as standing for ** entities, '3' for *** entities, '2' for **** entities, and '5' for ***** entities. Placing these interpretations on the sentences of system B, we obtain the following results: for '4 = 1 + 1' we obtain (**) = ((*)(*)), for '3 = 1 + 4' (***) = ((*)(**)), for '2 = 1 + 3' (****) = ((*)(***)), and for '5 = 1 + 2' (****) = ((*)(****)).

It might, however, be objected that on this interpretation of the sentences of system B we are placing the same interpretation on '1', '3', and '5' as is placed on them when the sentences of system A are given the standard interpretation. But, the objection continues, is it possible to interpret the sentences of system B in such a way that they express what I have referred to as necessary equalities while at the same time placing a nonstandard interpretation on each of the nonsyntactical symbols of system B? To this the answer is yes. To do so, however, it is necessary to do two things. One is to interpret '1' as standing either for *** entities or else for more than *** entities. This is necessary because if we interpret '1' as standing for ** entities, then, since '4 = 1 + 1' is a sentence of system B, we should have to interpret '4' as standing for **** entities, and this would require us to place the standard interpretation on '4'. The other thing it is necessary to do is to introduce equalities between numbers of asterisks other than those hitherto introduced and thus to introduce iconic symbols other than those thus far introduced. If, then, we interpret '1' as standing for *** entities, '4' as standing for *** ***, '3' for *** *** ***, '2' for *** *** *** ***, and '5' for *** *** *** *** ***, each of the sentences, as thus interpreted, of system B will express necessary equalities between entities, as the reader can see by performing the necessary calculations. (The asterisks are grouped in sets of three to make it easier to count them.) It will be noticed that on these interpretations the number of entities for which each numeral of the system stands is throughout three times as great as the number for which each stood on the previous interpretation. This means that if we divide by three the number of entities for which each numeral of the system stands on this new interpretation, we obtain the same number for which each numeral stood on the previous interpretation. Similar considerations would apply if we took some larger multiple of *, such as **** or *****, and gave the interpretations to the numerals of the system necessary to enable its interpreted sentences to express necessary equalities between numbers of entities, as the reader can see by placing the appropriate interpretations on the numerals of the system and performing the necessary calculations.

These considerations, however, afford no comfort for the conventionalist, for what they show is the reverse of what he must show. What he must establish is that these various equalities between numbers of entities are conventionally determined, in the sense that they issue from the adoption of certain linguistic conventions. But what our considerations indicate is that these equalities obtain regardless of which linguistic conventions we adopt. They therefore also indicate that, instead of the source of these equalities being the adoption of certain linguistic conventions, the interpretations we place on the symbols and sentences of a system must be tailored to the equalities if the former, as interpreted, are to apply to the latter. Thus, given that a certain interpretation is placed on such symbols and sentences, the question of whether they, as interpreted, apply to and express these equalities can be answered only by examining the equalities themselves. This examination is conducted by inspecting certain iconic symbols. If we use the iconic symbols I have been using, it consists in examining sets of asterisks to see whether there is the same number of asterisks immediately to the left of the '=' symbol as there is to the right. If there is, then the sentence in question, as thus interpreted, applies to or expresses a certain equality; if there is not, then it does not. But regardless of whether the sentence, as thus interpreted, expresses this equality, either there is or there is not the same number of asterisks immediately preceding the '=' symbol as there is immediately following it. Hence although the sentence, as thus interpreted, might express or apply to this equality, neither it nor its interpretation can be the source of the equality.

3. Geometric Necessities

So much for arithmetic. We turn now to consider geometry. The preceding considerations, with the necessary changes, apply to geometry as well as to arithmetic. One obvious difference between geometry and arithmetic is that the iconic symbols used in geometry must differ from those used in arithmetic, since the subject matter to which the sentences of geometry, as interpreted, are applied differs from that to which the sentences of arithmetic, as interpreted, are applied. Thus the iconic symbols inspected by the geometer interested in applying the interpreted sentences of Euclidean geometry are the familiar diagrams representing lines, circles, triangles, rectangles, and so on. Another difference between arithmetic and geometry worth commenting on has to do with the question of exactness or precision.

For our present purposes, the subject matter of interpreted arithmetic may be said to be equalities and inequalities between numbers of entities. Each distinct entity can easily be represented by a distinct iconic symbol. The iconic symbol I have used is an asterisk, but one could easily choose some other iconic symbol. The only limitation on our choice is that the symbol we use be such that it can function as an iconic symbol and be practically serviceable, i.e., easily constructed and manipulated. Since these iconic symbols represent any existent or thinkable entity, there is no need that they represent any specific kind of entity as opposed to others. Nor is it necessary that they do so to acquire or retain their iconic character. This character they acquire from the fact that each iconic symbol, as a distinct entity itself, represents one and only one distinct entity, which can be any existent or conceivable entity and need not be one specific kind of entity as opposed to others. Thus one asterisk represents one entity, two asterisks two entities, and so on. Given the nature of the subject matter of interpreted arithmetic and the simplicity of the iconic symbols that can be used, it is a relatively simple matter, provided that the number of entities and therefore of iconic symbols is not too great, to determine with precision whether we have an equality or an inequality. All that is necessary is that we count carefully the number of iconic symbols on each side of the '=' symbol. Someone skeptical about the possibility of acquiring certain or exact empirical knowledge might contend that we can never know with certainty that we have counted correctly. This, however, is to carry skepticism to a pointless and impractical extreme, for in actual practice we do reach a point, after a few checks to test the accuracy of our counting, at which we no longer have any doubt and at which further doubt would be unreasonable and practically pointless.

In geometry, on the other hand, the situation with respect to exactness or precision is somewhat different. This is the case because of the nature of the subject matter to which the interpreted sentences of geometry are applied. Thus the subject matter to which the interpreted sentences of Euclidean geometry are applied is such that the iconic symbols that most conveniently and also most accurately represent it are the familiar diagrams representing lines, circles, triangles, rectangles, and so on. In the case of arithmetic, as we have seen, a single iconic symbol represents any single existent or thinkable entity, two iconic symbols represent any two existent or thinkable entities, and so on, regardless of what these entities might be. This being the case, the iconic symbols of arithmetic can perform their iconic function only in terms of their number, not in terms of what may be referred to as their internal character or structure. Since, for example, a single asterisk represents any single entity that can possibly exist or be thought of, and does not represent certain existent or conceivable entities or kinds of entity to the exclusion of others, it cannot acquire its iconic function through having an internal character or structure similar to the internal character or structure of certain specific kinds of entity as opposed to others.

The situation in geometry is quite different. Its subject matter is less general and therefore less abstract than that of arithmetic. The terms and sentences of ordinary interpreted arithmetic apply to anything countable, whereas those of interpreted geometry do not. They apply only to certain countable entities and not to others. Thus 'circle', for example, as interpreted, applies to certain entities to which 'triangle' does not. The iconic symbol used to represent circles must therefore have an internal character or structure different from that of the iconic symbol used to represent triangles, since its internal character or structure must be similar to that of circles and different from that of triangles. As we shall see, it need not have an internal structure exactly similar to that of circles; but its internal character must be sufficiently similar to that of circles to enable it to function as an iconic symbol for circles and not for any of the other entities of geometry. It must therefore have a structure of a certain degree of complexity, and certainly of a greater degree of complexity than that required of a symbol if it is to function as an iconic symbol in arithmetic. But this opens the door to imprecision, for the greater the complexity of a symbol or entity, the greater the chance of imprecision in the description of it.

Thus suppose that we have a number of diagrams, some of which, so far as we can determine by inspecting them carefully, appear circular and others of which appear triangular. What is meant by saying that some appear circular and others triangular depends, at least in part, upon the definition of 'circle' and 'triangle' one accepts as one inspects them. Thus one may mean by 'circle' only a closed plane curve of such a nature that any point on it is equidistant from a point at the center, and by 'triangle' only a closed plane figure formed by three straight lines. On the other hand, one may use 'circle' and 'triangle' more precisely. Thus one may use 'circle' to refer only to a figure formed by a closed plane curve in such a way that its circumference is 3.14 times as long as its diameter, and 'triangle' to refer only to a plane figure formed by three straight lines whose internal angles contain half the number of degrees contained in a circle. Which of these two possible definitions of each term one accepts will determine whether the apparently circular and triangular diagrams are also accepted as genuinely circular or triangular. Thus suppose that I measure as carefully as I can both the ratio of the circumference of each apparently circular diagram to its diameter and also the number of degrees contained within the internal angles of each apparently triangular diagram. Suppose also that, upon doing so, I discover that the ratio of the circumference to the diameter of the various apparently circular diagrams are, respectively, 3.13, 3.15, 3.14, 3.12, and 3.16, and that the number of degrees contained in the internal angles of the apparently triangular diagrams are, respectively, 182, 179, 180, 178, and 181. If I assume that my measurements are correct, and if I accept the more precise definitions of 'circle' and 'triangle', I shall then accept only the third diagram of each group as genuinely circular or triangular and reject the others as only approximately circular or triangular. But if I accept the less precise definitions I may do either of two things. I may calculate the average of my measurements and then amend my less precise definitions so that they are transformed into the more precise definitions, i.e., I may reject the less precise definitions in favor of the more precise. If I do this, then I accept only the third diagram of each set as genuinely circular or triangular and reject the rest as only approximately circular or triangular. On the other hand, upon calculating the average of my measurements I may retain my less precise definitions and conclude only that the ratio of the circumference of a circle to its diameter is approximately 3.14 and that the internal angles of a triangle contain approximately 180 degrees.

If the more precise definitions are accepted, then the sentences "The ratio of the circumference of a circle to its diameter is 3.14" and "The internal angles of a triangle contain half the number of degrees contained in a circle" express analytic propositions. They also express analytic propositions if they express theorems of Euclidean geometry, provided that we treat each of the axioms and postulates involved in their deduction as definitions or at least as analytic and not synthetic. But, as we have seen, the fact that a sentence expresses an analytic proposition does not mean that it cannot also be used to express a synthetic proposition. The question here is therefore this: do these sentences also express synthetic propositions, and, more specifically, do they also express synthetic a priori propositions? The answer, I believe, is yes. In giving this answer, however, one might intend to make a stronger or a weaker claim. I am making only the weaker claim. This does not mean that I believe the stronger claim to be inadmissible. I do not know whether it is or not. It means only that I am much more confident of the truth of the weaker claim. The stronger claim is that each of the sentences in question expresses an exact or precise synthetic a priori proposition. Thus the first sentence may be read "The ratio of the circumference of a circle to its diameter is *precisely* 3.14" (leaving aside the obvious difficulties occasioned here by the irrationality of pi), and the second may be read "The internal angles of a triangle contain *exactly* half the number of degrees contained in a circle." Each of these sentences might express a synthetic a priori proposition. But then again they might not. I am confident neither that they do nor that they do not. Instead, I am confident only of the truth of the weaker claim. This is the claim that each of the sentences in question expresses an imprecise or inexact synthetic a priori proposition—that each expresses what may be referred to as a synthetic a priori 'approximate proposition' or 'approximation'. Thus the first sentence may be read "The ratio of the circumference of a circle to its diameter is *approximately* 3.14," and the second may be read "The internal angles of a triangle contain *approximately* half the number of degrees contained in a circle." These last two sentences require some explanation.

First, 'circle' and 'triangle', as they are used in these sentences, are used to refer to figures of a certain sort in or on a Euclidean plane or surface. 'Euclidean plane' and 'Euclidean surface', in this context, are used to refer to planes or surfaces that are flat, so far as we can determine through the most careful inspection of which we are capable. Thus these terms are used in a relatively imprecise or inexact sense. 'Circle' and 'triangle' are also used in such a sense. Thus 'circle' is to be used to refer to a figure formed by a closed plane curve, each point on the circumference of which is equidistant from a point at the center, and 'triangle' to refer to a closed plane figure formed by three straight lines, in each case so far as we can determine from the most careful inspection of which we are capable. These, or something equivalent, are the definitions of 'circle' and 'triangle' used in the synthetic a priori sentences "The ratio of the circumference of a circle to its diameter is approximately 3.14" and "The internal angles of a triangle contain approximately half the number of degrees contained in a circle."

The use of 'approximately' in these two sentences is itself imprecise, in the sense that it is to be interpreted as indicating that how close the approximation referred to in each sentence must be if the sentence is to be necessarily true is itself relatively indeterminate. Each sentence is obviously to be interpreted in such a way that the following two sentences express necessarily false propositions: "The ratio of the circumference of a circle to its diameter is 2.5" and "The internal angles of a triangle contain one-third the number of degrees contained in a circle." If we use 'circle' and 'triangle' in the way indicated in the preceding paragraph, each of these sentences expresses a necessarily false synthetic proposition, and the contradictory of each expresses a necessarily true synthetic proposition. Thus the following two sentences express true synthetic a priori propositions: "The ratio of the circumference of a circle to its diameter is not 2.5" and "The internal angles of a triangle do not contain one-third the number of degrees contained in a circle." From this it follows that the following singular sentences express necessarily false singular propositions: "The ratio of the circumference of this circle to its diameter is 2.5" and "The internal angles of this triangle contain one-third the number of degrees contained in a circle." If we use 'circle' and 'triangle' in the way indicated in the preceding paragraph, it is synthetically impossible that either of these propositions be true. This, I think, can easily be seen. But that either of the following sentences expresses a necessarily false synthetic proposition cannot so easily be seen: "The ratio of the circumference of this circle to its diameter is 3.15" and "The internal angles of this triangle contain 181 degrees." It is easy enough, that is, given that 'circle' and 'triangle' are used in the way indicated, to see that the previously mentioned singular sentences express synthetic impossibilities, but it is not at all easy to see that the latter two sentences express either synthetic necessities or synthetic impossibilities. From the necessary truth of our two synthetic a priori approximate propositions the necessary falsity of the former pair obviously follows. But neither the necessary truth nor the necessary falsity of the latter pair obviously follows; instead, they are borderline cases. So long as the sentences used to express them are interpreted as expressing synthetic a priori propositions, they cannot be seen to be either necessarily true or necessarily false. At least they cannot *easily* be seen to be one or the other. But the fact that some cases are borderline does not mean that all are. It is easy to see, given that 'circle' and 'triangle' are used in the way indicated, that it is synthetically impossible that the ratio of the circumference of any circle to its diameter be 2.5 and that the internal angles of any triangle contain one-third the number of degrees contained in a circle.

At this point it might be worth repeating that nothing in the preceding is to be interpreted as denying that any of the sentences of Euclidean geometry or of any other system of geometry are analytic. Each sentence of any of these systems of geometry can be treated as expressing an analytic proposition, either through simply defining its terms in such a way that it is true by definition or else through showing that it can be deduced from axioms or postulates that can themselves be treated as true by definition. But, again, it must also be remembered that the fact that a sentence can be used to assert an analytic proposition does not mean that it cannot also be used to assert a synthetic proposition. And in this connection it must also be remembered that many of the propositions Euclid derived as theorems of his system had been discovered by various mathematicians long before his time through constructing, inspecting, and measuring diagrams of various sorts. His great achievement consisted not so much in the discovery of these propositions as in showing how the scattered propositions discovered by previous geometers could be reduced to systematic order through deducing them from a relatively small number of definitions, axioms, and postulates.

It is perhaps also worth mentioning that in maintaining that at least some of the sentences of Euclidean geometry may be interpreted as expressing synthetic a priori propositions I do not intend to assert either that space as it is in itself is necessarily Euclidean or that the actual space of our experience is necessarily Euclidean. Space as it is in itself, taken completely in abstraction from what occupies it, is neither Euclidean nor non-Euclidean. What is Euclidean or non-Euclidean is not space as it is in itself taken in abstraction from what occupies it but rather actual or imaginary diagrams and figures and the two-dimensional and three-dimensional surfaces, shapes, and paths of actual and imaginary physical objects. If one abstracts completely from such diagrams, figures, surfaces, shapes, and paths, nothing remains that could be either Euclidean or non-Euclidean. Thus to say that space as it is in itself is either Euclidean or non-Euclidean can at best be only a misleading metaphorical way of saying that what occupies space is one or the other. This does not mean that space, taken completely in abstraction from what occupies it, is not real. Whether it is real and, if so, in what sense it is real are questions into which we cannot enter here. Similar considerations apply to the space of our experience, if by this is meant something different from space as it is in itself. Such space too, taken completely in abstraction from the diagrams and figures we construct or imagine and the surfaces, shapes, and paths of the objects we experience, is neither Euclidean nor non-Euclidean.

It will perhaps be remembered that I have maintained that the fact that a proposition is synthetic a priori does not mean that it is also factual or existential. Moreover, the fact that some of the sentences of Euclidean geometry can be interpreted as expressing synthetic a priori propositions does not mean that the sentences of non-Euclidean systems cannot also be interpreted in this way. Indeed, one might well argue that the fact that sentences that are analytic in one system, the Euclidean, can be interpreted as expressing synthetic a priori propositions is at least a prima facie reason for supposing that at least some of the sentences that are analytic in certain non-Euclidean systems can also be interpreted in this way. But regardless of whether they can be so interpreted, the fact is that the question of whether the actual space of our experience is Euclidean, in the only sense in which such a question has meaning, is an empirical question. This question can be answered only by discovering whether various terms of Euclidean and non-Euclidean geometries, as interpreted, denote anything actual and by discovering whether various interpreted sentences of Euclidean and non-Euclidean systems apply to actual states of affairs. As is well known, the answer seems to be that in certain respects actual space is Euclidean, in the sense that various of the terms and sentences of Euclidean geometry do apply, at least approximately, to various shapes and paths of actual objects, and that in certain respects it is non-Euclidean, in the sense that various terms and sentences of certain non-Euclidean systems also apply, again at least approximately, to various other shapes and paths of actual objects.

4. Synthetic Necessities and Impossibilities

Thus far we have devoted our attention primarily to the question of whether any of the sentences of various systems of mathematics can be interpreted as expressing synthetic a priori propositions. We turn now to consider briefly the question of whether any nonmathematical sentences can be given such an interpretation. If there is at least one such sentence, then conventionalism with respect to such sentences is false, since the conventionalist makes the extreme claim that there are *no* nonmathematical sentences that can be so interpreted. I shall therefore consider only one such sentence, namely, "No single area of a visual sense field can be both red and blue at the same time." I speak of visual sense fields rather than surfaces of physical objects to avoid certain irrelevant possibilities such as that of a surface of a physical object appearing red to one person and blue to another. As Waismann maintains, the sentence in question can be interpreted as expressing an analytic proposition. To give it such an interpretation, all one need do is adopt a rule to the effect that no single area of any visual sense field is to be labeled 'blue' so long as it is labeled 'red' and vice versa. But the adoption of such a rule leaves completely unanswered the question of whether any area of any visual sense field characterized by any of the shades of the color ordinarily referred to by means of 'red' can also at the same time be characterized by any of the shades of the color ordinarily referred to by means of 'blue'. This question ultimately can be answered only through having some acquaintance in experience with the colors ordinarily referred to by 'red' and 'blue'. Such acquaintance shows that no single area of any sense field can possibly be characterized at the same time both by some shade of red and also by some shade of blue, regardless of whether we adopt a rule to the effect that no single area of any sense field is to be labeled 'blue' so long as it is also labeled 'red'. Such acquaintance could afford a reason for adopting such a rule, but to say that the rule is the source of the incompatibility of red and blue is to get things backward.

We turn now to consider an objection to much of the argument of this chapter. This is that even if the considerations advanced were sufficient to show that certain sentences, when interpreted in certain ways, express objective analytic necessities, they are not sufficient to show that these sentences express synthetic necessities. Thus a defender of Lewis's position might argue that although the considerations advanced in this chapter establish the inadequacy of conventionalism, they are not sufficient to establish the inadequacy of Lewis's position, which admits that there are objective as well as conventional necessities but denies that there are any synthetic necessities on the ground that all objective necessities are analytic. Therefore, the objection continues, it is not enough to show that certain sentences, as interpreted, may be used to express objective necessities; instead, it is also necessary to show that they can be used to express synthetic necessities and not merely analytic objective necessities. And to establish this it is necessary to show that these sentences are not reducible to expressions of the law of identity. Nor, the defender of Lewis might continue, is it sufficient to point out that these sentences do not express identical propositions, for Lewis would grant that they do not, and, as we have seen, the fact that they do not does not mean that they are not reducible to the law of identity, since all nonidentical analytic propositions can be reduced to this law.

The reply to this objection is contained, at least implicity, in what has already been said. It will be recalled that I have argued that the source of the reducibility of a nonidentical analytic proposition to the law of identity, and its contradictory to a formal expression that violates the law of contradiction, is the definition of the subject term of the sentence expressing the proposition. This means that the source of the analyticity of a nonidentical analytic proposition is the linguistic decision or convention governing the use of the subject term of the sentence expressing the proposition. And this in turn means that all nonidentical analytic propositions are conventional rather than objective necessities. Now what I have argued is that certain sentences may be interpreted as expressing synthetic a priori propositions. This, however, does not preclude the possibility of interpreting them as expressing nonidentical analytic propositions; on the contrary, any sentence that may be interpreted as expressing a synthetic a priori proposition may also be interpreted as expressing a nonidentical analytic proposition. And, to repeat what by now is a familiar refrain, the fact that a sentence may be interpreted as expressing a nonidentical analytic proposition does not mean that it may not also be interpreted as expressing a synthetic a priori proposition. But no sentence that may be interpreted as expressing a synthetic a priori proposition may also be interpreted as expressing an identical proposition, since no such sentence has the form "All A are A" but can be reduced to this form only by adopting an appropriate linguistic convention governing the use of its subject term.

I have already given a number of examples of sentences that may be interpreted as expressing either nonidentical analytic propositions or synthetic a priori propositions but not as expressing identical propositions, such as "$2 = 1 + 1$," "The internal angles of a triangle contain half the number of degrees contained in a circle," and "No area of a visual sense field can be both red and blue." Each of these sentences may be interpreted as expressing a nonidentical analytic proposition simply by adopting the appropriate linguistic convention governing the use of '2', 'triangle', and 'red'. Only through doing so can each be reduced to an expression of the law of identity. But if we do not adopt these conventions but instead interpret these terms as suggested above, then these sentences express synthetic a priori propositions; or if, in addition to adopting these conventions we also interpret these terms as suggested above, then these sentences express synthetic a priori as well as nonidentical analytic propositions. Thus, for example, if we interpret 'triangle' as meaning, by definition, only a three-sided closed plane rectilinear figure, and not a three-sided closed plane rectilinear figure the internal angles of which contain half the number of degrees contained in a circle, the sentence "The internal angles of a triangle contain half the number of degrees contained in a circle" will express a synthetic a priori proposition. This is the case for two reasons. First, there is a synthetically necessary connection between, on the one hand, being a three-sided closed plane rectilinear figure and, on the other, having internal angles that contain half the number of degrees contained in a circle. Second, the contradictory of this sentence, given this interpretation of 'triangle', expresses, not a self-inconsistent proposition, but, instead, what may be termed a 'synthetic impossibility'. This is to say that the contradictory of this sentence, given this interpretation of 'triangle', is not reducible to a sentence of the form "Some A are not A" but rather expresses a necessarily false synthetic proposition to the effect that something can be a three-sided closed plane rectilinear figure without having internal angles containing half the number of degrees contained in a circle.

Since a synthetic a priori proposition is not reducible to the law of identity, its necessity cannot be established by accomplishing such a reduction. On the contrary, given its truth, its necessity can be established (to oversimplify somewhat) only through recognizing that nothing can have the property indicated by the subject term of the sentence expressing the proposition unless it also has the property indicated by the predicate term of that sentence. Similarly, since the contradictory of a true synthetic a priori proposition cannot be reduced to a proposition the form of which violates the law of contradiction, its necessary falsity cannot be established through accomplishing such a reduction. Instead (again to oversimplify somewhat), its necessary falsity can be established only through recognizing that anything that has the property indicated by the subject term of the sentence expressing the proposition necessarily has the property indicated by the predicate term of that sentence. It is only in these ways that synthetic necessities and impossibilities can be recognized and established.

Notes

1. Clarence Irving Lewis, *An Analysis of Knowledge and Valuation* (La Salle, Ill.: Open Court Publishing Co., 1946), pp. 48–50.

2. F. Waismann, *The Principles of Linguistic Philosophy*, ed. R. Harré (New York: St. Martin's Press, 1965), p. 68.

3. *An Analysis of Knowledge and Valuation*, p. 35.

4. *The Principles of Linguistic Philosophy*, p. 44.

5. *The Philosophy of Peirce: Selected Writings*, ed. Justus Buchler (London: Routledge & Kegan Paul, 1940), pp. 135–39.

3
Tokens, Types, and Meaning

THE term *proposition* was used throughout the last chapter. This was done for two reasons. One is that it was necessary to distinguish between assertable contents, judgments, and ideas or thoughts that are true or false on the one hand and the sentences used to express them on the other. The other is that it was necessary that we have some term to refer conveniently to the former in contrast to the latter, and for this purpose I chose 'proposition'. In introducing this term it was indicated that its use was not in any way intended to assert or presuppose the existence of propositions as a distinct irreducible ontological category. It was also indicated that the question of whether we do need to assert or presuppose the existence of propositions would be considered later. This question, however, is only part of a larger question we shall consider. Various philosophers have distinguished between sentences, statements, judgments, beliefs, propositions, facts, and states of affairs. The larger question is this: Do each of these constitute an indispensable irreducible ontological category or can some be dispensed with by reducing them to others? This question has to do with ontological simplicity.

1. Simplicity

Ontological simplicity is to be distinguished from aesthetic simplicity. The former is connected with truth, the latter with beauty, and, despite Keats, these are distinct. Someone with an austere aesthetic sensibility prefers a world populated with as few things and kinds of things as possible, whereas someone with a baroque or rococo sensibility prefers a world containing as many things and kinds of things as possible. Accordingly, in making an art object or in doing metaphysics a person with an austere aesthetic sensibility will tend to endeavor to produce something as simple as possible, whereas a person with a baroque or rococo sensibility will tend to attempt to produce something as ornate and as embellished as possible. Which of these two aesthetic sensibilities is preferable in matters of art and beauty has nothing to do with the question of simplicity in metaphysics. An ornate metaphysical system embellished with a vast multiplicity of categories and kinds of entity might well be preferred by someone with a baroque sensibility to a more austere system containing far fewer categories and types of thing and might indeed from an aesthetic point of view be more beautiful than the latter. Such a system might also be preferable from a religious or moral point of view, since it might be more compatible with the satisfaction of certain legitimate religious or moral interests. Indeed, one might even argue that a baroque sensibility is morally preferable in itself to an austere sensibility, on the ground that the former manifests a generous disposition that takes joy in the existence of a plethora of things and the latter a niggardly temperament that begrudges the existence of a well-populated world.

The preceding is not intended as an argument to the effect that in fact a baroque sensibility or temperament is aesthetically, religiously, or morally preferable to one more austere. Whether in fact it is so preferable is not here our concern. But even if it were, simplicity would still in metaphysics be preferable to the baroque and the rococo. This means that any attempt to justify metaphysical simplicity on aesthetic, religious, or moral grounds rests on a questionable foundation unless it is shown that simplicity is preferable aesthetically, religiously, or morally to the baroque and the rococo. But even if simplicity were preferable from these other points of view it would not follow that it is also preferable from a metaphysical point of view. From the fact that simplicity furthers more fully aesthetic, religious, or moral interests it would not follow that it also more fully furthers metaphysical interests. If, that is, from an aesthetic point of view an artist follows the maxim of not multiplying entities beyond necessity, for him this maxim will doubtless mean "Do not multiply entities beyond what is needed to produce a pleasing aesthetic object." This, however, is not what for the metaphysician this maxim means, since as a metaphysician his object is not to produce a pleasing aesthetic object. It is instead to discover the truth about some aspect of God, man, or the world.

This last means that the search for simplicity in metaphysics is to be justified ultimately in terms of the metaphysician's concern for truth. This justification differs from a justification in terms of religious, moral, or pragmatic concerns. We might have religious, moral, or pragmatic reasons for believing that something or other is the case, such as that God exists or that people are morally responsible for much of what they do. Such reasons are doubtless sometimes good reasons. But even if they are never such, a person might have a good moral reason, and indeed might even have a moral obligation, not to attempt to convince another that a certain belief the other holds is false, even though he has good reason to believe and be convinced that the belief in question is false. Thus suppose that one person, Thomas, has good reason to believe and is in fact convinced that another, Peter, is multiplying entities beyond necessity in believing that God exists. Let us suppose also that Thomas is correct from a metaphysical point of view and that in fact God does not exist. But let us also suppose that Thomas has good reason to believe and is also convinced that if Peter ceased believing in the existence of God his life would be completely shattered. If so, then Thomas has a good moral reason, indeed even a moral obligation, not to attempt to convince Peter that his belief is false. Although the holding of true beliefs and the possession of knowledge sometimes are good, such goods are not the only goods and from a moral point of view sometimes must be sacrificed when their existence is incompatible with the existence of greater goods. And that the prevention of the shattering of a person's life is a greater good than his not holding a false belief that God exists (assuming for our present purposes that it is false) seems unquestionable.

If the preceding considerations are acceptable, then there might be good religious, moral, or pragmatic reasons for multiplying entities beyond metaphysical necessity, for not attempting to convince others that certain of their beliefs are false, and even for not endeavoring oneself to discover certain truths if the consequences of their discovery and acceptance would probably be worse than those of remaining ignorant. In metaphysics, however, taken in abstraction from religious, moral, and pragmatic concerns, our concern is simply to discover the truth about various aspects of God, man, or the world. Insofar as this is our concern we must seek simplicity and endeavor not to multiply entities beyond metaphysical necessity. This kind of necessity differs from religious, moral, or pragmatic necessity. To satisfy certain religious, moral, or pragmatic interests it might sometimes be necessary to multiply entities beyond metaphysical necessity. If so, then from the standpoint of those interests such multiplication of entities is religiously, morally, or pragmatically necessary. This, however, does not mean that a multiplication of entities necessary to satisfy such interests is also necessary from the standpoint of metaphysics.

In metaphysics to multiply an entity beyond necessity is to posit or presuppose its reality even though we neither experience it nor need to make such a posit or presupposition in order adequately to explain or account for our experience or thought. Even though neither of these conditions is satisfied there might be religious, moral, or pragmatic justifications for positing or presupposing the reality of certain entities. But in metaphysics our only justification for doing so is either that we experience the entity in question or else have good reason to believe that unless we do posit or presuppose its reality we cannot account adequately for our experience or thought. If so, then in metaphysics we have no reason to believe that entities of type a exist unless we either experience them or else cannot account adequately for our experience or thought unless we do posit or presuppose their existence. Thus suppose that we can think of entities of three distinct types—type a, type b, and type c. Suppose also that we experience entities of type a but not any of types b or c. If so, we have reason to believe that entities of type a exist but not that entities of type b or type c exist. If, however, there is some aspect of our experience or thought that can be accounted for by positing the existence of entities of type b, then we have reason to believe that entities of type b as well as those of type a exist. But if there is no aspect of our experience or thought that can be accounted for by positing entities of type c, then we have no reason to believe that such entities exist. Since we have no reason to believe that entities of type c exist, a theory T_2 that posits their existence as well as the existence of entities of type b ought to be rejected in favor of a theory T_1 that posits only the existence of entities of the latter type. The reason for this is not aesthetic. As was said above, someone with baroque or rococo aesthetic sensibilities might well prefer T_2 to T_1 precisely because T_2 is more complex and posits the existence of entities of two distinct types rather than only one. Instead, the reason we ought to prefer T_1 to T_2 is that T_2 accounts for nothing not accounted for by T_1 and thus posits needlessly the existence of entities of a type in the existence of which we have no reason to believe. Theory T_2 thus multiplies entities beyond metaphysical necessity. It is for this reason, rather than for any aesthetic reason, that of two theories that equally account adequately for the data to be explained the simpler is to be preferred. The more complex of the two theories posits the existence of entities of a type in the existence of which we have no reason to believe, so that we have no reason to accept the more complex theory and some reason to accept the simpler. Here simplicity is preferable for metaphysical reasons.

We turn now to apply these considerations to the question of whether it is necessary to posit the existence of propositions and, more generally, to the question of whether it is necessary to treat sentences, statements, judgments, beliefs, propositions, facts, and states of affairs as indispensable irreducible ontological categories. Does each of these constitute such a category or can one or more be dispensed with by reducing it to some one or to some combination of the others? To answer this question it is necessary to consider the nature of each. We begin with a consideration of the nature and ontological status of sentences.

2. The Ontological Status of Tokens and Types

Sentences are either types or tokens. Considered as tokens, the following two sentences are two sentences. "The book is red." "The book is red." Considered as a type, only one sentence has been written. Thus two tokens of the same type have been written. But taken as a type, one sentence has been written twice. Tokens might, but need not, be sensible. The preceding two tokens are sensible, since they are visible. And if someone were to utter aloud a token of the same type it too would be sensible, since it would be audible. But tokens need not be sensible, since someone in thinking silently might use a sentence-token that has never been written or uttered, and such a token would be neither visible nor audible. Types, on the other hand, are never sensible and thus are never visible or audible. They are, however, thinkable. Thus I can think of the type-sentence 'The book is red' as being distinguishable from any of its tokens. This I can do even though it be necessary that I think of or at least use some token of this type as I think of the type. Visible tokens, since they are visible, are spatial. Audible tokens too may be said to be spatial in the sense that they exist or occur at the places at which they are audible. Insensible tokens, however, are not spatial, although the person who uses them in silent thought is in space. Sensible tokens are also temporal, since they exist or occur in time. Insensible tokens are also temporal, at least in the sense that their occurrence or use in acts of silent thinking, like such acts, is temporal. Types, on the other hand, are temporal or spatial only through their tokens. Thus the sentence-type 'The book is red' did not exist before people spoke English and will no longer exist when no visible tokens of it any longer exist and when no one any longer utters an audible token of it or uses any of its insensible tokens in thinking silently. So long, however, as sensible tokens of it exist and people in thinking silently use its tokens it too may be said to exist. It may also be said to exist at those places at which its sensible tokens exist and at those places occupied by the people who in thinking silently use its tokens. It is in these senses that types exist spatially and temporally through their tokens. We may go further and say that if no sensible token of a possible type ever exists and if no one in thinking silently ever uses a token of that possible type, then neither does it exist.

This last, however, does not mean that types are nothing over and above their tokens and are reducible without remainder to the latter. Types are not identical with tokens, since types have properties tokens do not have and vice versa, and no two entities can be identical if one has some property the other does not have. A type, for example, has tokens, whereas no token or collection of tokens does. A token, that is, is a token of a type, but no token can be a token of another token. And although a token is a member of a collection or class of tokens of the same type, its relationship to the collection is that of a member to a class and not that of token to type, which means that the relationship of a collection of tokens of a certain type to the particular members of the collection is that of a class to its members and not that of a type to its token. A token, that is, is a member of the class of tokens of its type and not a token of that class, and a class of tokens of a certain type, although it has as its membership the tokens of that type, is not itself the type of which they are the tokens. A token, then, is a token of a type and a member of a class of tokens of the same type; and a class of tokens of a certain type, although it is a collection of tokens of that type, is itself neither a token nor the type of token of which its members are the tokens. In addition, no type can be a token of another type. Although a species of type can be a specific form of a more general type, this does not mean that a type is a token of a type. Thus although the species of declarative sentence-types is a specific form of the genus consisting of sentence-types, this does not mean that any given sentence-type is a token of any specific or generic sentence-type. Instead, the relationship of a type to the species of type of which it is a type is analogous to the relationship of a determinate species of color such as crimson to the generic color such as red of which it is a determinate species. Thus although tokens are particular instances of types and particular members of the class of tokens consisting of those instances, types are not particulars but instead are analogous to universals.

The analogy between types and universals, along with the question of whether types are not merely analogous to, but in fact are, universals of a certain sort, will be pursued further later on. For the present it is sufficient to note that although their tokens are particulars they themselves are neither particulars nor classes of particulars consisting of their tokens. It will be helpful here, however, to press a bit further the analogy between types and tokens on the one hand and universals and their particular instances on the other. We shall see later that a particular instance of a universal is the type of particular it is because of the nature of the universal of which it is an instance. So also a token is the type of token it is because of the nature of the type of which it is a token. The token 'The book is red' is a different particular from both the token 'The book is red' and the token 'The book is green'. These three tokens are different particulars because they exist at different places and come into being at different times. But the first two tokens are the same in type and differ in type from the third. This fact cannot be accounted for simply by appealing to the fact that they are three distinct particulars existing at different places and coming into being at different times, for in these respects the first and second tokens are as distinct as particulars from one another as they are from the third. It can instead be accounted for only by appealing to the fact that the first two tokens are tokens of the same type whereas the third is a token of a different type.

The first two are tokens of the same type because they are composed of tokens of the same four type-words appearing in the same order, whereas in the third a token of a different type-word occurs as the last word-token. This means that two or more token-sentences can be tokens of the same type-sentence if and only if they are composed of tokens of the same type-words appearing in the same order. They are not composed of the same token-words. The token-words of one token-sentence are different tokens from those of another token-sentence. Nor can the difference between two type-sentences be explained by saying that their tokens are composed of different token-words, since two tokens of the same type-sentence are also composed of different token-words. Some reference to type-words is therefore necessary if we are to explain either (1) what makes two tokens of the same type-sentence tokens of the same type or (2) what makes two tokens of different type-sentences tokens of different types. This means that just as without tokens there could be no types, so also without types there could be no tokens. Neither is reducible to the other, and each is necessary to the being of the other.

Someone with nominalistic tendencies might, however, object that this conclusion is reached too quickly. It is important for someone with such proclivities, not only that such a conclusion not be reached too quickly, but also that it not be reached at all. Strictly speaking, the nominalist, as distinguished from the conceptualist, maintains that universals are names or words of a certain sort, whereas the conceptualist holds that they are concepts of a certain sort. This distinction is supported by the etymological consideration that the term *nominalism* was developed from the Latin term for *name*. Both positions agree that there are no extramental universals and thus that all real extramental entities are particulars. We shall consider conceptualism later. Here we shall consider only the question of what the ontological status of names or words must be for the nominalist, given his contentions that only particulars exist and that universals are only names or words of a certain sort. Since he admits that names or words exist, consistency would seem to require that he maintain also that they, like all other existent entities, are particulars. Thus for him universal names or words must be particulars of a certain sort, differing from singular words or names such as proper names by virtue of the fact that they, unlike the latter, represent, apply to, or can be predicated of a multiplicity of particulars. But if all names or words, regardless of whether they be universal or singular, are particulars, then types must be reducible to tokens, since types, unlike tokens, are not particulars.

It is hard, however, to see how a reduction of types to tokens can be accomplished. It would mean that all sentences and words are particulars. Thus the sentence 'The book is red' would be one particular and the sentence 'The book is red' would be another distinct particular. This, however, would conflict with the way in which we ordinarily think and speak, since ordinarily we should think and say that in the previous sentence one and the same sentence has been mentioned twice, not that two distinct sentences have been mentioned once each. Thus if the type/token distinction were in effect rejected by attempting to reduce types to tokens, we should be unable to use or mention the same sentence or word twice. We should, of course, be able to think of or refer to the same sentence or word twice, since we can think of or refer to the same particular twice. But we could not use or mention the same sentence twice in thinking of or referring to a sentence twice. Thus although I could think twice of the first mention of 'The book is red' in the sentence above, I could not use or mention that sentence again, so that in the present sentence the occurrence of 'The book is red' would be an occurrence of a distinct sentence from the first occurrence of 'The book is red' in the sentence above. Although 'The book is red' could be used in the present sentence to refer to and to mention the first occurrence of 'The book is red' in the sentence above, 'The book is red' as it occurs in the present sentence would be a different sentence from the sentence 'The book is red' as it occurs in the sentence above. This would mean that the same sentence could not be used on one occasion and mentioned on another. Instead, one sentence, 'The book is red', would be used to say something about the book in question, whereas a different sentence, 'The book is red', would be used to mention the first sentence. Although this does not mean that the use/mention distinction depends upon the type/token distinction in such a way that it too would be eliminated if the latter were, it does mean that one and the same sentence could not be used twice, mentioned twice, or used on one occasion and mentioned on another.

Moreover, if the type/token distinction were eliminated so that in effect tokens alone and not types exist, the same word could not be spelled either in the same or in different ways on two occasions of its use or mention. Thus in the tokens of 'The book is red' in the previous paragraph the word 'red' would not be spelled in the same way each time it occurs. This is the case because if the type/token distinction were eliminated the same word would not occur several times; instead, we should have a number of different words, rather than tokens of the same type-word, all spelled in the same way. In addition, if the type/token distinction were eliminated the same word could not be spelled differently on two occasions of its use. Thus *color*, spelled without the *u* in the American way, would be a different word from *colour*, spelled with a *u* in the British way. Finally, eliminate the type/token distinction and it becomes impossible for the same word to be spelled correctly on one occasion of its use and incorrectly on another, since without type-words we should simply have one word spelled in one way and another spelled in another. Thus the inscription *commited* would not be a misspelled token of the type-word *committed* but would instead be a different word spelled in a different way from another distinct word *committed*. It would also be a distinct word from another word, *commited*, spelled in the same way.

In addition, if the type/token distinction were eliminated the same sentence could not be used on different occasions to express either the same or different ideas, judgments, or beliefs or to state either the same or different propositions or facts. Thus I could not use the same type-sentence, 'The book is red', to make the same statement on two different occasions about the same book but instead should be using two different sentences rather than two different tokens of the same type-sentence. Nor could I, to revert to one of the themes of the previous chapter, use the same sentence on one occasion to assert an analytic and on another to assert a synthetic proposition. Instead, I should be using two different sentences, one to assert an analytic, the other to assert a synthetic proposition. Nor could the same word have two different meanings. Thus the same word 'red' could not have two different meanings, as in 'The book is red' and 'Lenin was red', since the same word would not occur in these two sentences. If, that is, there are no type-words, then what would be tokens of the same type if there were type-words would instead be different words with different meanings rather than uses of the same type-words with different meanings. Again, eliminate type-words and what would be tokens of the same type if there were type-words become different words with the same meaning and thus synonyms. Thus 'red' in 'This book is red' and 'red' in 'That book is red', since they would be different words with the same meaning, would be synonyms. If, then, there were only tokens and no types the same word could not have different meanings, and many words would be synonymous that we should not ordinarily think to be so.

Further, if there were only tokens and no types, then what would be a token of a type if there were type-words would have to be assigned a meaning on what would be each occasion of its use if there were type-words. Since, that is, 'red' in 'This book is red' would be a different word from 'red' in 'That book is red'—indeed, since 'red' in 'The book is red' would be a different word from 'red' in 'The book is red'—it would be necessary to assign a meaning to 'red' each time it is used. Otherwise it would have no meaning. To this the nominalist might respond that this would not in fact be necessary, on the ground that it would suffice to indicate that all words falling within the class of words sounded or spelled in a certain way are to be used in certain ways in certain contexts. Thus all words sounded and spelled as 'red' is are to be used in certain ways in certain contexts, so that it is not necessary to assign a meaning to each such word as it is used. In certain contexts such words are to be used to refer to a color of a certain kind, in others to refer to a political persuasion of a certain sort. Thus instead of saying that a certain meaning is assigned the type-word 'red' that governs the use of tokens of this type, the nominalist could say that a certain meaning is assigned in advance to all words sounded or spelled as 'red' is sounded or spelled, and instead of treating all such words as tokens of the same type he could treat them as different words having the same meaning and thus as being synonymous terms.

There seems, however, to be little to recommend such a way of describing the assignment of meaning to words. It would still conflict with the ways in which we ordinarily think and speak of words and their meanings and would not avoid the objections presented above. It would also, as presented, be incomplete if not inconsistent, taken as a nominalist account of the assignment of meanings to words. This is the case because it treats all words sounded and spelled as 'red' is as having the same meaning in certain contexts. Although each such word would be a distinct and different word, all would nonetheless have the same meaning. The meaning of each would therefore be common to all. It therefore would not itself be a particular but would instead be analogous to a universal or type, if indeed it would not in fact be a universal or type of a certain sort. Thus in eliminating type-words the nominalist would still be left with something that is not itself a particular, namely the meaning common to the words sounded or spelled in a certain way. To complete his nominalist program he would therefore need to show that there are no such common meanings. He would need to show, for example, that in the sentences 'This triangle is isosceles' and 'This triangle is isosceles' the words 'triangle' and 'triangle' do not, indeed cannot, have the same meaning. Although their meanings might be exactly alike, they cannot be the same; although, that is, the meaning of 'triangle' in the first sentence mentioned in the previous sentence is three-sided closed plane rectilinear figure and the meaning of 'triangle' in the second sentence mentioned is also three-sided closed plane rectilinear figure, the second meaning, although it might be exactly like the first, cannot be the same as the first in the sense of being identical with it. The nominalist, in short, must show that although two words can have meanings that are exactly alike, they cannot have the same meaning. He must therefore show that if two words are synonymous their synonymy cannot consist in their having the same meaning but consists instead in their having different meanings that are exactly alike.

That this can be shown is, to say the least, very much to be doubted. To do so it would be necessary to present some reason for maintaining that although two words, or two tokens of the same type, can have meanings that are exactly alike, they cannot have the same meaning. If two particulars, such as two pennies, were exactly alike, some reason could be given for claiming that they are nonetheless two particulars rather than one, such as that one has a different spatiotemporal location than the other. Such a reason, however, cannot be given for saying that the meanings of two words or of two tokens of the same type, though exactly alike, are two meanings rather than the same meaning. The token of 'triangle' occurring in the token-sentence 'This triangle is isosceles' is a different particular from the token of 'triangle' occurring in the token-sentence 'This triangle is isosceles' because they have different spatial locations. But if these tokens have exactly similar meanings but not the same meaning, the difference between these meanings cannot consist in the fact that the meaning of one has a different spatiotemporal location from that of the other. Although the two tokens have different spatial locations their meanings do not, since the latter, as distinct from the tokens, are not located in space at all. But if the difference in the meanings of these two tokens does not consist in a difference in their spatiotemporal locations, in what does it consist? If we assume that the meaning of each token is three-sided closed plane rectilinear figure, how does the meaning of either, as distinguished from the token of which it is the meaning, differ from that of the other? I suggest that it does not differ in the least, which, of course, is what we have been assuming throughout. But if the meaning of either token does not differ in the least from the meaning of the other, why claim that there are two meanings rather than one? Is not the nominalist, in his zeal not to multiply entities beyond necessity by reducing all categories of entity to the category of the particular, himself guilty in this case of multiplying meanings beyond necessity, just as, in his zeal to dispense with types in favor of tokens, he is guilty of multiplying words and sentences beyond necessity?

As distinguished from the nominalist, the conceptualist admits the existence not only of universal or common names or terms but also the existence of universal mental entities such as concepts. The realist admits the existence of everything the existence of which is also admitted by the conceptualist, but goes further than the latter does by also admitting the existence of extramental universals, the existence of which the conceptualist denies. At first glance it might seem that the conceptualist is confronted with difficulties similar to those facing the nominalist. For if types and meanings are universals or at least analogous to universals, yet are not mental entities such as concepts, then are they not extramental universals or at least extramental entities analogous to universals? And if they are, then does not the realist alone, as distinguished from the conceptualist, escape the difficulties confronting the nominalist discussed above?

The answer to these questions turns upon what we mean by 'mental' and 'extramental'. If we mean by 'mental' only phenomena such as sensations, feelings, emotions, perceptions, judgments, beliefs, and so forth, then types and meanings are not mental, since they are not phenomena of these sorts. On the other hand, to say of an entity that it is extramental may mean that if it exists it does so independently of the existence or occurrence of mental phenomena such as those mentioned above and of mental acts of any kind. In this sense of the term, types and meanings are not extramental, since they would not exist if no mental acts occurred. Although they are neither mental acts nor mental phenomena of the sorts mentioned above, they nonetheless depend for their existence upon the occurrence of mental acts and in this sense are mental rather than extramental entities. As such, their existence may consistently be admitted by the conceptualist even though they be universals or analogous to universals rather than particulars, since he denies only the existence of the extramental universals the existence of which the realist asserts. And to escape the difficulties confronting the nominalist canvassed above it is not necessary to assert the existence of extramental universals; instead, it is sufficient to recognize, as the conceptualist can consistently do, that types and meanings are not particulars. Thus if realism, as distinguished from conceptualism, is to be defended adequately, it must be shown that universals exist or have being independently of the existence or occurrence of any mental acts or phenomena of any sort. Although word-types and sentence-types are not concepts, their existence does depend upon the occurrence of mental acts and the possession of concepts, and for this reason they are not universals of the sort the existence or being of which the realist is interested in establishing even though they are not particulars. We shall discuss realism in some detail later on.

As was mentioned above, tokens, as contrasted with types and meanings, are particulars, and visible and audible tokens are also sensible. Moreover, taken in abstraction from their meanings and the types of which they are tokens, sensible tokens would still be sensible. In order, however, for a sensible particular to be a token it is necessary not only that it be sensible but also that it be a token of a type. As was said above, without types there could be no tokens, just as without tokens there could be no types. Thus what makes a given sensible particular a token, and a token of the type it is, is the type of which it is the token. Considered completely in abstraction from the type of which it is a token, and thus completely in abstraction from its nature as a token, a given sensible particular might be, indeed usually if not always is, a physical entity and as such is extramental. But considered as a token it is not a physical entity and nothing more. Instead, considered as a token it is considered as a token of a type. As such, it cannot be extramental, since it acquires its status as a token only as a consequence of a mental act consisting ultimately of a decision to assign some meaning to sensible physical entities of a certain type. Without such a mental act or decision a sensible physical entity would remain only an extramental particular; but as a consequence of such an act or decision it is transformed into something more than an extramental sensible physical particular—into a token of a certain type with a certain meaning.

Indeed, it is only as a consequence of such acts or decisions that what otherwise would be only a group of sensible physical particulars are transformed into and seen as a single particular. Thus considered completely in abstraction from its status as a token, 'The book is red' is not a single particular but rather a group of four particulars, 'The', 'book', 'is', and 'red'. What transforms these four distinct particulars into one particular is our treating or taking them as together constituting a token of the type-sentence 'The book is red'. Unless we so treat or take them, they remain four distinct particulars, and if we no longer treat or take 'The book is red' as a token of the type 'The book is red' it dissolves into a group of four distinct particulars. This means that 'The book is red', like any other sentence-token consisting of more than one token-word, since it acquires its status as a distinct particular only through being treated or taken as a token of a type, and thus only as a consequence of a mental act, is not an extramental particular. It is only the distinct token-words constituting the token-sentence that are extramental particulars. Not even this, however, is strictly the case, since considerations analogous to those just advanced in connection with token-sentences apply also to token-words. Thus the printed word 'red', taken completely in abstraction from its status as a token of the type-word 'red', is not a single distinct particular but rather a group of three distinct particulars, 'r', 'e', and 'd'. What transforms them into a single particular, 'red', is our treating or taking them as together constituting a token of the type-word 'red'. It is therefore only token-letters, not token-words, that are extramental particulars, since a collection of token-letters is transformed into a single distinct particular only through our treating or taking them as together constituting a token of a certain type, and thus only as a consequence of a mental act. Similar considerations apply even to certain token-letters, such as lowercase tokens of 'i'. Taken completely in abstraction from its status as a token, 'i' is not a single particular but two particulars, one of which is a dot. It is transformed into a single particular only through treating or taking it as a token of the type-letter 'i'.

But although some sensible tokens, taken completely in abstraction from their types and meanings and thus in abstraction from their status as tokens, would not be distinct particulars, others would be. Thus 'red' as sounded would still be a distinct particular even when taken in such abstraction. Sounded token-sentences consisting of more than one word or syllable, however, would not be. What transforms the series of distinct particular sounds uttered when a token of 'The book is red' is spoken into a single particular is our taking or intending such a series as a spoken token of the type-sentence 'The book is red'. For someone who utters or understands an utterance of a token of 'The book is red' the spoken token is, or at least can be, taken as a single distinct particular. But when one does not understand a spoken language it is difficult if not impossible for him to determine which of the distinct particular sounds he hears constitute distinct particular spoken token-words and token-sentences and which do not. He will doubtless believe that certain groups of such distinct particulars constitute such tokens and that others do not, but which do and which do not he is unable to determine. It is because of this that he does not understand the language in question when spoken even though he can read it with some facility. The phenomenon described, regardless of whether one accepts the interpretation or account of it presented here, is doubtless familiar to those who hear a language spoken that as spoken they do not understand even though they be able to read it. Until they learn the language as spoken they are unable to determine which groups of distinct particular sounds constitute particular tokens of words and sentences and which do not.

3. Meaning and Meaninglessness

If the preceding considerations are acceptable, then which sensible particulars and groups of such constitute particulars that are also tokens and which do not can be determined only by determining which are instances of types and which are not. Moreover, if a type of token is to be a word-type or a sentence-type it must have some meaning. Thus 'abecdi' and 'abecdi' can be taken as tokens of the type 'abecdi', yet they are not word-tokens of a word-type because, given that 'abecdi' is a nonsense-locution, neither they nor the type of which they are tokens have a meaning. Similarly, 'Book the is red' and 'Book the is red', although they can be taken as tokens of the type 'Book the is red', are not sentence-tokens of a sentence-type. Although each of the four words—'Book', 'the', 'is', 'red'—has a meaning, the string they form, 'Book the is red', so long as each word in the string is used with its usual sense, does not and cannot be used to say anything about anything. For a token to be a word-token or a sentence-token and a type to be a word-type or a sentence-type it must have some meaning. Otherwise it is meaningless and lacks sense and is therefore senseless or nonsense; although it is a token or a type, it is at best a nonsense-locution or a meaningless string of meaningful words and not a word or a sentence. Thus just as a particular, to be a token, must be a token of a type, so also a token or a type, to be a token or a type of a word or a sentence, must have a meaning. Just as some particulars that could be tokens are not, so also some tokens and types that could be tokens or types of words or sentences are not. To be such tokens or types they must have a meaning. If so, then no words or sentences are meaningless.

To some this last will doubtless seem at least an extravagant, if not in fact a false, claim. One thinks immediately of various versions of the verifiability and falsifiability criteria of empirical meaningfulness. To say, however, that every word and sentence has a meaning is not to say that every word is applicable to some empirical phenomenon or that every sentence is empirically verifiable or falsifiable. Strictly speaking, the sentence "Material objects exist independently of being perceived" is not verifiable or falsifiable empirically, since no one can perceive material objects existing unperceived nor can anyone have any experience that would establish that they do not exist unperceived. Yet certainly such a sentence is meaningful. Moreover, the sentence "I shall continue to have experiences after the death of my body" is verifiable if it is true but neither verifiable nor falsifiable by means of an appeal to experience if it is false. Yet certainly it too is meaningful. The various versions of the verifiability and falsifiability criteria of empirical meaningfulness might be unobjectionable if taken simply as specifying the conditions that must be satisfied if strictly empirical claims are to be verified or falsified. Logical empiricists, however, did not always so take them but instead used them to dismiss as meaningless certain metaphysical claims on the ground that they are neither analytic nor verifiable or falsifiable empirically. Such a dismissal has a ring of irrelevance about it, since few metaphysicians would think in the first place that all their metaphysical claims are either analytic or else verifiable or falsifiable empirically. To say that many such claims are neither analytic nor verifiable or falsifiable empirically is one thing and would be acceptable to many metaphysicians who make them; but to say that they are therefore meaningless is another thing and is unacceptable.

To say, however, that all words have meaning is not to say that they all have the same kind of meaning. Husserl's distinctions between independent and nonindependent meanings and between complete and incomplete meanings are helpful here.[1] To oversimplify somewhat, for Husserl categorematic words have complete meanings, syncategorematic words only incomplete meanings. Thus 'book' and 'red' have complete meanings independently of the sentences in which they occur, whereas 'the' and 'is' do not but require completion by combining them with categorematic words. Nonetheless, they, along with the categorematic words occurring in a sentence, help to determine the meaning of the latter. Thus just as 'The book is red' and 'The pencil is red' have a different meaning from 'The book is blue' because 'book' has a different meaning than 'pencil' and 'red' than 'blue', so 'A book is red' and 'The book was red' have a different meaning from 'The book is red' because 'a' has a different meaning than 'the' and 'is' than 'was'. The fact that a difference between the syncategorematic words occurring in distinct sentences can lead to a difference in the meanings of the sentences even though there is no difference in the categorematic words means that syncategorematic as well as categorematic words have meaning even though the meaning of the former requires completion by the latter. Otherwise it would be impossible for a difference in syncategorematic words to lead to a difference in meaning between distinct sentences. If, that is, 'the' does not have a meaning different from 'a', then the meaning of 'The book is red' could not differ from that of 'A book is red', since the other words of these two sentences do not differ and occur in the same order.

Syncategorematic words, then, do have meaning even though it be a nonindependent meaning that requires completion by combining such words with categorematic words. There is also a sense in which categorematic words may be said to have nonindependent meanings and to require completion by combining them with syncategorematic words. Such combinations are necessary if something is to be said about something. A string of categorematic words such as 'book pencil red blue', like a string of syncategorematic words such as 'a the is was', says nothing about anything, and both sets of words are senseless if taken as sentences. Neither string of words is a sentence, since neither says anything about anything, nor can either be transformed into a sentence by capitalizing the first letter of the first word and placing a period after the last. Just as the syncategorematic words occurring in the second set of words must be combined with categorematic words if they are to be used to say something about something, so also the categorematic words occurring in the first set must be combined with syncategorematic words if they are to be used to say something. In this sense categorematic as well as syncategorematic words may be said to have nonindependent meanings and to require completion by combining them with words of the other type. There is still a sense, however, in which categorematic words have independent meanings and syncategorematic words do not, since the former can possibly be applied to and used to name or refer to objects and properties of various sorts whereas the latter cannot.

We saw above that any set of words consisting entirely of either categorematic or syncategorematic words is senseless if taken as a sentence, since no such set says anything about anything. We also saw earlier that some combinations of categorematic and syncategorematic words are also senseless and say nothing about anything, such as 'Red the is book'. In order that such combinations say something about something they must be combined in an acceptably grammatical way. The sentence 'The book are red', though ungrammatical since it has a singular subject and a plural verb, is acceptably grammatical in the sense intended, since it can be used to say something about something and would be understood even by grammatical purists to have the same meaning as 'The book is red'. Any acceptably grammatical combination of words that says something about something constitutes a sentence and therefore has meaning. Thus 'The book is eating', since its categorematic and syncategorematic words are combined in a grammatically acceptable way, is a sentence and therefore has meaning even when its words are taken in a straightforward literal sense. It clearly says something about something: it says about the book that it is eating. Rather than being senseless, such a sentence is false, since it is impossible for a book literally to eat. No sentence can be false unless it is meaningful, and the sentence in question, if used to say of any book that it is literally eating, would clearly be false.

Similarly, acceptably grammatical combinations of words containing categorematic words used to express self-inconsistent concepts are also meaningful and might also be true. Thus although "There is a square-circle on the wall" is necessarily false, "There are no square-circles" is necessarily true. The first sentence could not be false and the second true if they were meaningless; but since we do know that the first is false and the second true they cannot be meaningless. Yet no sentence can be meaningful, indeed no sentence can be a sentence, unless its categorematic and syncategorematic words have a meaning. And in fact 'square-circle' does have a meaning. It names anything that has all the properties essential to something's being a square and all the properties essential to something's being a circle. But since nothing can possibly have both sets of properties, since nothing can both be and also not be round and both have and also not have four sides, square-circles cannot possibly exist and therefore 'square-circle' cannot possibly name anything existent. Moreover, we could not know that words such as 'square-circle' express self-inconsistent concepts if they were meaningless, since if they had no meaning they could not express such concepts. It is only because we know that they express such concepts that we know that they cannot possibly name anything existent and that sentences used to assert the existence of entities to which such concepts would apply if they were consistent are necessarily false and that those used to deny the existence of such entities are necessarily true.

The preceding means that grammatically acceptable combinations of words containing categorematic words that express self-inconsistent concepts differ in an important way from such combinations containing nonsense-locutions in place of such words. Given that 'abecdi' is a nonsense-locution, "There is an abecdi on the wall" and "There are no abecdis" are both senseless, and therefore neither is either true or false. Each of these combinations of tokens would be meaningful and would be a sentence if for 'abecdi' we substitute some categorematic (but not some syncategorematic) word, since the substitution of a categorematic (but not a syncategorematic) word would produce sense. Whether a categorematic or a syncategorematic word is required to yield sense depends upon whether the combination of words produced when such a substitution is made is acceptably grammatical. Thus in the case of "There abecdi a square-circle on the wall" and "There abecdi no square-circles" the substitution of 'is' in the first and 'are' in the second would yield sense, whereas the substitution of a single categorematic word in each would not, or at least probably would not. The only type of acceptably grammatical combinations of words containing nonsense-locutions are those in which they are mentioned but not used. Thus "The locution 'abecdi' is a nonsense-locution," in which 'abecdi' is mentioned but not used, is a perfectly meaningful sentence. It is also true, which it could not be if it were senseless. This means that even some combinations of words containing nonsense-locutions can be meaningful and either true or false, but only if such locutions are mentioned rather than used. But combinations of words containing words expressing self-inconsistent concepts can be meaningful and either true or false regardless of whether such words are used or mentioned. Thus "There is a square-circle on the wall," in which 'square-circle' is used and not mentioned, is false and hence meaningful.

4. Supposition

The theory of the supposition of terms developed by late medieval scholastics applies nicely to and might help to explain further the distinction I have been attempting to make between nonsense-locutions and words expressing self-inconsistent concepts. We need not go here into various of the refinements of this doctrine. Instead, a consideration simply of the distinction between personal, simple, and material supposition will suffice.[2] According to Ockham, 'supposition' means 'taking the position, as it were, of something else."[3] Thus the kind of supposition a term has on a given occasion of its use is determined by the kind of thing it is being used to take the position or place of or to stand for. A word has personal supposition when it is used to stand for any or all of the objects it signifies, simple supposition when it is used to stand for a concept or mental content, and material supposition when it is used to stand for a spoken or written sign.

The term 'nonsense-locution', like the expressions 'word expressing a self-consistent concept' and 'word expressing a self-inconsistent concept', can have all three kinds of supposition, for it can be used to refer to nonsense-locutions, to the concept of nonsense-locution, or to itself, as when it is mentioned and not used. This is the case because the term 'nonsense-locution' is not itself a nonsense-locution. Instead, it has a meaning and expresses a concept that applies to a multiplicity of entities, namely nonsense-locutions. But no nonsense-locution can have either personal or simple supposition, since no such locution applies to anything or expresses a concept. Nonsense-locutions can, however, have material supposition, since they can be used to refer to themselves, as is done when it is said that 'abecdi' is a nonsense-locution containing six letters. It might be mentioned in passing that in order that a term be used with material supposition to stand for itself—which is to say that in order that a term be mentioned rather than used—it need not be italicized or placed in quotation marks. Such conventions are modern devices not adopted by the medievals and, indeed, not universally adopted even today. Thus a term can be used with material supposition to stand for itself—can be mentioned rather than used—regardless of whether it is italicized or placed in quotation marks.

Words expressing self-inconsistent concepts, like nonsense-locutions, cannot have personal supposition, since they, like nonsense-locutions, apply to nothing. But the reason they have no application is different from the reason nonsense-locutions have none. Nonsense-locutions apply to nothing because they do not express concepts, which is to say that they cannot have personal supposition because they do not have simple supposition. Words expressing self-inconsistent concepts, on the other hand, cannot apply to anything precisely because they express self-inconsistent concepts. Thus although they cannot have personal supposition they do have simple supposition, and it is because of the kind of simple supposition they have that they cannot have personal supposition. They therefore stand, so to speak, in between nonsense-locutions and words expressing self-consistent concepts. The latter can have all three kinds of supposition precisely because they express self-consistent concepts and therefore can but need not apply to things, depending upon whether the concepts they express apply to anything. Thus the word 'mermaid', since it expresses a self-consistent concept, could but does not in fact have personal supposition because the concept it expresses could but does not in fact apply to anything. Words expressing self-consistent concepts, then, can have all three kinds of supposition; those expressing self-inconsistent concepts can have simple and material but not personal supposition; and nonsense-locutions can have only material supposition.

This means that sentences containing nonsense-locutions can be meaningful and true only if the latter are used with material supposition, that sentences containing words expressing self-inconsistent concepts can be true only if the latter are used with either material or simple supposition, and that sentences containing words expressing self-consistent concepts can be true regardless of whether the latter are used with material, simple, or personal supposition. Thus "The nonsense-locution 'abecdi' has six letters," in which 'abecdi' is used with material supposition, is both meaningful and true, and "The nonsense-locution 'abecdi' has five letters," in which 'abecdi' is also used with material supposition, is meaningful but false. But "The concept abecdi is self-consistent," in which 'abecdi' is used with simple supposition, and "There is an abecdi on the wall," in which 'abecdi' is used with personal supposition, are both meaningless and therefore neither true nor false, since 'abecdi', being a nonsense-locution, expresses no concept at all and applies to nothing and therefore can have neither simple nor personal supposition. On the other hand, "The word 'square-circle' expresses a self-inconsistent concept," in which 'square-circle' is used with material supposition, is true, whereas "The word 'square-circle' expresses a self-consistent concept," in which 'square-circle' is also used with material supposition, is false. Similarly, both "The concept square-circle is self-consistent" and "The concept square-circle is self-inconsistent," in which 'square-circle' is used with simple supposition, are both meaningful even though the first is false and the second true. But "There is a square-circle on the wall," in which 'square-circle' is used with personal supposition, necessarily is false, since 'square-circle' expresses a self-inconsistent concept and therefore can apply to nothing. Since sentences containing words that express self-consistent concept can be either true or false regardless of the type of supposition with which such words are used, there is no need to give examples.

All the sentences considered so far which contain words expressing self-inconsistent concepts have been affirmative. It might seem, however, that if we consider negative as well as affirmative sentences, then true sentences containing such words used with personal supposition are possible. Thus "There are no square-circle" can be true only if 'square-circle' is used with personal rather than with simple or material supposition, since someone who uses such a sentence to express a judgment or to make a statement is saying that there are no square-circles, not that there is no word 'square-circle' or no concept of square-circle. There is, however, a way of avoiding this consequence, which consists of substituting for such a sentence the sentence "The concept square-circle has no application," in which 'square-circle' is used with simple supposition, or of substituting for such a sentence the sentence "The word 'square-circle' has no application," in which 'square-circle' is used with material supposition. If such substitutions are made, then the terms used to express the corresponding self-inconsistent concepts are used with either simple or material rather than with personal supposition. Similar considerations apply to sentences used to assert the nonexistence of self-consistent entities such as mermaids. Thus for the sentence "There are no mermaids," in which 'mermaids' is used with personal supposition, we can substitute the sentence "The concept mermaid has no application," in which 'mermaid' is used with simple supposition, or the sentence "The term 'mermaid' has no application," in which 'mermaid' is used with material supposition.

It might, however, be objected that such substitutions cannot be made because sentences used to assert the nonexistence of entities such as square-circles or mermaids are not equivalent in meaning to sentences asserting the nonapplicability of the corresponding concepts or words. For, the objection continues, such sentences are used to make statements about the entities the nonexistence of which they assert and not about the concepts of these entities or the words used to express these concepts. To this objection two responses can be made. The first is that it must be admitted that in such sentences no explicit mention is made of the concepts or words corresponding to the entities the nonexistence of which is asserted. As was indicated above, such sentences are used to assert the nonexistence of square-circles or mermaids, not of the concepts square-circle or mermaid or the words 'square-circle' or 'mermaid'. This, however, does not mean that for such sentences we cannot substitute sentences about the corresponding concepts or words. For what could possibly be meant by saying that there are no square-circles or mermaids other than that the corresponding concepts or words have no application? Nor will it do to say that the sentences "There are no square-circles" and "There are no mermaids" would still be true even if there were no words 'square-circle' and 'mermaid', since if these words and the corresponding concepts did not exist the sentences in question could not exist and therefore could not be true. This brings us to the second response to the objection. Why insist that in such sentences 'square-circle' and 'mermaid' are used with personal supposition in such an irreducible way that for these sentences we cannot substitute others in which these terms are used with either simple or material supposition? One might answer that such sentences are used to refer to such entities as square-circles or mermaids and not to the corresponding concepts or words. The difficulty confronting this answer is that the use of such sentences is precisely to deny that there are any such entities. To say that there are no square-circles or that there are no mermaids is to say that there are no entities to which the concepts square-circle or mermaid or the words 'square-circle' or 'mermaid' apply. It is a way of saying that these concepts and words apply to nothing at all.

Similar considerations apply to the corresponding affirmative existential sentences "There are square-circles" and "There are mermaids." For these sentences too, in which 'square-circle' and 'mermaid' might also seem to be used with personal supposition, we can substitute corresponding sentences in which these terms are used with simple or material supposition. Such sentences would, of course, be false, but then so also are the original sentences for which they are substitutions. For all sentences beginning with "There are . . . ," which we may label 'explicitly existential sentences', whether they be true or false, affirmative or negative, we can substitute sentences in which the words that in the original sentences might seem to have personal supposition instead clearly have simple or material supposition. When such substitutions are made there might be less of a temptation to suppose that in order that a negative explicitly existential sentence be true there must be entities of the sort the existence of which the sentence explicitly denies. If, that is, we suppose that in "There are no square-circles" the word 'square-circle' has personal supposition, we might be tempted to suppose that in some sense there are square-circles even though the sentence is used to deny explicitly that there are any. This temptation vanishes, or at least is diminished, if we interpret such a sentence as meaning that the concept or word 'square-circle' applies to nothing at all so long as it is used with personal rather than with simple or material supposition. For then we see that 'square-circle' stands for the concept square-circle if used with simple supposition, for the word 'square-circle' if used with material supposition, but for nothing at all if used with personal supposition.

If the preceding considerations are acceptable, then, as was maintained above, nonsense-locutions can have material but not simple or personal supposition, words expressing self-inconsistent concepts can have material and simple but not personal supposition, and words expressing self-consistent concepts can have all three kinds of supposition. To say, however, that nonsense-locutions and words expressing self-inconsistent concepts cannot have certain kinds of supposition is not to say that they cannot be used as though they had the kind of supposition which in fact they cannot have. Thus someone who does not know that 'abecdi' is a nonsense-locution might believe that it expresses some self-consistent concept that applies to existent entities and use the sentences "The concept abecdi is self-consistent" and "There is an abecdi on the wall" to state what he believes to be facts. If so, then in the first sentence he is using 'abecdi' with simple supposition and in the second with personal supposition. From this, however, it does not follow that it does in fact have simple or personal supposition, for the fact that someone happens to believe that what is in fact a nonsense-locution expresses a concept that applies to existent entities does not mean that it does. Whether a given term has simple or personal supposition depends upon whether it does in fact express a concept and upon whether that concept does apply to existent entities and not upon whether someone happens to believe that it does and uses it as though it did in fact have a supposition that in fact it does not have.

The preceding means that a necessary but not a sufficient condition of the truth of a sentence is that its terms be used with the correct supposition. Thus "The concept abecdi has six letters" is false because 'abecdi' is used with simple rather than material supposition. Only words and nonsense-locutions, not concepts, can have a given number of letters. But "The nonsense-locution 'abecdi' has five letters," in which 'abecdi' is used with the correct supposition, is nonetheless also false because in fact 'abecdi' has six letters. Since, that is, words and nonsense-locutions, concepts, and entities of other types each have properties peculiar to things of their type, no sentence can be true unless its terms are used with the proper supposition. This, however, is a necessary condition only of the truth of a sentence, not of its meaningfulness. Thus just as "The book is eating" is false but not meaningless, so "The concept abecdi has six letters," though false, is still meaningful. We know that it is false rather than meaningless because we know that 'abecdi' has no simple supposition and also because we know that no concept can have six letters. Thus although the use of words with the correct supposition is only a necessary and not a sufficient condition of the truth of a sentence, it is a sufficient but not a necessary condition of the meaningfulness of a sentence, given that the sentence is otherwise acceptably grammatical. Hence any acceptably grammatical sentence is meaningful if its words are used with the correct supposition.

To some the account of meaning presented above might seem over-generous, since the only expressions it rules out as meaningless are nonsense-locutions used with simple or personal supposition, combinations of words that are not acceptably grammatical, and sentences containing nonsense-locutions used with simple or personal supposition. An explanation but not a justification of the claim that there are meaningless words and sentences, other than those containing nonsense-locutions used with simple or personal supposition, might be that it is sometimes made to justify a rejection of the claims that would be made by the use of sentences of certain sorts if they were meaningful. This explanation of the claim, however, cannot constitute an acceptable justification of it, since it is difficult, if not indeed impossible, to know what claims would be made by the use of certain sentences if these sentences are in fact meaningless. Rather than adopt such a questionable if not impossible method, it seems better to adopt the simpler and more straightforward method of attempting to show that certain claims are false or at least questionable while admitting that the sentences by means of which they are made are meaningful. Certainly to admit the meaningfulness of a sentence is not to admit the truth of the claims made through its use.

5. Denotation and Comprehension

I have argued that words expressing self-inconsistent concepts, unlike nonsense-locutions and like words expressing self-consistent concepts, are meaningful. Whether a concept is consistent or inconsistent depends entirely upon the nature of its content. Considered in itself simply as a concept completely in abstraction from its content, no concept is either consistent or inconsistent, since so considered it has no nature by virtue of which it could be either. Indeed, so considered, no concept has a nature by virtue of which it could differ from any other concept. One concept differs from another only by virtue of a difference in their contents, which is to say that if two concepts have exactly the same content they are not two concepts but one. Thus concept a can differ from concept b only if there is some difference in the content of the two concepts. Moreover, no concept can be a concept unless it has some content. A completely contentless and therefore empty concept is impossible, so that the concept of such a concept is a self-inconsistent concept that cannot possibly apply to any concept.

Given the preceding, it follows that the self-inconsistent concepts square-circle and round-triangle necessarily have not only contents but also different contents. The first is the concept of something that both does and does not have four sides, the second the concept of something that both does and does not have three sides. It is because of a difference in their contents that the corresponding terms 'square-circle' and 'round-triangle' have different intensions. And it is because both concepts have self-inconsistent contents that neither applies to anything actual and thus that both have the same zero denotation.

In addition to the distinction between the intension and the denotation of a term, C. I. Lewis also distinguishes between the comprehension and the denotation of a term. Lewis explains the distinction by saying that "the *denotation* of a term is the class of all actual things to which the term applies," whereas "the *comprehension* of a term is the classification of all possible or consistently thinkable things to which the term would be correctly applicable."[4] Thus in addition to the concept of a class, which is the denotation of a term and consists of the actual things to which the term applies, Lewis introduces the concept of a classification, which is the comprehension of a term and consists of the "consistently thinkable things to which the term would correctly apply" if these things existed.[5] This distinction, however, as Professor Körner has argued, is spurious, although my reasons for thinking it spurious differ somewhat from his.[6]

Everything of importance that can be said by talking about the comprehension of a term and the classification it comprehends can also be said by talking instead simply about the denotation of a term and the class it denotes. This is obvious in the case of terms expressing self-inconsistent concepts such as 'square-circle', since the comprehension of such terms and the classification they comprehend, necessarily being zero, is identical with their denotation and the class they denote, which also necessarily is zero. In the case of such terms there is therefore no difference at all between their comprehension and their denotation, between the classification they comprehend and the class they denote. Even in the case of terms expressing self-consistent concepts there is no point in making the distinction. Thus instead of speaking of the comprehension of a term such as 'mermaid' that expresses a self-consistent concept but has a zero denotation and of the classification it comprehends, one could instead say simply of such terms that they, by virtue of their expressing self-consistent concepts, could but do not in fact denote a class of actual things. And instead of speaking of the comprehension and the classification comprehended by terms that do denote actual things, one could instead say simply of such terms that it is logically possible that they denote a greater number of actual things than in fact they do. Thus it is logically possible that the term 'man' denote a greater number of actual things than in fact it does, since it is logically possible that more men exist than in fact do exist.

The concepts of the comprehension of a term and of the classification it comprehends are therefore dispensable, since everything that can be said by using such concepts can also be said without using them, simply by talking instead about the denotation of a term and the class it denotes. If so, then to continue to use such concepts is to continue to multiply concepts beyond necessity. But not only are such concepts useless—in addition their continued use involves the danger of multiplying not only concepts but also entities beyond necessity. This danger might not be apparent in the case of terms expressing self-inconsistent concepts such as 'square-circle', since the classification comprehended by such terms is necessarily identical with the class they denote by virtue of the fact that such terms have both a zero comprehension and a zero denotation. But it is readily apparent in the case of self-consistent concepts such as 'mermaid' and 'man'. Thus although the term 'mermaid' has zero denotation it does not have zero comprehension but instead comprehends "the classification of all consistently thinkable things to which the term would correctly apply," which consists of all animals that are women from the waist up and fish from the waist down. Since no such animals exist the term has zero denotation; but since such animals are consistently thinkable it does not have zero comprehension. And although the term 'man' denotes only the class of actual human beings, it comprehends the classification of consistently thinkable human beings regardless of whether they actually exist. Thus the classification comprehended by 'man' includes not only all actual but also all consistently thinkable human beings.

The use of the concepts of the comprehension of a term and of the classification it comprehends therefore involves the risk of inclining people to suppose that there are two types of thing—those that are not only consistently thinkable or logically possible but also actual and those that are logically possible but not actual. Not only does it involve this risk: it might also presuppose that there are in fact two such types of thing. Thus Lewis explicitly says that "the denotation of a term is, obviously, included in its comprehension; but the converse relation does not hold."[7] The first part of this quotation, however, seems to be a slip, since the denotation of a term expressing a self-inconsistent concept, rather than being included in its comprehension, is instead identical with it, both being zero. It also seems strange to speak of the denotation of a term such as 'mermaid' as being included in its comprehension, since such terms have zero denotation. Since, that is, such terms denote nothing but do comprehend a certain classification of consistently thinkable things, to say that their denotation is included in their classification is like saying that nothing can be included in something. But even in the case of terms that denote a given class of actual things it seems strange to say that their denotation is included in their comprehension, since this suggests that a given class of actual things is included in a larger classification consisting not only of actual but also of possible nonactual things. There is no problem with saying that both the class of male human beings and the class of female human beings are included in the class of human beings, since both subclasses and the larger class in which they are included consist only of actual things. But if the denotation of a term denoting a class of actual things is included in but not identical with its comprehension, then its classification must consist of possible nonactual as well as actual things.

There is no problem with saying that the realm of the possible includes but is not identical with the realm of the actual, provided that this be interpreted as meaning only (1) that nothing can exist unless it is possible and (2) that some possibilities are never actualized. To think the latter, however, it is not necessary to introduce the concepts of the comprehension of a term and the classification it comprehends in addition to the concepts of the denotation of a term and the class it denotes. Instead, all one need do is to say that it is logically possible that the class denoted by a given term include more members than in fact it does or that the number of things denoted by the term be greater than in fact it is. And in the case of terms such as 'mermaid' that express self-consistent concepts but denote nothing, all one need do is to say that it is logically possible that such terms denote something although in fact they do not. Such ways of speaking involve less risk of inclining people to suppose that there must be nonactual possible things as well as actual things. If, that is, we use only the concepts of the denotation of a term and of the class of actual things it denotes without also using the concepts of the comprehension of a term and the classification it comprehends, we are less likely to suppose that there must be a realm consisting of nonactual as well as actual possible things in which the realm of actual things is included.

One might attempt to defend Lewis by responding that the introduction of the concepts of the comprehension of a term and of the classification it comprehends need in no way lead one to suppose that more things exist than in fact do exist. This is especially the case in view of the fact that these concepts differ from those of the denotation of a term and the class it denotes in such a way that it is only consistently thinkable or logically possible things and not actually existent things that are included in the classification comprehended by a term but not in the class it denotes. This is to say that the classification comprehended by a term does not contain a single existent thing that is not included in the class the term denotes, and so long as this is recognized there need be no danger of supposing that a larger number of things exist than in fact do exist. There would be no point whatever in the introduction of the concepts in question if one supposed that everything included in the classification comprehended by a term exists, for then it would include nothing not included in the class the term denotes. Instead, the concepts in question are necessary, or at least useful, precisely because the classification comprehended by a term expressing a self-consistent concept includes nonexistent consistently thinkable things as well as the existent things, if any, denoted by the term. So long, then, the response concludes, as one recognizes that the classification comprehended by a term contains nothing existent not also included in the class denoted by the term, there is no danger of supposing that more things exist than in fact do exist.

It must, I think, be conceded that someone who understands the point of the introduction of the concepts in question is in no danger, as a consequence of their introduction, of believing that a greater number of actual things exist than in fact do exist. Nonetheless, the introduction of these concepts might still lead someone who understands its point to believe in the existence of nonactual possible things. Such a person might therefore raise the question of how many possible things of a given type exist. He might, for example, raise the question of how many possible mermaids exist or of how many possible but nonactual human beings exist. The question of how many actual things of a given type exist has a determinate answer even though we might never be able to discover it. Thus the question of how many actual human beings exist has a definite answer even though we be unable to determine the number. But the question of how many possible mermaids or possible human beings exist has no answer. This question would still be unanswerable even if we did not use the word 'exist' but instead raise the question in a different way by asking how many possible nonexistent mermaids there are. Even if we suppose that there are possible nonexistent mermaids, as someone who asked seriously such a question would seem to suppose, the question of how many there are is still a question without an answer. This, however, is not to say that it is a meaningless question. If it were meaningless we could not know that it is unanswerable. But we do know that it is unanswerable.

In order to prevent or at least to diminish the likelihood of the raising of such essentially unanswerable questions, it seems better to say simply and straightforwardly that there are no possible nonexistent things and to eschew the introduction of the concepts of the comprehension of a term and of the classification it comprehends. As was indicated above, such concepts in any event are dispensable, since everything that can be said through using them can also be said by using instead the concepts of the denotation of a term and of the class it denotes. Thus even if the use of such concepts did not involve the risk of leading people to multiply entities beyond necessity, it would still involve the multiplication of concepts beyond necessity.

Nor is the use of such concepts necessary to account for the possibility of thinking of nonexistent things. From the fact that one can think of such things it does not follow that there is some classification in which they are included. I can think of a mermaid reclining seductively on the couch, but from this it does not follow that there is a consistently thinkable but nonexistent thing included in the classification comprehended by the term 'mermaid'. This does not follow any more than the fact that I can think of a square-circle's being on the blackboard means that there is a consistently thinkable but nonexistent thing included in the classification comprehended by the term 'square-circle'. The sentence "There is a square-circle on the blackboard," though necessarily false, is nonetheless meaningful. Indeed, as we have seen, if such a sentence were meaningless we could not know that it necessarily is false. But since we do know that it necessarily is false we do know that it is meaningful. Yet if we know that it is meaningful we can think of a square-circle's being on some blackboard even though we be unable, knowing *what* it means, to believe that any square-circle can be on any blackboard. But if we can nevertheless *think* of a square-circle's being on the blackboard without supposing that the term 'square-circle' comprehends a classification consisting of consistently thinkable or logically possible but nonexistent square-circles, we can also think of a mermaid's reclining on the couch without supposing that the term 'mermaid' comprehends a classification consisting of logically possible but nonexistent mermaids. If so, then regardless of whether the concepts of the comprehension of a term and of the classification it comprehends might be necessary or useful for other purposes, they are not necessary to account for the fact that we can think of nonexistent intentional objects, regardless of whether these objects be such that it is logically possible or logically impossible that they exist.

Notes

1. Edmund Husserl, *Logical Investigations,* trans. J. N. Findlay (London: Routledge & Kegan Paul, 1970), Investigation IV, secs. 4 and 5, vol. 2, pp. 499–503; see also C. I. Lewis, *An Analysis of Knowledge and Valuation* (La Salle, Ill.: Open Court Publishing Company, 1946), pp. 78–82.

2. For a clear simple account of these types of supposition, see William of Ockhan, *Philosophical Writings: A Selection,* translated, with an introduction, by Philotheus Boehner, O.F.M. (Indianapolis: Library of Liberal Arts, 1964), pp. xxxiv–xxxv, 70–73.

3. Ibid., p. 69.

4. *An Analysis of Knowledge and Valuation,* p. 39.

5. Ibid., p. 40.

6. Stephan Körner, *Conceptual Thinking: A Logical Inquiry* (New York: Dover Publications, 1959), pp. 47–50.

7. Lewis, *Analysis,* p. 41.

4

From Statements to Facts

EVEN though some will doubtless find questionable or even false certain of the things said about sentences in the previous chapter, everyone will nonetheless admit that there are sentences. But not everyone will admit that in addition to sentences there are also statements, judgments, beliefs, propositions, facts, and states of affairs. Not everyone, that is, will admit that each of these constitutes a distinct irreducible ontological category. Does each of these in fact constitute such a category, or is some one or more of them dispensable because reducible to some other or to some combination of the others? We begin with statements.

1. Sentences and Statements

Sentences and statements are entities of distinct types, and neither type is reducible to the other. The reason this is so is not simply that there are interrogative, imperative, and exclamatory as well as declarative sentences. Even if all sentences were declarative, sentences and statements would still be entities of distinct types. Moreover, the distinction between declarative sentences and those of other types is mainly grammatical, and statements can be made by using sentences of other grammatical types as well as by using declarative sentences. In addition, the same statement can be made by using different declarative sentences, and the same declarative sentence can be used to make different statements. Thus 'The book is red' and 'The color of the book is red', though different sentences, can both be used to make the same statement; and 'My wife is at home' and 'My wife is at home', though both tokens of the same sentence-type, when used by different persons to make a statement are used to make different statements. This last in turn means that one token of a given sentence-type can be used to make a true statement whereas another token of the same sentence-type can be used to make a false statement. Finally, a person can utter or write a token of a sentence without making any statement at all, as when an actor in a play speaks his lines without making any statements.

This last does not mean that for a person to make a statement he must believe that the sentence he uses to make it is true. Instead, a person can lie by making a statement he believes to be false through using a sentence he believes to be false. This in turn means that in order for someone to make a statement it is not necessary that he believe that the statement he makes is true. People can make statements regardless of whether they believe them to be true, false, or doubtful. Moreover, a person can utter or write a sentence he believes to be true without thereby making a statement, as when an actor in a play, without making any statements at all, speaks lines including sentences he believes to be true. Thus to make a statement it is neither necessary nor sufficient that a person believe that the sentence he uses in making it is true. In addition, a person can make a statement without using any sentences at all, as can be done by nodding the head or pointing a finger.

Still another difference between sentences and statements is that token-sentences can be visible or audible, whereas statements cannot be. In making a statement a person might use some sensible sentence-token, but neither the statement he makes nor his act of making it is identical with such sensible tokens or their occurrence. This follows from what has already been said. It does not, however, mean that there is nothing at all analogous in the case of statements to the type/token distinction in the case of sentences. Thus just as two tokens can be tokens of the same type-sentence, so two people, perhaps by uttering two distinct tokens of the same type-sentence, can make the same statement, as when each, by uttering a distinct token of the sentence-type 'The book is red', states that the book in question is red. Here two distinct acts of making a statement occur, but the same statement is made by means of each act. We must therefore distinguish between statements on the one hand and making statements on the other. The making of a statement is a particular temporal act, whereas the statement made is not. The same person can make the same statement on a number of different occasions, and different people can also make the same statement either at the same or at different times. The making of a statement is therefore analogous to a token of a type, whereas the statement made is analogous to a type. Just as tokens are particulars, so the making of a statement is a particular act; and just as types are not particulars but are analogous to universals, so also statements are not particulars but instead, like types, are analogous to universals.

The analogy between tokens and the making of statements on the one hand and between types and statements on the other can be pursued a bit further. Just as no particular can be a token unless it is a token of a type, so no act of making a statement can occur unless a statement is made. Just as there could be no tokens without types, so no acts of making statements could occur if no statements were made. Just as two tokens of the same type are distinct particular tokens because they exist or occur at different places or times, so two acts of making the same statement are distinct particular acts either because they are performed by different people or else because they are performed at different times by the same person. And just as two tokens are tokens of the same or of different types because of the nature of the types of which they are tokens, so two acts of statement making are acts of making the same or different statements because of the nature of the statements made. This last requires explanation.

The occurrence of acts requires the existence of agents. If no agents existed no acts could occur. In order, however, for an agent to act it must do something, and the nature of its act is determined by the nature of what it does. Two agents are agents of the same type to the degree that they perform acts of the same type, of different types to the degree that they perform acts of different types. Two distinct patricular agents would still be distinct particular agents even if they both performed acts of only the same type. Their difference as distinct particular agents, however, would issue from something other than the type of acts they perform, since they do not differ insofar as the type of act they perform is concerned. Instead, they are both agents of the same type because they perform only acts of the same type. For them to be agents of different types they must to some degree perform acts of different types. But if they are to perform acts of different types they must do things of different types. Although two distinct particular acts can differ as particular acts even though they be acts of the same type, they cannot differ in type unless in performing one the agent does something not done in performing the other. An act of running and an act of walking do not differ insofar as each is considered only as an act and as nothing more; instead, they differ in kind only because of a difference in kind in what the agent does in performing the two acts. Similarly, an act of asking a question and an act of making a statement do not differ in kind insofar as each is considered only as an act and as nothing more; instead, they differ in kind only because in performing one the agent does something he does not do in performing the other. It is only because there is a difference in kind between asking a question and making a statement that the two acts differ in kind.

Similar considerations apply to differences of kind between acts of making statements. Two particular acts of statement making can differ as distinct particulars even though they do not differ in kind, provided (1) that they be performed by different persons or (2) that they be performed at different times if performed by the same person. Leaving aside such matters as the logical form of the statements made and the degree of certainty or force with which they are made, two acts of statement making can differ in kind only if in one some statement is made that is not made in the other. Thus suppose that two people, or the same person at different times, with the same degree of certainty make the statement 'The book is red'. If so, then the act of statement making of the one does not differ in kind from that of the other even though they do differ as distinct particular acts, and the source of the identity in kind between these two particular acts is that in each the same statement is made. Had one made instead the statement 'The book is green', his act of statement making would differ in kind from that of the other, and this difference would issue from the difference between the statements made. Since 'The book is red' and 'The book is green' differ as statements, any act of making one of these statements necessarily differs in kind, i.e., not just as a distinct particular act, from any act of making the other, and any two or more distinct particular acts of making the statement 'The book is red' are the same in kind because in each the same statement is made.

In the preceding we have been abstracting from the logical form of a statement and from the degree of certainty or force with which a statement is made. But even when we do not make such an abstraction we can also arrive at the point just made. There are four things to be considered: the act of making a statement, the statement itself, the logical form of the statement, and the degree of certainty or force with which the statement is made. The logical form of a statement is a property of the statement, not of the act of making it; and the degree of certainty or force with which a statement is made is a property of the act of making it, not of the statement itself. This means that although the logical form of a statement determines to some degree the kind of statement it is, the degree of certainty or force with which the statement is made does not. Instead, the latter determines to some degree only the nature of the act of making the statement. Thus suppose that two people make the same statement, 'The book is red', and that one makes it with more certainty or force than the other does. If so, then although the act of the one differs in nature to some degree from that of the other, the nature of the statement made by the one does not in the least differ from that made by the other. Instead, they both make precisely the same statement. The identity and nature of the statement they make, however, do not issue simply from its logical form, since two statements can have the same logical form without thereby losing their status as distinct statements. Thus although the two statements 'The book is red' and 'The book is green' have the same logical form, since they are both simple affirmative categorical statements, they are nonetheless distinct statements. But since they have the same logical form, their distinctness cannot issue from their logical form. From what then does it issue?

It cannot issue from a difference in the degree of certainty or force with which they are made, for they remain distinct even though they both be made with the same degree of certainty or force. Moreover, two people can make the same statement even though one makes it with more certainty or force than the other. Nor can it issue from the fact that two distinct statements can be made only through two distinct acts of statement making, for the same statement can be made through two such distinct acts, as when two people make the same statement. Nor can it issue from the fact that one statement is made by one person and the other by another, for the same person can make distinct statements and two people can make the same statement. Nor can it issue from the fact that they are made through using distinct sentence-tokens, since the same statement can also be made by using distinct sentence-tokens and, indeed, must be made by using distinct tokens if it is made more than once. Nor can it issue from the fact that they are made by using tokens of distinct sentence-types, for, as we saw above, the same statement can be made by using tokens of distinct sentence-types, and different statements can be made by using tokens of the same sentence-type. Nor can it issue from the fact that the two statements are made at different times or places, for the same statement can be made at different times and places and distinct statements at the same time or place. Instead, it can issue only from a difference in the intrinsic nature of the two statements, which is to say that two statements can be distinct only if one has an intrinsic nature the other does not have. In the absence of such a difference of intrinsic nature there is only one statement, not two.

A sufficient but not a necessary condition of the existence of a difference in the intrinsic nature of two statements is that one have a different logical form from the other. Thus 'A book is red' differs from 'The book is red' because one has a different logical form from the other. But, as we saw above, two statements can have the same logical form and yet differ intrinsically. Thus 'The book is red' and 'The book is green' differ intrinsically even though they have the same logical form. Given that two statements have the same logical form, one can differ from the other only if anyone who makes them either (1) says different things about the same thing, (2) says the same thing about different things, or (3) says different things about different things. If one person at different times or two people at the same or different times say the same thing about the same thing, then they make the same statement. Thus the following pairs of statement-forms intrinsically differ from one another even though they all have the same logical form: (1) 'a is F' and 'a is G', (2) 'a is F' and 'b is F', (3) 'a is F' and 'b is G'. Hence the following statements all differ intrinsically from one another even though they all have the same logical form: 'The book is red', 'The book is green', 'The pencil is red', 'The pencil is green'. And the following two sentences can be used to make the same statement because they can both be used to say the same thing about the same thing: 'The book is red' and 'The color of the book is red'.

The preceding provides an additional reason for regarding statements, like types, as being analogous to universals rather than particulars. As we shall see later, it is conceivable that two particulars have all their properites in common, with the exception of those that issue solely from their spatiotemporal location, even though in fact this might never happen. Even though it might never happen, two particulars would still be distinct particulars if one exists or occurs at a different time or place from the other even though each has all and only the properties the other has with the exception of those that issue solely from their spatiotemporal location. But universals, considered in abstraction from their exemplification by particulars, have no spatiotemporal location and therefore cannot differ from one another by virtue of a difference in their spatiotemporal location. Instead, they can differ only by virtue of a difference in their intrinsic nature. The color red differs from the color green not because one has a different spatiotemporal location from the other but because one has a different intrinsic nature, or rather *is* a different nature, than the other. Similarly, the statement 'The book is red' differs from the statement 'The book is green' not because one has a different spatiotemporal location than the other but because one has a different intrinsic nature than the other. Although acts of statement making are particular events and as such have a spatiotemporal location, the statements made are not particulars and have no spatiotemporal location. Instead, just as the color red can be exemplified at different places and times and just as the same type can have a variety of tokens existing or occurring at different times and places, so also the same statement can be made at a variety of places and times.

Statements, then, like types, are not particulars but instead, again like types, are analogous to universals. Although this contention is incompatible with nominalism, it nonetheless can consistently be accepted by those who reject the realist contention that there are extramental universals. This is the case because just as there can be no types without tokens, so also there could be no statements if no statement were ever by anyone made. In the last chapter it was maintained that there could be no tokens without types and no types without tokens, so that neither category is reducible to the other. Thus if there were no sentence-tokens there could be no sentence-types and vice versa. Similarly, the categories of statements and statement making require one another, so that neither is reducible to the other. In an act of statement making a person performs an act of making a statement, not an act of making an act of statement making, so that if statements were not distinct from statement making there could be no statement making. An act of statement making is like any other act of making something. Unless something distinct from the act of making is made there can be no act of making. Yet an act of statement making is not an act of making a particular of a certain type, since the same statement made by one person in an act of statement making can also be made by him or by another in another act of statement making. But although the same statement can be made by a number of distinct particular acts of statement making, no statement can exist unless it is made by some particular act of statement making. To be a statement is to be a statement made, so that a statement never made is not a statement, just as to be an act of statement making is to be an act of making a statement, so that an act of statement making in which no statement is made is not an act of statement making.

One thing that might incline some to suppose that statements do not depend for their being upon acts of statement making is that the truth-value of statements, unlike that of sentence-types, cannot change and is therefore timeless. If someone at the time of the event in question were to make a statement by uttering a token of the sentence "Washington is crossing the Delaware", he would utter a true sentence and make a true statement. But if someone in the twentieth century were to make a statement by uttering a token of the same sentence he would utter a false sentence and make a false statement. One and the same type-sentence can therefore be true on one occasion of its use through the utterance of a true token of it and false on another occasion of its use through the utterance of a false token of it. But the truth-value of a statement cannot change. Thus the statement made by someone at the time of Washington's crossing the Delaware would still be true if made by someone today, although to make it today the past rather than the present tense would have to be used. Indeed, the statement in question would also have been true had someone, by using the future tense, made it prior to Washington's crossing the Delaware, even though it be granted that prior to the event in question no one could have known with certainty that it would occur.

But, it might be objected, if the truth-value of statements cannot change, then it is independent of the times at which they are made. Regardless of when they are made, true statements are true and false statements false. But how can the truth-value of statements be independent of the times at which they are made and therefore of the acts of making them if statements themselves depend for their being upon the particular acts of making them, so that if no such acts occurred there could be no statements? A similar question can be raised about a priori statements, whose truth or falsity is independent of what happens in time. How are such statements possible if statements depend for their being upon particular temporal acts of statement making, so that if there were no such acts there could be no statements?

2. Tenses, Time, and Truth

The answer to these questions would seem to lie in the distinction already made between a statement on the one hand and the act of making it on the other. Whereas acts of statement making are temporal, the statements made by means of these acts are not. But since truth and falsity are properties of statements, not of the acts of making them, the truth or falsity of a statement is as timeless as the statement itself. Thus although there would be no statements at all if there were no acts of statement making, the truth or falsity of a statement is independent both of the act of making it and of the time at which it is made. Thus take the statement "The pencil with which I am writing is yellow." In making this statement I refer to a certain pencil and say of it that it is yellow. Since the pencil to which I refer is in fact yellow, the statement I make about it is true. If anyone were to say of this pencil, either before it comes into being or after it ceases to be, what I say of it by stating that it is yellow, he would thereby make a true statement. He would also make the same statement about it that I make, even though, as we saw, he would doubtless express the statement by using a sentence in the future tense if he makes it prior to the pencil's coming into being and in the past tense if he makes it after the pencil ceases to be. The truth or falsity of the statement in question, however, whether it be expressed by using the future, present, or past tense, in no way depends upon the act of making it.

The preceding can perhaps also be expressed in the following way. No statements would exist if no acts of statement making occurred. Thus if no acts of statement making occurred no statements would be either true or false, since then there would be no statements to be either. But if someone were to make a given statement its truth or falsity would not depend upon his making it but rather upon what he states by making it. Thus suppose the statement I make in the present by using the present-tense sentence "The pencil with which I am writing is yellow" were never in fact by anyone made. If so, then it would not exist. Nonetheless, if this statement, as distinguished from the sentence by means of which it is made, were ever at any time to be made by anyone it would be true. The fact that it would be true if it were ever at any time made by anyone means that its truth does not depend upon its being made by someone at some time. The situation here is analogous to someone's drawing a triangular figure. If no triangular figures existed in nature and if no one ever drew such a figure, then no triangular figures would exist. Given, however, that someone does at some time draw a triangular figure, then the figure he draws necessarily has three sides, since otherwise it would not be a triangular figure. The figure he draws necessarily has three sides because it is triangular, not because he draws it, since he could draw some figure other than a triangular figure. Although, that is, it is not necessary that he draw a figure or that, if he does, he draw a triangular figure, and thus although it is not necessary that the particular triangular figure he draws exist, it is necessary that it have three sides if it is to be triangular. Even if no triangular figures ever existed it would still be necessary that a figure have three sides if it is to be triangular.

Although, then, there would be no statements if there were no acts of statement making, the truth or falsity of a statement is a timeless property of the statement, not of the act of making it. There are two factors that might incline some to doubt the timelessness of the truth or falsity of statements, both connected with the sentences used to express certain statements. One of these factors has to do with the use of tensed sentences to express statements about temporal states of affairs. As mentioned above, the statement I make by using the past-tense sentence "Washington crossed the Delaware" would be made prior to the occurrence of that event by using the future-tense sentence "Washington will cross the Delaware" and would be made at the time of its occurrence by using the present-tense sentence "Washington is crossing the Delaware." The first sentence would express a false statement if used prior to or contemporaneously with Washington's crossing the Delaware, the second a false statement if used contemporaneously with or after his crossing it, and the third a false statement if used prior to or after his crossing it. In order that these three sentences express the same statement they must be used at the proper times—the first after his crossing the Delaware, the second prior to his crossing it, and the third contemporaneously with his crossing it.

The preceding means that although differently tensed sentences, when used at the proper times, can express the same statement, they also do more. In addition to expressing the same statement, they also locate temporally the act of the speaker's using them relative to the events about which they are used to say something. Thus a sentence in the future tense indicates that the speaker's act of using it is temporally prior to the event about which it is used to say something, a sentence in the present tense indicates that the speaker's act of using it is contemporaneous with the event in question, and a sentence in the past tense indicates that the speaker's act is subsequent to the event in question. It is important, however, to recognize that they only indicate and do not make a statement about the temporal positon of the speaker's act of using them. If they made a statement about rather than only indicated the temporal position of the speaker's act they would express different statements, since they would then be used to make a statement not only about the event about which they are used to say something but also about the temporal position of the speaker's act relative to this event. Since, however, they only indicate and do not make a statement about the temporal position of the speaker's act relative to that of the event about which they are used to say something, they can all be used to make the same statement regardless of their tense.

Tensed sentences therefore have a double function. One is to say something about some event or temporal state of affairs. The other is to indicate the temporal position of the speaker's act of using them relative to that of the event about which they are used to say something. Doubtless tensed sentences could be replaced by tenseless sentences which could also be used to make the same statements. Such tenseless sentences, however, would fail to fulfill the double function fulfilled by tensed sentences, since they would fail to indicate the temporal position of the speaker's act of using them relative to that of the event about which they are used to say something. The use of such tenseless sentences would therefore fail to provide as much information as the corresponding tensed sentences provide. Although their use would provide as much information about the event about which they as well as the corresponding tensed sentences can be used to say something, they would provide no information at all about the temporal position of the speaker's act of using them relative to that of the event about which they are used to say something.

Tensed sentences are like sentences containing indexical expressions such as pronouns in that the truth or falsity of the statements expressed by means of them depends at least in part upon the relation of the speaker to that about which he says something. Thus the same type-sentence "I am walking," if used simultaneously by two speakers, can express a true statement as used by one and a false statement as used by the other, depending upon whether the two speakers are in fact walking. Similarly, the same type-sentence "This is green," if used simultaneously by two speakers, can express a true statement as used by one and a false statement as used by the other, depending upon whether the objects they refer to by means of 'this' are in fact green. In the first case 'I' refers to the speaker; in the second 'this' refers to something in the vicinity of the speaker. Thus if two speakers use the same type-sentence "I am walking" to make a statement, they are making different statements, since although each says the same thing about the subject to which he refers they refer to different subjects. Similarly, if two speakers use the same type-sentence "This is green" to make a statement they might be making different statements, since although each says the same thing about the thing to which he refers they might be referring to different things. Since the same indexical type-sentence on one occasion of its use can express a true statement and on another a false statement, a failure to keep in mind the distinction between sentences and statements might lead one to suppose that the truth-value of statements, like that of type-sentences, can change and thus to deny the timelessness of the truth or falsity of statements.

Indexical sentences, however, are unlike tensed sentences in that in the former there is an explicit reference by means of the index-word occurring in the sentence to the subject to which it refers, whereas, as we have seen, in a tensed sentence the tense of the sentence only indicates and does not explicitly refer to the temporal position of the speaker relative to that of the event about which he says something. To use indexicals, as in "I am walking," "You are walking," "He is walking," and "This is green," is to refer explicitly to the subjects about which these sentences are used to make statements and not merely to indicate the relationship of the speaker to these subjects. To use the first person is not only to indicate that something is being said about the speaker but also to refer explicitly to him, to use the second person is not only to indicate that something is being said about the person addressed but also to refer explicitly to him, to use the third person is not only to indicate that something is being said about some third person other than the speaker or the person addressed but also to refer explicitly to him, and to use 'this' is not only to indicate that something is being said about something in the vicinity of the speaker but also to refer explicitly to it.

The second factor mentioned above that might lead some to doubt the timelessness of the truth or falsity of statements has to do with the temporality of the events and states of affairs about which something is said by making empirical statements. It might readily be granted that a priori statements are timelessly true or false on the ground that those who make such statements are purporting to specify necessary relationships between nontemporal entities or properties. Thus it might readily be granted that the 'is' of "The square on the hypotenuse is equal to the sum of the squares on the sides" is a timeless 'is' on the ground that such statement is a priori. But, someone who makes such a concession might ask, how can statements about events and temporal states of affairs also be timelessly true when such events and states of affairs are not themselves timeless? The answer to this question is at least implicit in what has already been said. Although the truth of an empirical statement such as "The Declaration of Independence was signed in 1776" depends upon the occurrence of the event in question at the time in question, if anyone were to make the statement expressed by this sentence either before, after, or simultaneously with the occurrence of this event he would make a true statement. Thus just as the time at which an a priori statement is made is irrelevant to its truth or falsity, so also the time at which an empirical statement is made—whether before, after, or simultaneously with the occurrence of the event about which the statement is made—is also irrelevant to its truth or falsity. It is in this sense that the truth or falsity of empirical as well as a priori statements are timeless.

Some philosophers deny the timelessness of the truth or falsity of empirical statements on the ground that such statements are neither true nor false if made prior to the occurrence of the events or states of affairs about which they are made. Such philosophers admit that once a statement acquires a truth-value, by being made contemporaneously with or subsequent to the event about which it is made, its truth-value cannot change, so that if it is made again at a later time its truth-value remains the same. They therefore admit that a statement made by using a sentence in the present or past tense has a truth-value and that the past-tense sentence must have the same truth-value as the corresponding present-tense sentence. But they deny that statements about future events or states of affairs are either true or false and thus that the corresponding future-tense sentences have a truth-value. Since, they conclude, empirical statements acquire a truth-value only at the time of the occurrence of the events about which they are made, they cannot be timelessly true or false even though their truth-value remains constant once it is acquired.

There would seem to be two major reasons for espousing such a position, neither of which is compelling. One is connected with a failure to distinguish in this instance between truth and knowledge. We can grant that today I cannot know, at least not infallibly, that tomorrow it will rain in Miami. Yet the statement that tomorrow it will rain in Miami is today true or false, depending upon whether it does in fact do so tomorrow. If tomorrow it does rain in Miami, then today I make a true statement if I say that it will, even though I cannot know today that it will and thus cannot know today that my statement is true. This brings us to the second reason. It seems sometimes to be supposed that if a statement about some future event or state of affairs has a truth-value prior to the occurrence of the event in question, then its doing so causally or in some other way determines or necessitates the occurrence of that event. Sometimes this supposition is expressed by claiming that if a person can know prior to its occurrence that a given future event is going to occur, then his knowledge causally determines its occurrence. At least the beginning of the correct answer to this supposition was made long ago by St. Augustine in his *De libero arbitrio voluntatis*.[1] The truth or falsity of a statement, as distinguished from the act of making it, is in no way causally related to the event or state of affairs about which it is made. Although there is a relation of dependence between the two, this relation is not causal. Moreover, it is the truth or falsity of the statement that is dependent upon the occurrence of the event about which it is made and not vice versa. Rather than my stating today that tomorrow it will rain in Miami causing it to do so, the truth or falsity of the statement I make depends upon whether tomorrow it does in fact rain in Miami. If tomorrow it does, then today my statement is true; if tomorrow it does not, then today my statement is false. And since I cannot know that a statement is true unless in fact it is true, whether today I can know that tomorrow it will rain in Miami depends upon whether it does in fact do so. Thus even if I could know today that tomorrow it will do so, my knowledge, rather than causally determining that tomorrow it will rain, is instead dependent upon its raining tomorrow.

3. Judgments and Beliefs

We turn now to consider judgments and beliefs. We begin with judgments. With of course the necessary changes, much of what has been said about statements applies also to judgments. Since the same type-sentence can be used to express different judgments and the same judgment can be expressed by different type-sentences, judgments, like statements, must be distinguished from the sentences by means of which they are expressed. And since the same judgment can be made at different times by the same person and either at the same or at different times by different persons, judgments must be distinguished from acts of judgment making. The latter, like acts of statement making, are temporal, whereas judgments, like statements, are timeless, as is their truth or falsity. Whereas acts of judgment making, like acts of statement making, are particular temporal events, judgments, like statements, are not, but instead are analogous to universals in that the same judgment can be made at different times and places by different persons. Since the reasons supporting these claims about judgments are the same as those presented above in support of the corresponding claims about statements, there is no need to repeat them here.

But, the question naturally arises, if judgments in all these respects are like statements, how do they differ? They differ in at least two major respects. One is that a person, as we saw above, can make a statement he believes to be false, whereas no one can make a judgment he believes to be false. This can be put by saying that whereas a person can make a statement he judges to be false, no one can make a judgment he judges to be false. To make a judgment involves believing that it is at least probably true, whereas this is not involved in making a statement. Lying statements can be made, but no lying judgments can be made. The second major repsect in which the two differ is connected with the first. This is that judgments can be made even though they are not stated and therefore without making statements, whereas statements cannot be made unless judgments are also made. This is true even of lying statements, since to make a lying statement is to make a statement one believes or judges to be false. It is to make a statement one believes to be contrary to what one judges to be the case. Thus whereas statements presuppose judgments, judgments do not presuppose statements. Judgments could still be made even if no statements were ever by anyone made, but no statements could be made if no judgments were ever by anyone made. In this sense judgments are more fundamental than statements. This, however, does not mean that statements are reducible to judgments, since in making a statement one does something else in addition to what one does in making a judgment. In making a judgment one judges that something is the case, whereas in making a statement one expresses a judgment or, in the case of a lying statement, the contrary of what one judges or believes to be the case. Moreover, one cannot express a judgment unless one makes some statement, and the statement made is true only if the judgment it expresses is true. To express a judgment, however, it is not necessary to use a sentence, since, as we saw above, a person can make a statement without using a sentence by using such means as pointing a finger or nodding the head.

If the preceding considerations are acceptable, then sentences, statements, and judgments constitute distinct ontological categories none of which are reducible to the others. Judgments are expressed by making statements which in turn are usually made by using sentences. The truth-value of the sentence-token used is determined by that of the statement it is used to make, which in turn is determined by that of the judgment it expresses unless the statement made is a lying statement, in which case the truth-value of the sentence-token used and of the statement made is the opposite of that of the judgment that would be expressed by the statement were the latter not a lying statement. But, as we have seen, sentence-tokens can be used without making statements, statements can be made without expressing judgments made by the person who makes the statement, and judgments can be made without being expressed. If so, then sentences, statements, and judgments constitute distinct ontological categories that are not reducible to one another.

This brings us to beliefs. As in the case of judgments, much of what was said earlier about statements applies, with the necessary changes, also to beliefs and for much the same reasons, which need not be repeated. Yet beliefs differ from sentences, statements, and judgments. I take it as evident that beliefs are distinct from sentences and statements, since beliefs can be held without being stated. Even when they are stated they are still distinct from the statements made to state them and the sentences used to make these statements. Moreover, a statement, rather than expressing some belief held by the person who makes it, can instead express the opposite of what he believes, as when a person makes a lying statement. Beliefs also differ from judgments. One difference is that beliefs are held, whereas judgments are made, so that although there are acts of judgment making there are no acts of belief making, even though one might come to hold a given belief as a consequence of an act of making a judgment. Acts of judgment making, like acts of statement making, are particular events episodic in nature, whereas the holding of a belief can continue over a considerable span of time. Thus even though a given belief might come to be held only as a consequence of an act of judgment making, the holding of the belief is distinct from the act of judgment making. But although the holding of a belief is distinct from any acts of making judgments or statements, to hold a given belief is to be disposed to make the corresponding judgments or statements in certain situations. A person's holding a given belief can therefore be said to be a disposition that manifests itself by his making the corresponding judgments or statements in certain situations. Conversely, knowledge of a person's making certain judgments or statements in certain situations gives us some reason to believe that he holds the corresponding beliefs.

The distinction between beliefs on the one hand and judgments and statements on the other has been drawn in terms of factors other than a difference in their content. This is because the content of a belief is precisely the same as that of its corresponding judgment or statement. If, that is, I believe that the pencil with which I am writing is yellow, the content of my belief is exactly the same as that of my judgment or statement if I judge or state that the pencil with which I am writing is yellow. This can be put by saying that to believe that p, to judge that p, and to state that p differ only by virtue of one's being a belief, one's being a judgment, and one's being a statement. They do not differ by virtue of any difference in their content, since there is no such difference. Were there a difference between the content of a belief and that of its corresponding judgment or statement the latter would not correspond to the former, which is to say that a judgment or statement corresponds to a belief only if they have the same content as the belief. If a judgment or statement could not have the same content as its corresponding belief, then the holding of a belief could not be a disposition to make the corresponding judgment or statement in certain situations, and no belief could be stated by making a statement that corresponds to it.

Since the content of a belief is precisely the same as that of the corresponding judgment or statement, and since the same judgment or statement can be made by different people, it follows that the same belief can be held by different persons. Just as two people make the same judgment or statement if they judge or state the same thing about the same thing, so also two persons hold the same belief if they believe the same thing about the same thing. And just as judgments and statements have a timeless truth-value and can be considered completely in abstraction from any consideration of the people who make them, so also in the case of beliefs. Finally, just as there would be no judgments or statements if there were no acts of judgment making or statement making, so also there would be no beliefs if none were ever by anyone held. Since, in short, the content of a belief is precisely the same as that of its corresponding judgment or statement, much of what was said above about the latter can be said also about the former, and for the same reasons.

Since the content of a belief is the same as that of its corresponding judgment or statement, it can be considered in abstraction from any consideration of whether it is the content of a belief as opposed to a judgment or statement, a judgment as opposed to a belief or statement, or a statement as opposed to a belief or judgment. If I believe that the pencil with which I am writing is yellow, you judge that it is, and he states that it is, the content of my belief is the same as that of the judgment you make and the statement he makes. Therefore my belief cannot be true unless your judgment and his statement are also true, and none of the three can be true unless their common content is true. The truth-value of a belief is not determined by the fact that it is a belief or by the fact that it is held by some particular person, since beliefs can be false regardless of who happens to hold them. Similarly with judgments and statements. Their truth-value is not determined by the fact that they are judgments or statements or by the fact that they are made by some particular person, since they too can be false regardless of who happens to make them. If I believe that p, you judge that p, and he states that p, the truth-value of my belief, your judgment, and his statement is dependent entirely on that of their common content p and not on the fact that I believe, you judge, and he states that p. It is because p is true that my belief, your judgment, and his statement are true, and p would be true regardless of whether I believe, you judge, or he states that it is.

4. Propositions and States of Affairs

We have just arrived at the concept of a proposition. A proposition, as distinct from a belief, judgment, statement, or sentence, is a content the truth or falsity of which ultimately determines the truth or falsity of beliefs, judgments, statements, and sentences. If I believe, you judge, and he states by using a token of the sentence "The Eiffel Tower is in London" that the Eiffel Tower is in London, there is a content common to my belief, your judgment, and his statement. This content is the proposition expressed by the sentence "The Eiffel Tower is in London". It is not a belief since, as we have seen, a belief, to be, must be held by someone, and it is possible that no one believe that the Eiffel Tower is in London. But it is a possible content of a belief, since it is possible for someone to believe that the Eiffel Tower is in London. Nor is it a judgment or statement, since again, as we have seen, a judgment or statement, to be, must be made by someone, and it is possible that no one ever judge or state that the Eiffel Tower is in London. But it is a possible content of a judgment or statement, since it is possible for someone to judge or state that the Eiffel Tower is in London. As was said above, beliefs, judgments, and statements must by someone be held or made if they are to be. But their content, which we may now refer to as their propositional content, when considered completely in abstraction from its being the content of some belief, judgment, or statement, is something that can by someone be believed, judged, or stated regardless of whether in fact anyone ever does do so.

It is considerations such as these that have led various philosophers to introduce the concept of propositions as entities distinct in kind from beliefs, judgments, statements, and sentences. I have argued that the latter constitute distinct irreducible ontological categories—that there are in fact beliefs, judgments, statements, and sentences and that no member of any of these four categories can be identical with or reduced to any member or combination of members of any of the other three categories. The question therefore arises of whether the concept of a proposition, like these other four concepts, is also the concept of a distinct irreducible ontological category. Is this concept the concept of such a category, or can it instead be dispensed with by reducing it to some other concept or combination of concepts? Are we, in asserting that there are propositions, multiplying entities beyond metaphysical necessity? To answer these questions it will be helpful to introduce a concept not heretofore discussed. This is the concept of states of affairs.

States of affairs are neither true nor false. Instead, they either obtain or do not obtain. If one believes, judges, or states that a given state of affairs obtains when in fact it does or that it does not obtain when in fact it does not, then one's belief, judgment, or statement is true. But if one believes, judges, or states that a given state of affairs obtains when in fact it does not or that it does not obtain when in fact it does, then one's belief, judgment, or statement is false. States of affairs are either contingent, necessary, or impossible. If the argument of Chapter Two is sound, necessary states of affairs are either synthetically or analytically necessary, and impossible states of affairs are either synthetically or analytically impossible. Every necessary state of affairs necessarily obtains, no impossible state of affairs can possibly obtain, and a contingent state of affairs might or might not obtain. If one asserts of a necessary state of affairs that it obtains or of an impossible state of affairs that it does not obtain, then one's assertion necessarily is true. But if one asserts of a necessary state of affairs that it does not obtain or of an impossible state of affairs that it does obtain, then one's assertion necessarily is false. And if one asserts of a contingent state of affairs either that it does obtain or else that it does not obtain, then one's assertion might or might not be true, depending upon whether the state of affairs in question does or does not obtain.

An example of a necessary state of affairs is the internal angles of a Euclidean triangle's containing half the number of degrees contained in a circle. This state of affairs necessarily obtains regardless of whether in fact any Euclidean triangles ever exist, in the sense that if at any time at any place a Euclidean triangle does in fact exist its internal angles necessarily contain half the number of degrees contained in a circle. Although it is not necessary that a Euclidean triangle exist at any time at any place, if such a triangle does at some time at some place exist it is necessary that its internal angles contain half the number of degrees contained in a circle. Thus although some actual figure's being a triangle is a contingent state of affairs, if it is a triangle its having internal angles that contain half the number of degrees contained in a circle is not a contingent but is rather a necessary state of affairs. An example of an impossible state of affairs is the internal angles of a Euclidean triangle's containing one-third the number of degrees contained in a circle. Since this is an impossible state of affairs, no actual figure that happens to be a Euclidean triangle can have internal angles containing one-third the number of degrees contained in a circle. All states of affairs that are neither necessary nor impossible are contingent and therefore might or might not at some time obtain.

Contingent states of affairs are therefore temporal in the sense that they might obtain at certain times and not obtain at certain other times. And some contingent states of affairs, such as a centaur's running in a pasture, are only possible and never actual, in the sense that although they might at some time obtain in fact they never do. But necessary and impossible states of affairs are timeless in the sense that there is no time at which the former might not and the latter might obtain. If, then, there is something the existence of which is necessary, its existence is timeless in the sense that there is no time at which it might not exist. In the case, however, of anything the existence of which is contingent, its existence or nonexistence is contingent in the sense that there is some time at which it might or might not exist. The obtaining, then, of necessary states of affairs and the nonobtaining of impossible states of affairs is timeless, whereas the obtaining or nonobtaining of any contingent state of affairs is temporal.

States of affairs are distinct from and not reducible to beliefs, judgments, statements, or sentences. The state of affairs consisting of my writing now with a yellow pencil either obtains or does not obtain but is neither true nor false, whereas the belief, judgment, or statement expressed by the sentence-token "I am writing now with a yellow pencil" is true or false, as is the sentence-token used to express them. Beliefs, judgments, statements, and the sentence-tokens used to express them are not themselves states of affairs, although someone's believing, judging, or stating by using some sentence-token that a given state of affairs obtains is a state of affairs that obtains at a given time. Although, then, a person can believe, judge, or state by using some sentence-token that a given state of affairs obtains, the state of affairs itself is not a belief, judgment, statement, or sentence. It is instead that which is believed, judged, or stated to obtain. It seems clear, then, that the concept of states of affairs is distinct from and not reducible to the concepts of beliefs, judgments, statements, and sentences. Rather than being reducible to the latter, the concept of a state of affairs is the concept of something the obtaining or the nonobtaining of which can be the content of a belief, judgment, or statement. As such, states of affairs are unlike beliefs, judgments, and statements in that whereas there would be no beliefs if no one ever held them and no judgments or statements if no one ever made them, the obtaining or the nonobtaining of a state of affairs in no way depends upon anyone's believing, judging, or stating either that it does or that it does not obtain. This applies even to those states of affairs that consist in someone's believing, judging, or stating that some state of affairs obtains, since in order that such states of affairs obtain it is not necessary that anyone believe, judge, or state that they do. Although such states of affairs would not obtain if no one believed, judged, or stated that some state of affairs obtains, since their obtaining consists in someone's believing, judging, or stating that some state of affairs obtains, their obtaining still does not depend upon anyone's believing, judging, or stating that they do.

It was said above that the concept of a state of affairs is the concept of something the obtaining or the nonobtaining of which can be the content of a belief, judgment, or statement. But earlier it was also said that the content of a belief, judgment, or statement is a proposition. A question therefore arises concerning the relationship of the obtaining or the nonobtaining of a state of affairs to a proposition. From the fact that they are both the content of a belief, judgment, or statement it does not follow that they are identical, since it is possible that a belief, judgment, or statement have two contents, one the obtaining or the nonobtaining of a given state of affairs, the other a proposition. It is also possible that a proposition be the content of a belief, judgment, or statement in a different sense from that in which the obtaining or the nonobtaining of a state of affairs is. As we shall see, the obtaining or the nonobtaining of a state of affairs cannot be identical with a proposition. *That* a given state of affairs obtains, however, is a proposition. That a given state of affairs, such as the Eiffel Tower's being in London, obtains is a proposition (1) that is either true or false and (2) that can be entertained, denied, believed, accepted, or stated. To believe, judge, or state that a given state of affairs obtains is to believe, accept, or state a proposition that is either true or false.

We must therefore distinguish between (1) states of affairs, (2) the obtaining and the nonobtaining of a state of affairs, and (3) that a given state of affairs obtains (or does not obtain), which is a proposition. (3) presupposes but is not reducible to (2), which presupposes but is not reducible to (1). States of affairs, such as the Eiffel Tower's being in London, can be entertained as intended objects of thought but cannot be believed, judged, or stated. They obtain or do not obtain, but are distinct from and not reducible to their obtaining or their not obtaining. If this were not the case one could not entertain as an object of thought some state of affairs, such as the Eiffel Tower's being in London, without considering also the question of whether it does or does not obtain. Moreover, in order to consider this latter question it is necessary first to have as the intended object of one's thought the state of affairs the obtaining or the nonobtaining of which one is to consider. One must first think of a state of affairs before one can think of it as obtaining or as not obtaining. In addition, without states of affairs there would be nothing to obtain or not to obtain, and no proposition could be either true or false. It is in this sense that they are presupposed by their obtaining or nonobtaining and by propositions. The concept of states of affairs is therefore distinct from that of their obtaining or not obtaining and from that of propositions.

But although the concept of states of affairs is presupposed by that of their obtaining or not obtaining, it is a necessary fact that any absolutely determinate state of affairs either obtains or else does not obtain. Moreover, just as the obtaining of a state of affairs is distinct from the state of affairs that obtains, so also it is distinct from the proposition that it obtains. The obtaining of a given state of affairs, like the state of affairs that obtains, is neither true nor false, whereas the proposition that a given state of affairs obtains is true or false. But although the two are not identical, they are necessarily related. First, propositions presuppose the obtaining and the nonobtaining of states of affairs, in the sense that no proposition could be true or false in the absence of the obtaining and the nonobtaining of states of affairs. It is because various states of affairs do or do not obtain that various propositions are true or false. Second, for any given state of affairs there is a pair of propositions, one to the effect that it obtains, the other to the effect that it does not obtain. Which of the two is true depends upon whether the state of affairs in question does or does not obtain. Thus the proposition that the state of affairs consisting of the Eiffel Tower's being in London does in fact obtain is true if and only if this state of affairs does in fact obtain. Since it does not in fact obtain, the proposition in question is false.

5. Nominative, Predicative, and Propositional Acts

The preceding considerations mean that a state of affairs and its obtaining or nonobtaining is the content of a belief, judgment, or statement in a different sense from that in which a proposition is. A state of affairs and its obtaining or nonobtaining may be said to be the nominative content and a proposition to be the predicative content. The predicative content presupposes but is not presupposed by the nominative content. This is the case because, as was indicated above, one can think of a given state of affairs and of its obtaining without believing, judging, or stating that it does in fact obtain, whereas one cannot believe, judge, or state that it obtains without first having thought of it. In this sense the nominative content of a belief, judgment, or statement is more fundamental than the predicative content. It is also more fundamental in the sense that it is only by virtue of a difference in their nominative component that two propositions of the same quality and quantity can differ. Thus the proposition that the state of affairs consisting of the Eiffel Tower's being in London does in fact obtain differs from the proposition that the state of affairs consisting of the Eiffel Tower's being in Paris does in fact obtain only by virtue of a difference in the nominative component of the two propositions. It might be objected that the first proposition also differs from the second by virtue of the fact that the first is false and the second true. To this the reply is that two propositions of the same quality and quantity can differ in truth-value only if there is a difference in their nominative component.

What is meant by saying that a state of affairs and its obtaining or not obtaining is the nominative content and a proposition the predicative content of a belief, judgment, or statement can also be explained as follows. When one simply thinks of some state of affairs or of its obtaining or not obtaining without also thinking either that it does or that it does not obtain, one simply intends it as the object of one's thought and does not predicate of it either that it does or that it does not obtain. The linguistic expression of such a thought would be something such as "the Eiffel Tower's being in London" or "the obtaining (or nonobtaining) of the state of affairs consisting of the Eiffel Tower's being in London." Neither of these phrases is a sentence, and neither can be used to make a statement, at least not if one adheres to the rules of English grammar. Neither has a subject and a predicate, and neither says anything about anything. The most that such acts of thinking and their corresponding linguistic expression do is to nominate something as a possible subject of predication. They are therefore nominative rather than predicative acts of thinking and phrases, and as such their nominative contents are neither true nor false. But when such nominative acts of thinking are accompanied by predicative acts, as when I think that the state of affairs consisting of the Eiffel Tower's being in London does not obtain, the state of affairs in question and its nonobtaining are not simply nominated as possible subjects of predication but instead are actually made the subject of a predication. I think, that is, not simply nominatively *of* the state of affairs consisting of the Eiffel Tower's being in London or *of* the nonobtaining of this state of affairs, but also *that* it does not obtain. I predicate of it that it does not obtain.

As contrasted with nominative acts of thinking and their linguistic expression, predicative acts of thinking and their linguistic expression are true or false. As we saw above, the nominative act of thinking of the state of affairs consisting of the Eiffel Tower's being in London or of the obtaining or the nonobtaining of this state of affairs is neither true nor false. Neither are the linguistic expressions of these nominative acts, such as "the Eiffel Tower's being in London" and "the obtaining (or nonobtaining) of the state of affairs consisting of the Eiffel Tower's being in London." But the predicative act of thinking that the state of affairs consisting of the Eiffel Tower's being in London does in fact obtain is either true or false, as is its linguistic expression. Whereas "the Eiffel Tower's being in London" and "the obtaining (or nonobtaining) of the state of affairs consisting of the Eiffel Tower's being in London" are not sentences, do not express propositions, and are neither true nor false, "the state of affairs consisting of the Eiffel Tower's being in London does in fact obtain" is a sentence, does express a proposition, and is either true or false. This can be put by saying that whereas the expressions "that the Eiffel Tower's being in London is true or false" and "that the obtaining or nonobtaining of the state of affairs consisting of the Eiffel Tower's being in London is true or false" can be neither true nor false, "that the state of affairs consisting of the Eiffel Tower's being in London does in fact obtain is true or false" is either true or false. If we omit the "that" occurring at the beginning and the "is true or false" occurring at the end of these three expressions, we obtain in the first two cases nonsentential phrases and in the third a sentence. It is because of this that the first two expressions, unlike the third, are neither true nor false. One cannot obtain a sentence by placing "that" at the beginning of a nonsentential phrase and "is true or false" at the end. Such operations yield a sentence only if the expression before which "that" is placed and after which "is true or false" is placed is already a sentence or at least can be used as one.

The form of sentence used above as expressing propositions is admittedly pedantic. Only philosophers, and then only in their philosophical moments, would think of using "the state of affairs consisting of the Eiffel Tower's being in London does in fact obtain" to express a proposition. Ordinarily they, like everyone else, would express such a proposition by using instead some such simple sentence as "The Eiffel Tower is in London." There is nonetheless some point in using such pedantic forms of sentences. It is that they indicate more clearly than do the simple sentences we ordinarily use the relationships between states of affairs, the obtaining or nonobtaining of states of affairs, and propositions. The use of such pedantic sentences indicates more clearly than does the use of the simple sentences we ordinarily use that to deny, believe, accept, or state a proposition is to deny, believe, judge, or state that some nominated state of affairs does (or does not) obtain. Their use here is intended only for this purpose and is in no way intended as a recommendation that in our everyday speech we replace the simple sentences we ordinarily use to express propositions with such pedantic sentences. Such philosophical recommendations that ordinary language be altered are seldom accepted in practice even by the philosophers who make them and even less often by other philosophers and by people who are not philosophers, who never become apprised of such recommendations in the first place. The purpose, then, of the use of pedantic locutions in philosophy is not to alter the use of ordinary language in everyday life but rather is to enable us to see certain relationships more clearly than we would be likely to do if we used only the ordinary language of everyday life. This alone is the point of the pedantic locutions used above.

We distinguished above between nominative and predicative acts. Acts of both sorts are moments or aspects of what we may now refer to as propositional acts. Every propositional act involves both a nominative and a predicative act and has both a nominative and a predicative aspect. The nominative act or moment consists of thinking of some state of affairs and of its obtaining or not obtaining, the predicative act or moment of denying, believing, judging, or stating that the nominated state of affairs does (or does not) obtain. The complete propositional act consists of both the nominative and the predicative act. It consists, that is, of thinking of some nominated state of affairs and denying, believing, judging, or stating either that it does or that it does not obtain. The content of the complete propositional act is the proposition that the nominated state of affairs does (or does not) obtain.

Propositions, however, can constitute the content of nominative as well as propositional acts. This happens when a proposition is simply intended as an object of thought without being accepted or rejected. Thus one can think of the proposition that the Eiffel Tower is in London without accepting or rejecting it. Such an act, even though it has a proposition as its object, is a nominative rather than a propositional act. Although the proposition constituting the object of the act is nominated as something susceptible of predication as true or false, no such predicative act is performed. This is to say that simply to think of or to entertain a proposition without performing the predicative act of accepting or rejecting it is to perform a nominative act without also performing a propositional act. Such acts differ from the nominative acts of thinking of a state of affairs and of its obtaining or not obtaining, since the objects of these nominative acts are neither true nor false, whereas the objects of the acts in question, being propositions, are either true or false. In such an act one thinks, for example, not simply of the Eiffel Tower's being in London or of the obtaining or the nonobtaining of this state of affairs, but of the proposition that it does in fact obtain. Whereas neither this state of affairs nor its obtaining or nonobtaining can be either true or false, the nominated proposition can be. But in the nominative nonpropositional act of thinking of or entertaining it no judgment of its truth or falsity is made. For this reason such acts are nominative rather than propositional even though they have propositions as their intended objects.

If our argument up to this point is sound, then we must admit the category of propositions as a distinct category in addition to and not reducible to those of sentences, statements, judgments, beliefs, and states of affairs. Unlike states of affairs and their obtaining or not obtaining, propositions are either true or false and cannot be identical with or reduced to states of affairs or their obtaining or not obtaining. Neither are they identical with or reducible to sentences, statements, judgments, or beliefs even though the latter, like propositions, are either true or false, since their truth or falsity is determined by that of the propositions that constitute their content. Whether, that is, a sentence, statement, judgment, or belief is true is determined by whether the proposition stated, accepted, believed, or expressed by means of the sentence is true. But if the category of propositions is not identical with or reducible to any of these other categories it must itself, like them, be accepted as an irreducible ontological category unless there is some other category with which it is identical or to which it is reducible. One possible candidate for such a category is that of facts. The same question, however, can be raised concerning this category. Is it an irreducible ontological category or can it be reduced to some one or to some combination of these other categories?

6. Facts

To answer this question it will be helpful to distinguish between different senses of the term 'fact'. In one sense of the term it is used to designate anything that exists or has being independently of its being thought of by anyone. The term is used in this sense more widely in nonphilosophical than in philosophical contexts and discourse. Later we shall have to introduce a more precise terminology, but for the purposes of this section it will suffice if we refer to facts in this sense of the term as 'existent entities' or 'real entities'. In this sense of 'fact' the Eiffel Tower, since it exists independently of being thought of by anyone, is a fact, whereas mermaids and square-circles, since they do not, are not facts. Although acts of thinking of mermaids or square-circles, since they can occur without themselves being thought of, are facts, the intended objects of such acts are not, since they have no being independently of being for someone intentional objects. If anything does in fact exist independently of its being for anyone an intentional object, then there are facts in the sense in question. If some such things, such as numbers, are timeless, then so also are some facts in this sense of 'fact'; and if some are temporal, so also are some facts in the sense in question.

A second sense of the term 'fact' is that in which it is used to designate states of affairs that obtain. In this sense of the term those states of affairs that obtain are facts; those that do not obtain are not facts. The term is also perhaps used more widely in this sense in nonphilosophical than in philosophical contexts and discourse. In this sense of the term, the Eiffel Tower's being in Paris is a fact, since that state of affairs does obtain, whereas the Eiffel Tower's being in London is not a fact, since that state of affairs does not obtain. In this sense of 'fact', facts are either necessary or contingent. Since necessary states of affairs, such as the internal angles of a Euclidean triangle's containing half the number of degrees contained in a circle, necessarily obtain, such states of affairs are necessary facts. Since all necessary states of affairs necessarily obtain, all such states of affairs are facts. Since, however, contingent states of affairs might or might not obtain, some are facts and some are not. Those that do obtain are facts; those that do not are not facts. But no impossible states of affairs can be facts, since no such states of affairs can possibly obtain. Since various necessary and contingent states of affairs do obtain, there are various necessary and contingent facts. To admit the category of facts in this second sense, however, is not to introduce another ontological category in addition to that of states of affairs that obtain, since the term 'fact' in this sense is only another name for such states of affairs and designates nothing distinct from or in addition to them.

A third sense of the term 'fact' is that in which it is used to designate the obtaining or the nonobtaining of a state of affairs, as distinct from the state of affairs that does or does not obtain. In this sense of the term, the obtaining of the state of affairs consisting of the Eiffel Tower's being in Paris is a fact distinct from the fact consisting of that state of affairs, which is a fact in the second sense of 'fact'. Similarly, in this third sense of the term the nonobtaining of the Eiffel Tower's being in London is a fact, even though the state of affairs consisting of the Eiffel Tower's being in London is not a fact in the second sense of 'fact', since it does not obtain. In this third sense of the term, the obtaining of a state of affairs that does obtain is a fact distinct from the state of affairs that obtains, which is a fact in the second sense of 'fact'; and the nonobtaining of a state of affairs that does not obtain is also in this third sense a fact even though the state of affairs that does not obtain is not a fact in the second sense. In this third sense of 'fact' the obtaining of necessary and the nonobtaining of impossible states of affairs are necessary facts, the obtaining or the nonobtaining of contingent states of affairs contingent facts.

To some it might seem that the term 'fact' is never used in this third sense, either in philosophical or in nonphilosophical contexts or discourse. If, however, we substitute for the pedantic "the obtaining (or the nonobtaining) of the state of affairs consisting of the Eiffel Tower's being in Paris" the ordinary expression "the existence (or the nonexistence) of the Eiffel Tower in Paris," we can more easily see that 'fact' is sometimes used in this third sense. People do, that is, sometimes say such things as "the existence of the Eiffel Tower in Paris is a fact" and "the nonexistence of the Eiffel Tower in London is a fact." To admit, however, the category of facts in this third sense is not to introduce another category in addition to that of the obtaining or the nonobtaining of states of affairs, since facts in this sense are nothing other than the obtaining or the nonobtaining of states of affairs.

A fourth sense of the term 'fact' is that in which it is used to designate true propositions. In this sense of the term the following two sentences are equivalent in meaning: "That the Eiffel Tower is in Paris is a true proposition" and "That the Eiffel Tower is in Paris is a fact." So also are these two sentences: "It is true that the Eiffel Tower is in Paris" and "It is a fact that the Eiffel Tower is in Paris". To generalize, any sentence that can be used to express a true proposition can also be used to express a fact and vice versa. Thus "The Eiffel Tower is in Paris" expresses a true proposition if and only if it expresses a fact. The use of a sentence "p" to express a true proposition is emphasized if we use the forms "That p is true" and "It is true that p," whereas its use to express a fact is emphasized if we use the forms "That p is a fact" and "It is a fact that p." A true sentence, however, when used without either of these forms of emphasis, expresses at once a true proposition and a fact. This last, however, can be misleading in that it might suggest that the expressed true proposition and the expressed fact are distinct when in point of fact they are identical. The true proposition expressed by the true sentence "p," rather than being distinct from the fact expressed by "p," is instead identical with this fact. The true proposition expressed, for example, by "The Eiffel Tower is in Paris," rather than being distinct from the fact expressed by this sentence, is instead identical with it. To say, that is, of a given state of affairs that does obtain that it does obtain or of one that does not obtain that it does not obtain is at once to state a true proposition and also a fact, or rather something that is both, since the proposition stated is identical with the fact stated. Therefore to admit the category of facts in this fourth sense is not to introduce a category distinct from and in addition to that of true propositions. Instead, the term 'fact', used in this fourth sense, is only another name for what is designated by the expression 'true proposition'.

It might, however, be objected that facts cannot be identical with true propositions. One reason that might be given in support of such an objection is that facts, unlike propositions, can be neither true nor false. Thus whereas the sentence "The true proposition that the Eiffel Tower is in Paris is true" is true, the sentence "The fact that the Eiffel Tower is in Paris is true" is not true, since facts can be neither true nor false. Since these two sentences are identical except for the fact that 'true proposition' occurs in the first and 'fact' in the second, and since the first but not the second is true, facts cannot be identical with true propositions. Since, that is, "That p is a true proposition" can be true whereas "That p is a true fact" cannot be true, true propositions cannot be identical with facts. Moreover, since "True propositions are true" is true whereas "Facts are true" is not, facts and true propositions cannot be identical. Since, in short, truth and falsity are predicable of propositions but not of facts, true propositions and facts cannot be identical.

The reply to this objection begins with a consideration of the use of alternative expressions that might or might not have the same reference. Certain sentences containing one of these expressions might be correctly formed and true, yet be transformed into incorrectly formed sentences if the expression in question be replaced by its alternative expression. One of the two alternative expressions, that is, might be combinable with other expressions in such a way as to yield a correctly formed and true sentence, whereas if the other expression were combined with these other expressions an incorrectly formed sentence would result. From this, however, it does not follow that the two expressions do not have the same denotation. Whether they do or not can be determined only through attempting to discover something denoted by one but not by the other. If nothing can be discovered that is denoted by one but not by the other, we lack sufficient reason for believing that they differ in their denotation. If in the absence of such a sufficient reason we nonetheless assert that they differ in denotation, we are guilty of multiplying entities beyond metaphysical necessity, since we then assert the existence of a difference in denotation, and thus the existence of at least two distinct entities or types of entities, without having sufficient reason for so doing. Now 'fact' and 'true proposition', as the objection we are considering clearly establishes, are not always combinable with precisely the same other expressions in such a way as to yield correctly formed and true sentences. Certain sentences containing 'true proposition' in combination with certain other expressions are correctly formed and true, yet are transformed into incorrectly formed sentences if 'fact' be substituted for 'true proposition'. From this, however, it does not follow that either of these expressions denotes anything not denoted by the other. To show that one denotes something not denoted by the other it is necessary to do more than show that when one is combined with certain other expressions certain correctly formed and true sentences result that do not result when the other is combined with these expressions. Unless more than this can be shown the two alternative expressions, although not always correctly combinable with precisely the same other expressions, might nonetheless be only alternative ways of speaking.

The question therefore arises as to whether either 'fact' or 'true proposition' designates anything not designated by the other in locutions such as "p is a fact" and "p is a true proposition." To answer this question it might be helpful if we raise a similar question concerning the first three senses of 'fact'. Are these three senses simply alternative ways of speaking or does each indicate something not indicated by either of the others? Facts in the first sense are existent or real entities; facts in the second sense are states of affairs that obtain; and facts in the third sense are the obtaining or the nonobtaining of states of affairs. Now there clearly is a difference between an existent entity, a state of affairs that obtains, and the obtaining or the nonobtaining of a state of affairs. The Eiffel Tower is an existent entity, its being in Paris is a state of affairs that obtains, and the obtaining of this state of affairs is distinct from the latter. The Eiffel Tower as an existent entity is distinct from the state of affairs consisting of its being in Paris, since it could be an existent entity even if this state of affairs did not obtain. It could, for example, be dismantled and reassembled in London, in which case it would still be an existent entity even though the state of affairs consisting of its being in Paris would then no longer obtain. Similarly, the state of affairs consisting of the Eiffel Tower's being in Paris is distinct from the obtaining of this state of affairs, since it is possible that it not obtain, as it would not if the Eiffel Tower were in London.

It seems clear, then, that each of the first three senses of 'fact' indicates something not indicated by either of the others. It seems clear also that each indicates something not indicated by the fourth sense of 'fact', since in the fourth sense a fact is a true proposition, and neither a real entity, a state of affairs that obtains, nor the obtaining of a state of affairs is a true proposition. But does 'fact' in the fourth sense indicate anything not indicated by 'true proposition'? We saw above that there are good reasons for maintaining that states of affairs and their obtaining or their not obtaining, which are neither true nor false, are distinct from propositions, which are true or false. From this, however, it does not follow that there is also some good reason for believing that 'fact' in the fourth sense indicates anything not indicated by 'true proposition'. If there is such a reason I do not know what it is. Those who think that there is such a reason can establish that there is in fact such a reason only by explaining what it is that 'fact' in the fourth sense but not 'true proposition' indicates. As we have seen, the fact that 'true proposition' can be combined with certain other expressions with which 'fact' cannot be combined to yield correctly formed and true sentences does not mean that either expression indicates anything not also indicated by the other. Instead, this fact is compatible with the position that these two expressions are simply alternative ways of indicating the same thing. If this position is correct, then the distinction between facts and true propositions is only a verbal distinction to which nothing nonlinguistic corresponds. If so, then just as facts in the first sense are real entities, facts in the second sense are states of affairs that obtain, and facts in the third sense are the obtaining or the nonobtaining of states of affairs, so facts in the fourth sense are true propositions. Although the distinction between these four senses is not merely verbal, that between 'fact' and 'true proposition' is.

The result of these considerations is that the category of facts is not an irreducible ontological category. Instead, the term 'fact' has at least four distinct senses, according to which facts are either real entities, states of affairs that obtain, the obtaining or the nonobtaining of states of affairs, or true propositions. This, however, does not mean that there are no facts. If there are real entities, states of affairs that obtain, and true propositions, then there also are facts. But if our argument is sound, facts, in the various senses of the term, are not entities distinct from and in addition to real entities, states of affairs that obtain, and true propositions. Nor does the fact that facts do not constitute a distinct ontological category mean that the term ought no longer to be used. From the fact that neither of two alternative expressions indicates anything not indicated by the other it does not follow that either ought no longer to be used.

The elimination of facts as a distinct irreducible ontological category leaves us with sentences, statements, judgments, beliefs, states of affairs, and propositions, none of which are reducible to any of the others. Since each of these constitutes a distinct irreducible ontological category, a question arises as to precisely what the ontological status of each is. We have already dealt with this question as it relates to sentences, and nothing more need to said here about their ontological status. Nor need any more be said here about acts of statement making and judgment making, which are particular acts performed by individual persons, or the holding of a belief by a person, which is a disposition to act in certain ways in certain situations, including the making of statements and judgments and the utterance of sentence-tokens expressing the belief. The difficult question that remains concerns the ontological status of the content of statements, judgments, and beliefs. Such contents, as we saw above, are propositions, states of affairs, and the obtaining or the nonobtaining of the latter.

Note

1. Saint Augustine, *On Free Choice of the Will,* trans. Anna S. Benjamin and L. H. Hackstaff (Indianapolis: Library of Liberal Arts, 1964), B. 3, Chaps. 4–5, pp. 88–95.

5
Intentionality and Reality

To answer the question raised at the end of the last chapter it will be helpful to consider first a related set of issues. These are the intentionality of thinking and thoughts and the distinction between intentional objects and existent entities and their relationship to one another. These issues can be grouped together under the general heading of intentionality and reality.

1. Intentional Objects and Existent Entities

Since it is impossible to think without thinking of something, every thought is essentially intentional. Although one can think of the concept of nothing, one cannot think of nothing, except in the sense of not thinking of anything at all, which is identical with not thinking. Every act of thinking therefore necessarily has an intentional object, which is that of which the thinker is thinking. But from this it does not follow that in every act of thinking some entity exists of which one is thinking. Intentional objects might but need not be existent entities. If I think of the Eiffel Tower the intended object of my thought is also an existent entity. But if I think of the mermaid reclining on the couch the intended object of my thought, which is the mermaid, is not an existent entity. The intended object of a thought is also an existent entity only if it exists independently of the act of thinking of it. Indeed, to exist is nothing other than to be independently of being thought and thus of being an intended object of thought. There is no harm in speaking of intentional objects as entities, provided that one remembers that an intentional entity is not necessarily an existent entity. But to avoid confusion it is perhaps better to reserve the term 'entity' for existent entities and to use the term 'object' when speaking of intentional objects.

From the fact, however, that intentional objects are not necessarily existent entities it does not follow that nonexistent intentional objects are

127

nothing, for they are still intentional objects. Without such objects, as was indicated above, there could be no thoughts, since one cannot think of nothing. Moreover, such objects determine, at least partly, the nature of thoughts. Just as two concepts do not differ as concepts taken completely in abstraction from their contents or objects, so also two thoughts differ from one another, at least in part, by virtue of a difference in their intentional objects. Thus the thought of a mermaid differs from the thought of a centaur by virtue of a difference in the intentional objects of the two thoughts. One is the thought of an animal that is a woman from the waist up and a fish from the waist down, the other the thought of an animal that is a man from the waist up and a horse from the waist down. Without this difference in the nature of the intended objects of the two thoughts, neither would differ from the other.

The fact, however, that thoughts differ from one another by virtue of a difference in their intended objects does not mean that the latter must exist. Instead, thoughts, by virtue of their essential intentionality, have the peculiarity of differing from one another by virtue of a difference in their intended objects regardless of whether the latter exist. Even when the intended objects of two thoughts are also existent entities, as in the case of the Eiffel Tower and the Taj Mahal, the difference between the two thoughts issues entirely from a difference in their intentional objects, since the thought of the Eiffel Tower would still differ from the thought of the Taj Mahal even if neither of these intentional objects were also existent entities. Moreover, these two existent entities do not differ insofar as they are considered only as existent entities in complete abstraction from any consideration of their individual properties. Neither, that is, differs from the other by virtue of the fact that each exists. To say of one that it exists and also of the other that it exists is to say the same thing about both and therefore is not to distinguish one from the other. The latter can be done only by specifying properties possessed by one but not by the other or by indicating that one has some spatiotemporal location the other does not have. As soon as this is done a difference between intentional objects appears regardless of whether there are in fact existent entities possessing the specified properties or the indicated spatiotemporal locations.

Whether, then, intentional objects are also existent entities has nothing whatever to do with the question of whether the intended objects of two thoughts differ. The thought of a mermaid differs from the thought of a centaur, even though the thinker who has the two thoughts believes that neither intended object is also an existent entity, because the thought of a mermaid is a thought of an intended object different in nature from the intended object of the thought of a centaur. And the thought of a mermaid reclining on the couch is a different thought from that of a mermaid swimming in the sea, even though the thinker who has the two thoughts believes that neither intended object is also an existent entity, because the two thoughts differ in content. Intentional objects that are not also existent entities therefore can differ from one another fully as much as existent entities can. Moreover, just as the difference between existent entities does not issue from a difference between the thoughts of them, so also the difference between intentional objects, rather than issuing from a difference between the thoughts of which they are the objects, instead determines the difference between the thoughts. But whereas existent entities exist independently of thoughts of them and thus independently of their status as intentional objects, intentional objects do not. This can be put by saying that existent entities would still be existent entities even if they were not also intentional objects. Although their status as intentional objects depends upon their being thought, their status as existent entities does not. But since intentional objects that are not also existent entities do not exist at all, they would have no status at all if they were not thought. Their being, which is intentional being, depends entirely upon their being thought. To have intentional being, i.e., to be an intentional object, is to be the object of a thought. Although there would (or at least might) be existent entities if there were no thoughts, there could be no intentional objects in the absence of thoughts.

Some philosophers would object immediately to the ascription to intentional objects of even such an attenuated form of being as intentional being. Certain of these philosophers might be satisfied somewhat if instead of speaking of the intentional being of intentional objects we spoke instead of their intentional inexistence, as Professor Chisholm, following Brentano, and others do.[1] This, however, would amount only to a change of language, not a change of thought, if 'intentional inexistence' has the same meaning as 'intentional being'. The only advantage the expression 'intentional inexistence' might have over 'intentional being' is that the former expression perhaps indicates more directly than the latter does that intentional objects that are not also existent entities do not exist. But 'intentional being' has the advantage of indicating that intentional objects, even when they are not also existent entities, still are something and not nothing. So long as one keeps in mind that to say that intentional objects have intentional being in no way commits one to the claim that they therefore are also existent entities, there seems little if any harm in speaking of their intentional being. It is hard to know what more one can do to satisfy those who might object to speaking of the intentional being of intentional objects other than to repeat what has been said above: intentional objects have intentional being because one cannot think without thinking of something regardless of whether that of which one thinks is an existent entity, and since that of which one thinks is necessarily something rather than nothing it must have some form of being. But the only form of being it necessarily has by virtue of its status as an intentional object is intentional being. Whether an intentional object is also an existent entity is a further question, and if it is not then it does not exist. If this does not satisfy the critic then I do not know what would other than to concede that there are no intentional objects in the first place, since if there are no such objects then nothing can have intentional being.

One might attempt to eliminate talk of such objects by developing an adverbial theory of thought analogous to adverbial theories of sensing.[2] Thus instead of saying that one is thinking of a mermaid or a centaur one would say instead that one is thinking mermaidly or centaurly. Such forms of speech, however, soon become cumbersome if not ludicrous. Thus instead of saying that one is thinking of the Eiffel Tower or the Taj Mahal one would say instead that one is thinking Eiffel Towerly or Taj Mahally. But how can one say in adverbial fashion that one is thinking of a mermaid on the couch or of a centaur in the pasture? Doubtless these things could be said in an adverbial way even though such a way of speaking would be quite cumbersome, if not in fact patently ludicrous. The motive animating such ways of speaking would doubtless be a desire to avoid speaking of intentional objects. But what is it to think mermaidly or centaurly other than to think of a mermaid or a centaur? One cannot succeed in transforming 'thinking' from a transitive into an intransitive verb simply by developing an adverbial way of speaking. The term 'thinking' is a transitive verb because thinking is essentially intentional, and one cannot transform thinking into something that is not intentional simply by developing a way of speaking according to which 'thinking' becomes an intransitive verb. One can think well or badly, clearly or confusedly, validly or invalidly, but to think well or badly one must think of something. Thus although adverbial modifiers can be applied to acts of thinking, they indicate how one is thinking and not that of which one is thinking. This suggests that attempts to develop adverbial theories of thinking might rest ultimately upon a confusion of how one is thinking with that of which one is thinking. Since thinking is an act, 'thinking' is a verb. And since thinking is an act it can be done in various ways, such as successfully or unsuccessfully, which means that 'thinking' can be adverbially modified. But since thinking is essentially an intentional act it necessarily has an intentional object, and because of this 'to think' is the infinitive form of a transitive verb. Thus although one can think clearly or confusedly about mermaids, one cannot think clearly and mermaidly unless this latter locution be interpreted only as a rather bizarre way of saying that one is thinking clearly about mermaids. If one who uses such an adverbial way of speaking intends thereby to say that one can think clearly and mermaidly without thinking of anything at all, then he manifests thereby a failure to think clearly about thinking about mermaids or about anything else.

Another possible objection to the introduction of intentional objects concerns their relationship to existent entities and has to do with the principle of the indiscernibility of identicals. If intentional objects were never existent entities and existent entities never intentional objects, then no problems would arise in connection with this principle. But problems do arise if intentional objects are also sometimes existent entities. For if identicals are necessarily indiscernible, then x and y cannot be identical if either has some property the other lacks. But an intentional object necessarily has some property, namely that of being an intended object of thought, which an existent entity need not have; and an existent entity also necessarily has some property, namely that of not depending for its being upon its being an intended object of thought, which no intentional object can possibly have. Therefore no intentional object can be identical with any existent entity. But if this is the case, and if to think of an existent entity it is necessary that it be the intended object of one's thought, then no one can ever think of an existent entity. And if no one can ever think of an existent entity, i.e., have it as the intended object of one's thought, then no one can ever have knowledge of existent entities. The result will then be a form of extreme subjective idealism according to which one can have knowledge only of the intended objects of one's thoughts and not of existent entities, which is only one step removed from if not equivalent to a form of extreme skepticism or agnosticism according to which no one can ever have knowledge of existent entities. It is therefore important that a solution be found to the problem in question.

The solution, I suggest, is to be found by advancing considerations similar to those involved in one possible solution to the similar problem of the identity of the Evening Star with the Morning Star. The concept of the Evening Star is the concept of a certain heavenly body appearing at a certain place in the heavens in the evening, that of the Morning Star of a certain heavenly body appearing at a certain place in the heavens in the morning. The two concepts are therefore distinct concepts; neither is identical with the other. But through empirical means it is discovered that these two distinct concepts both apply to the same entity to which a third concept also applies—that of the planet Venus existing continuously from evening to morning to evening and traversing a certain path in the heavens. Because of the nature of the concepts of the Evening Star and the Morning Star, nothing can satisfy the first concept unless it appears in the evening and nothing can satisfy the second unless it appears in the morning. But both these concepts could still be satisfied even if that which satisfies the one were not in fact identical with that which satisfies the other. It is a contingent empirical fact that the same entity that satisfies a third concept, that of the planet Venus, also satisfies the other two concepts. But since the three concepts are distinct and not identical concepts, that which satisfies all three can do so only by virtue of its possessing three distinct properties—that of appearing at a certain place in the heavens in the evening, that of appearing at a certain place in the morning, and that of existing continuously and appearing successively in both places.

Similar considerations apply to the concepts of an intentional object and an existent entity. Something is an intentional object by virtue of its being an intended object of thought, an existent entity by virtue of its existing independently of being thought. The two concepts are thus distinct concepts, and something can satisfy one without satisfying the other. The intended object of my thought when I think of a mermaid satisfies the concept of an intentional object but not that of an existent entity, and a material object never intended in thought by anyone satisfies the concept of an existent entity but not that of an intentional object. But some things, such as the Eiffel Tower, satisfy both concepts. Just as it is one and the same identical object, the planet Venus, that is both the Evening Star and the Morning Star, so also it is one and the same identical object, the Eiffel Tower, that is both an intentional object and an existent entity. But whereas the planet Venus would still be both the Evening Star and the Morning Star if it were only an existent entity and never an intentional object, it is analytically true that nothing can be both an intentional object and an existent entity unless it is an intentional object as well as an existent entity. The planet Venus, that is, is both the Evening Star and the Morning Star because it exists at certain places at certain times and not because at some time it is the intended object of someone's thought, whereas nothing can be both an existent entity and an intentional object unless at some time it is the intended object of someone's thought.

This last can be put by saying that whereas the planet Venus is both the Evening Star and the Morning Star by virtue of its having certain objective properties, nothing can be an intentional object as well as an existent entity by virtue of its having such properties. The planet Venus is the Evening Star because it exists at a certain place in the heavens in the evening, the Morning Star because it exists at a certain place in the morning, and it would exist at these places at these times even if it were never for anyone an intentional object. Nothing, however, is an intentional object simply by virtue of its status as an existent entity or by virtue of any of the properties it possesses as such an entity. Instead, it acquires its status as an intentional object only as a consequence of an act of thought on the part of some thinker for whom it thereby becomes such an object. Its being an intentional object is therefore not a property an existent entity as such possesses, but is rather a property it acquires only as a consequence of some act of thought on the part of some thinker. This, however, does not mean that the property of being an intentional object is not in fact a property of an existent entity that is also an intentional object. Since it is the existent entity the Eiffel Tower that is the intended object of my thought when I think of it, being the intended object of my thought becomes a property of the existent entity the Eiffel Tower when I think of it.

The fact that an existent entity acquires the property of being an intentional object only as a consequence of the act of another agent, i.e., of the thinker who thinks of it, and not as a consequence of its own nature or action, is not an especially singular phenomenon. For existent entities sometimes acquire objective properties as a consequence of the action of other agents. Thus the point of a pin becomes hot when held in a flame. What is singular about the acquisition by an existent entity of the property of being an intentional object is that this property is not an objective property of the existent entity but becomes and remains a property of it for only so long as it remains an intentional object. Other properties of existent entities are also sometimes somewhat ephemeral, as is the heat of the point of a pin that has been held in a flame. Its point is hot for a few seconds, then cold again. Yet, leaving aside the question of the objectivity of the so-called secondary qualities, all properties of existent entities other than that of being an intended object, and those that issue from this property alone, are objective properties of the entity, in the sense that it has these properties regardless of whether it is also ever for anyone an intentional object.

Part of what this means is that no act of thought by means of which an existent entity becomes for someone an intentional object can ever by itself effect any changes in it, so that none of its objective properties are ever in any way altered simply as a consequence of its becoming an intentional object. Another way of putting this is to say that no act of thought by means of which an existent entity becomes an intentional object can ever by itself be causally efficacious in effecting some change in the objective nature of that entity. Its objective nature and status as an existent entity therefore remain what they are regardless of whether it ever for anyone becomes an intentional object. A flame can heat the point of a pin or consume a piece of paper and is therefore causally effective in producing changes in the objective nature or status of existent entities. But no act of thought can ever by itself produce any change in the objective nature or status of any existent entity it transforms into an intentional object. This means that there is nothing in the nature of an act of thought that can possibly prevent the thinker whose act it is from knowing the objective nature as it is in itself of any existent entity that becomes for him an intentional object. Such knowledge would be impossible if acts of thought necessarily produced some change in the objective nature of existent entities by transforming them into intentional objects, for then we could never know the objective nature of such entities as they are in themselves but instead could know only their nature as changed in some way as a consequence of their becoming intentional objects. There might be other factors that prevent us from knowing the objective nature of existent entities as they are in themselves, but their becoming intentional objects is not such a factor.

To say, however, that acts of thought cannot by themselves produce changes in the objective nature of the existent entities that become their intentional objects is not to say that they are never necessary conditions of the production of such changes. Thus if I am intentionally to heat the point of a pin the point must not only be an existent entity but must also be for me an intentional object. But its being for me an intentional object is only a necessary and not a sufficient condition of my intentionally heating it, since it can for me be an intentional object without my attempting to heat it. For me intentionally to heat it I must not only intend it in thought but also choose to heat it. Although, then, an existent entity's being also an intentional object is never a sufficient condition of the production of a change in its objective nature, it is sometimes a necessary condition. This would be the case even if some people had telekinetic powers that enabled them intentionally to produce objective changes in existent entities without using bodily means, since such entities would first have to be intentional objects for such people if they are intentionally to produce such changes. Such changes could be produced telekinetically in existent entities without the latter becoming intentional objects only if the people who produce them do so unintentionally.

The objective nature, then, of an existent entity is not in the least affected simply by virtue of the fact that the entity becomes for someone an intentional object. Although an existent entity cannot be an intentional object unless it is such an object for someone, its status as an existent entity is not in the least dependent on its being for anyone an intentional object. Moreoever, an existent entity is also an intentional object only for so long as for someone it is an intended object of thought. This means that an entity that exists for thousands of years, such as some rock in some desert, that becomes throughout its existence an object of thought for only one person and then for only a fleeting second, never to be thought of again by anyone, is an intentional object only for that fleeting second. It means also that the same identical existent entity can intermittently become at various moments throughout its existence an intentional object without being such an object throughout its existence. Furthermore, the same identical existent entity can be an intentional object not only twice or more for the same person, as when I think of the Eiffel Tower yesterday and then again today, but also either at the same or at different times for two or more people, as when I yesterday, you today, and he tomorrow all think of one and the same Eiffel Tower. Although our ways of identifying it, beliefs about it, images, if any, of it, and attitudes, if any, toward it, might all in varying degrees differ, we can all think of one and the same identical Eiffel Tower, and if we do then one and the same existent entity is an intentional object for each of us so long as we think of it.

One and the same thing, then, can be both an existent entity and an intentional object, just as one and the same planet can be both the Evening Star and the Morning Star. It is an existent entity by virtue of its possessing one property, that of not being dependent for its being upon being thought, an intentional object by virtue of its possessing another property, that of being an object of thought, just as the planet Venus is the Evening Star by virtue of its possessing one property, the Morning Star by virtue of its possessing another property. As an existent entity it has existent being, as an intentional object intentional being. There are thus two distinct modes of being—one existent being, the other intentional being. As was indicated above, some entities, such as the Eiffel Tower, have being in both senses, whereas others, such as a rock that never becomes for anyone an intended object of thought, have only existent and not intentional being. And some intentional objects, such as the mermaid reclining on the couch, have only intentional and not existent being. More needs to be said about such objects.

2. Intentional Objects and Intentional Acts

It was maintained above that an existent entity can intermittently at different times be an intentional object for the same person or for different persons and at the same time be an intentional object for different persons. Thus I can think of the Eiffel Tower at different times and different people can think of it at the same or at different times. Yet the Eiffel Tower, as an existent entity, continues to have being as an existent entity regardless of whether anyone at any time ever thinks of it. This last, however, is not true of intentional objects that are not also existent entities. The question therefore arises of whether one and the same identical nonexistent intentional object can be an intended object of thought at different times and for different persons. The answer would seem to be that it can be. Thus I can think today of the same nonexistent mermaid reclining on the couch of which I thought yesterday, and you as well as I can also think of her. If this were not the case we could not both raise the question of what couch she is reclining on nor could we both agree that she does not exist. More generally, if the same person could not think more than once or if more than one person could not think of the same nonexistent intentional object, then fiction would be impossible. If, that is, Shakespeare as he wrote the last act of *Hamlet* could not think of the same nonexistent intentional object Hamlet of which he thought as he wrote the first act, then the fictional death of the fictional character Hamlet in the last act could not be the death of the same fictional character of that name appearing in the first act. And if literary critics could not think of the same nonexistent intentional object, then it is hard to see how the vast body of literature about the fictional character Hamlet could have developed.

It is true that to some degree different people identify fictional characters differently and have different beliefs about, images of, and attitudes toward them. But the same thing, as we have seen, is also true of intentional objects that are also existent entities. Thus two or more people can have as their intentional object the same existent entity the Eiffel Tower even though they differ to some degree in their ways of identifying it and in their beliefs about, images of, and attitudes toward it. Moreover, just as true and false statements can be made about existent entities, so also such statements can be made about fictional characters. Thus it is true that Laertes was the brother of Ophelia, false that Polonius was the father of Hamlet. And two or more people can agree that the first statement is true and the second false, which they could not do unless they were thinking of the same nonexistent intentional objects. Although such statements are true or false ultimately because of decisions Shakespeare made in writing *Hamlet,* they are still statements about fictitious characters, not about decisions made by Shakespeare. In saying, that is, that Laertes was the brother of Ophelia, one is saying something about a fictitious character, not about some decision made by Shakespeare, for one could believe that Laertes was her brother without believing that Shakespeare was the author of *Hamlet* but not without having Laertes as the intended even though nonexistent object of one's thought. In general, then, to think of a fictitious character is to do just that, for a fictitious character is one object of thought, the decision of an author another, and one can think of the former without thinking of the latter.

But even if one could not think of a fictitious character without also thinking of the decision of some author to create the character, one still could not describe adequately such a decision without some mention of the nature of the fictitious character created by means of it. Just as it is impossible to think without thinking of something, so also it is impossible to create without creating something. Creating, like thinking, is essentially intentional or transitive, and two distinct acts of creation can no more be adequately described or even distinguished from one another without some mention of the object created than two acts of thought can be so described or distinguished without some mention of their intended objects. Insofar as two acts of creation are described simply as two acts of creation, nothing is said about one that is not said about the other, which is to say that two acts of creation do not differ from one another insofar as each is considered only as an act of creation and nothing more. And although some reference to one act of creation as an act on the part of Shakespeare and to another as an act on the part of Cervantes might suffice to distinguish each act from the other, it would not suffice to distinguish either act from any other act of creation on the part of the same author. Shakespeare created the character Horatio as well as Hamlet, Cervantes the character Sancho Panza as well as Don Quijote, and it is hard to see how we could distinguish between these separate acts of creation on the part of the same author without some mention of the characters created. Certainly no complete description of them could be given without some mention of the characters created by means of them. Moreover, most of us know much more about the characters in question than we do about the acts by means of which they were created. Indeed, most of us know nothing at all about these particular acts, as distinguished from others by the same authors, other than that they were the acts by means of which the characters in question were created. We have, that is, only an indirect knowledge of such acts by way of our knowledge of the characters in question, and most of us probably suppose that such acts occurred only because we know that the characters in question are fictions created by the authors in question.

If the preceding is correct certain consequences follow. One is that the nature of certain existent entities is partly determined by the nature of intentional objects regardless of whether the latter are also themselves existent entities. Here the expression 'existent entity' is being used to refer to acts as well as things. This, however, might be misleading, since acts are not entities in the same way in which things are. Instead, acts presuppose agents, since they are acts of agents who might also perform still other acts. One might therefore prefer to say that it is only agents who exist and not the acts they perform and that the latter instead are events that occur. This being the case, it might be better to use an expression such as 'actual entity' to refer to acts and other events. Such an expression, however, has already been appropriated by Whitehead, and its use here might lead those familiar with his use of it to read his meaning into it. This being so, perhaps the most felicitious language we can use here is the scholastic terminology used by Descartes in the Third Meditation when he speaks of formal reality and objective reality. Roughly speaking, intentional objects have objective reality, whereas things, agents, events, and acts that have being regardless of whether they also are intentional objects have formal reality. Existent entities therefore constitute a species of formal reality; some formal realities, such as things and agents, are also existent entities but some, such as events and acts, are not. Because their being is not dependent upon their being intentional objects, events and acts as well as things and agents have formal reality even though the former, unlike the latter, are not existent entities. Events and acts occur regardless of whether they are objects of thought; they are actual regardless of whether they are also intentional objects. They are therefore formal realities even though they, unlike things and agents, are not existent entities. With these terminological remarks in mind, we return to the point at issue.

This is that the nature of certain formal realities is partly determined by the nature of certain intentional objects regardless of whether the latter are also formal realities. The nature of an act of thinking is partly determined by the nature of its intended object regardless of whether the latter is also a formal reality. Thus the nature of an act of thinking of a mermaid differs at least in part from that of an act of thinking of a centaur by virtue of a difference in the intended objects of the two acts, even though neither object is also a formal reality. But since acts of thinking are formal realities regardless of whether they are also intentional objects, this means that the nature of certain formal realities is determined at least in part by the nature of certain intentional objects regardless of whether the latter are also formal realities. The only formal realities, however, of which this is true are those that have intentional objects. As was indicated above, the objective nature of existent entities that do not have intentional objects can be affected by nonexistent intentional objects only indirectly through the action of some agent for whom such intentional objects are objects. Thus the decision of someone who thinks of mermaids to write about mermaids leads him to place certain marks on a sheet of paper. In this way the sheet of paper, which is an existent entity that has no intentional objects, is affected by someone's having a nonexistent intentional object as his intended object of thought. It is, however, only indirectly as opposed to being directly affected by the latter's thinking of such a nonexistent object, since his thinking of such an object is only a necessary and not a sufficient condition of his placing on it the marks he does. Should he, upon thinking of mermaids, decide not to write about them, the marks in question would not be made.

The only formal realities, then, whose natures are at least partly determined directly by intentional objects regardless of whether the latter are also formal realities are those that have such objects as their intended objects. Even this, however, might be found objectionable by those averse to the idea that something nonexistent can determine directly, even though only partly, the nature of a formal reality. Yet, given that there are nonexistent intentional objects, the only way of escaping such a conclusion would seem to be to deny that there are any formal realities of the kind in question. Such a denial, however, would involve denying that acts of thinking of nonexistent intentional objects do in fact occur. But that such acts do occur seems undeniable. Even if such acts always had themselves, in addition to their nonexistent intentional objects, as their objects, they would still be formal realities. Even, that is, if every act of thinking of something always had itself as part of its intentional object, it would still be a formal reality. This would mean that every act of thinking of something would always have some formal reality, namely itself, as part of its intentional object even though some other part of its object were a nonexistent object. In point of fact, however, it is not the case that every act of thinking has itself as part of its intentional object, for I can think of a mermaid without thinking of my thinking or thought of the mermaid. Although people sometimes do think of their thinking of some intentional object while they are thinking of the latter, it is by no means necessary that they do so. Although, then, a formal reality such as an act of thinking can be at least part of its own intentional object, it need not be but instead can have something other than itself as its only object.

It is also possible to think of something without thinking of one's way of identifying it or of any of one's beliefs about, images of, or attitudes toward it. The latter constitute what may be referred to as the content of an act of thinking, as distinct from its object. When I think of the Eiffel Tower the intentional object of my thought is the Eiffel Tower itself, not my way of identifying it or any beliefs about, images of, or attitudes toward it I might have. It is true that I could not think of the Eiffel Tower or have anything else as an intentional object without identifying it in some way and perhaps also without having some beliefs about it. Although, that is, I can think of something without having any images of it or attitudes toward it (unless indifference itself be counted as an attitude), it is hard to understand what thinking of something, i.e., having it as the intended object of one's thought, could consist in if one neither identified it in some way nor had any beliefs at all about it. Nonetheless, my way of identifying some intended object of thought and my beliefs about it, like any images of it or attitudes toward it I might have, constitute the content of my consciousness and need not be part of its object. The object of my consciousness, as distinct from its content, is that around which the content is centered; it is that which I identify in some way, have beliefs about, and perhaps also have images of and attitudes toward. But although every act of thinking has some content as well as some object, the content need not be part of the object. Although I might think of some part of the content as I think of the object, I need not do so in order to think of the latter. The object and the content of consciousness thus function differently or play different roles in acts of thinking. To think of the former is not to think of the latter, and if one thinks of the latter as well as or instead of the former the object of one's consciousness is to that degree different from what it is if one thinks of the former and not also of the latter.

But even if in order to think of some object it were necessary to think also of one's act of thinking and of some part of its content, the object itself would not be reducible to the act of thinking or to its content or to any part of its content. Both the act and its content are essentially intentional in nature and intend the object. It is the object of which one thinks and which one identifies in some way, has beliefs about, images of, and attitudes toward. Without an intentional object one could not think of, identify, have beliefs about, images of, or attitudes toward anything at all; and no act of thinking, no identification, no belief, no image, no attitude can be completely described without some mention of its intentional object, which means that its nature is determined at least in part by the nature of its intentional object. Every act of thinking and its content therefore presuppose some intentional object the nature of which determines at least in part their nature. But although every act of thinking, identifying, and imaging and every holding of a belief or an attitude is a formal reality, its intentional object need not be. If it is not, then certain formal realities presuppose certain objective realities that are not also formal realities, and their nature is determined at least in part by the nature of these objective realities. But this coin, as we have seen, also has another side, which is that in the absence of these formal realities there could be no objective realities, regardless of whether the latter are also formal realities. Without acts of thinking there could be no intentional objects, regardless of whether the latter are also existent entities. Although an existent entity would still be an existent entity if there were no acts of thinking, it could not be an intentional object. Thus just as certain formal realities presuppose objective realities, so also objective realities presuppose certain formal realities.

3. The *Cogito*

This brings us to certain truths contained in the Cartesian *cogito*. Although something's being an objective reality does not mean that it is also a formal reality, it does mean that there is some formal reality, since without some formal reality there can be no objective reality. Although, that is, the fact that something is an intentional object does not mean that it is also an existent entity, it does mean that there is an act of thinking, since without acts of thinking there could be no intentional objects. But since there is at least one intentional object, namely the mermaid reclining on the couch of which I am now thinking, there is at least one act of thinking. And since without agents there could be no acts, there is at least one agent, namely the agent thinking of the mermaid. Although for each distinct act there might be a distinct agent, there is at least one thinking agent or subject, since there is at least one act of thinking. Since, that is, thinking is an act, since acts require agents, and since an act of thinking is now occurring, a thinking agent or subject now exists. Regardless of whether the intentional object of the present act of thinking is also a formal reality, its objective reality presupposes the formal reality of the present act of thinking, which in turn presupposes the formal reality of some thinking agent or subject. Without a formally real act of thinking there could be no objective reality or intentional object, and without a formally real thinker there could be no act of thinking. Since there can be no thinking without a thinker, and since an act of thinking is now occurring, a thinker now exists. Although I might not know who this thinker is or what, if anything, it is other than a thinker, I do know that it exists.

But although I might not know who this thinker is, I can refer to it by means of a personal pronoun. The question is: What such pronoun ought I to use? There are six possibilities. I can use the first, second, or third person singular or the first, second, or third person plural. Let us try first the second person singular and say "You are thinking." If I use this sentence seriously with its usual sense, then I suppose the existence of two people, the speaker and the person addressed. I presuppose the existence of another if I address seriously the words "You are thinking" to him in the sense that it would be pointless to use such a form of words unless I believe the person addressed does in fact exist. The person addressed is therefore for me an intentional object. From this, however, it does not follow that he is an existent entity. From the fact, that is, that I believe that another person exists and that he is thinking, it does not follow either that he does in fact exist or that he is in fact thinking if he does exist. Thus the statement "You are thinking" is false if the person addressed does not exist or if he does exist but is not thinking. The use of this sentence by the speaker, however, to make a statement about another presupposes the existence of the speaker in the sense that he could not so use it if he did not exist. Although the existence of the person addressed is a necessary condition of the truth of the statement, it is not a necessary condition of the making of the statement. The existence of the speaker, on the other hand, is a necessary condition of his making the statement but not of its truth.

Similar considerations apply to the third person singular and to the first, second, and third person plural forms of the statement in question. Thus if I seriously address the words "He is thinking" to another, I presuppose the existence of three persons—myself, the person addressed, and the person about whom the statement is made. Similarly, the statement "We are thinking" presupposes the existence of the speaker and of at least one other person; "You all are thinking" presupposes the existence of the speaker and of at least two other persons; and "They are thinking," said to another, presupposes the existence of the speaker and of at least three other persons, at least one of whom is addressed and at least two of whom are referred to. These statements are all like "You are thinking" in that a necessary condition of their truth is that someone other than the speaker be thinking at the time the speaker makes them. "We are thinking" and "You all are thinking" are also like "You are thinking" in that a necessary condition of their truth is that the persons addressed be thinking. "He is thinking" and "They are thinking," it is true, are not like "You are thinking" in this respect, but they are like it in that they, like it, are true only if someone other than the speaker is thinking. But although the existence of someone other than the speaker is a necessary condition of the truth of any of these statements, it is not a necessary condition of the speaker's making them. The existence of the speaker, on the other hand, is a necessary condition of his making any of these statements but not of their truth, except in the case of "We are thinking," which is true only if the speaker as well as another is thinking. In all these statements the intentional object of the speaker is someone other than himself, again with the exception of "We are thinking," in which he as well as others constitute his intentional object, and it is possible that the others who are his intentional objects are not existent entities. Regardless, however, of whether they are existent entities, and thus of whether these statements are true, the speaker's making them requires his formal reality as an existent entity.

In this last respect these statements are like "I am thinking," said either silently or aloud. Indeed, in this respect they are like any statement or judgment made by anyone or any act of thinking on the part of anyone, since any statement or judgment or act of thinking requires the formal reality as an existent entity of the thinker who makes the statement or judgment or performs the act of thinking. The statements in question, however, differ from "I am thinking" in that their intentional objects might not also be existent entities, again with the exception of "We are thinking" insofar as its subject term refers to the speaker as well as to others, whereas the intentional object of "I am thinking" necessarily is also an existent entity, since it is identical with the entity the existence of which is a necessary condition of the making of that statement or judgment. Although it is not necessary that there exist an entity that thinks "I am thinking" or that such an entity think such a thought, it is necessary that the intentional object of such a thought be an existent entity, since the act of thinking "I am thinking" requires the existence of some formal reality that is also the intentional object of such an act. Thus if I know that I am thinking, I thereby have sufficient knowledge to know also that I exist.

It might, however, be objected that there is nothing special about my knowing that I am thinking being sufficient to enable me to know also that I exist. For one thing, if I know that another is thinking, then also I have sufficient knowledge to know that he exists. For another, if I know that I am writing or walking or doing anything else, then I have sufficient knowledge to know that I exist. Therefore, as Professor Hampshire has argued, I can know that I exist equally as well on the basis of my knowledge that I am writing or walking as on the basis of my knowledge that I am thinking. In this respect "I am thinking" does not differ essentially from "I am writing" or "I am walking."[3] It must, of course, be granted that if I know that another is thinking or that I am writing or walking, then I have sufficient knowledge to know also in the first case that another exists and in the second that I exist. There is nonetheless an important difference between the act of thinking that another is thinking or that I am writing or walking on the one hand and the act of thinking that I am thinking on the other. This difference is that my thought necessarily is true if I think that I am thinking whereas it is not if I think that another is thinking or that I am writing or walking. Although another exists if he is thinking and I exist if I am writing or walking, my knowledge that I am thinking that another is thinking or that I am writing or walking is not sufficient by itself to enable me to know that another is in fact thinking or that I am in fact writing or walking. From the fact, that is, that I think that another is thinking or that I am writing or walking it follows neither that he is in fact thinking nor that I am in fact writing or walking. But whereas my knowledge that I am thinking that another is thinking does not suffice by itself to enable me to know that he exists, my knowledge that I am thinking that I am writing or walking is sufficient to enable me to know that I exist. I can think that another exists even though in fact he does not, but I cannot think that I am writing or walking if I do not exist. In order, however, that my knowledge that I am thinking that I am writing or walking suffice to enable me to know that I exist it is not necessary that I in fact be doing either. Regardless of whether I am doing either, if I know that I think that I am doing either I have sufficient knowledge to know also that I exist.

The preceding considerations mean that the judgment "I am thinking" does in fact differ essentially from the judgment that another is thinking and from the judgment that I am doing something other than thinking such as writing or walking. It is possible that my judgment is false if I think that another is thinking or if I think that I am writing or walking. But it is not possible that my judgment is false if I think that I am thinking. Whereas the judgments that another is not thinking and that I am not writing might be true, the judgment that I am not thinking cannot be true at the time I make it. If, then, I think that another is not thinking or that I am not writing, my judgment is not necessarily false. But if I think that I an not thinking my judgment is necessarily false. Although it is not necessary that another be thinking or that I be writing if I am to think that he is thinking or that I am writing, it is necessary that I be thinking if I am to think that I am thinking. Each time, then, I think that I am thinking, the intentional object of this act of thinking necessarily is also an existent entity, since if it were not I could not think that I am thinking, and the thought I think in thinking that I am thinking necessarily is true, since I could not think that I am thinking unless I were in fact thinking. Moreover, each time I think that I am not thinking the intentional object of my act of thinking necessarily is also an existent entity, since if it were not I could not think that I am not thinking, and the thought I think in thinking that I am not thinking necessarily is false, since I could not think that I am not thinking unless I were in fact thinking.

If the preceding considerations are acceptable, then it is a mistake to maintain, as some have done, that Descartes was justified in concluding from the cogito only that thinking is occurring, not that he exists. Since thinking is an act, and since acts are acts of agents, if I know that an act of thinking is occurring I thereby have sufficient knowledge to know also that some agent is thinking and thus that a thinking agent or subject exists. The concept that thinking can occur even though there is no thinking subject doing the thinking is a concept that cannot possibly apply to any instance of thinking. If so, one cannot possibly know that thinking is occurring without thereby having sufficient knowledge to know that some thinker is thinking.

It is also a mistake to attempt, as the empiricist Hume did, to discover the thinking subject by means of acts of introspection. By means of such acts one can succeed in discovering only various contingent contents of consciousness which, once discovered, become the intentional objects of such acts of introspection. Failing by such means to discover the thinking subject, one might easily, with Hume, conclude that there is no thinking subject as distinguished from the various empirical contents of consciousness discovered by means of acts of introspection. And if one begins, also as Hume did, by accepting the empiricist assumption that all ideas are copies of impressions, the failure to discover by means of acts of introspection an impression of the thinking subject leads naturally to the conclusion that since we have no impression of such a subject we have no idea of it either. Such an empirical introspective search, however, is misdirected from the beginning, since a thinking subject, rather than being discoverable by means of such a search, is instead a necessary condition of the possibility of conducting it, since it is precisely a thinking subject that is mistakenly going in search of itself by means of an act of introspection. Since, that is, introspection is an act, there must be an agent that performs the introspective act. We therefore know that there is a thinking subject, not because it is discovered by means of an empirical introspective search, but because there could be no such search if there were no thinking subject conducting it.

This last means that the thinking subject reached by means of the *cogito* must be distinguished from the empirical self discovered by means of acts of introspection performed by thinking subjects. The empirical self of one person discovered by means of such acts differs from that of another, since what such acts discover in the case of one person differs to some extent from what they discover in the case of another. But the thinking subject reached by means of the *cogito* as performed by one thinker does not differ in the least, insofar as it is only a thinking subject, from that reached by means of it as performed by another thinker. From the fact, that is, that I am thinking it follows only that I exist as a thinking subject. Nothing at all follows about what I am other than that I am a thinking subject. Nor does anything at all follow about who I am. By means of the *cogito* alone Descartes could not discover that he was a Frenchman born in 1596 nor could Hume discover that he was a Scotsman born in 1711 nor could either discover any other empirical facts about himself. This was clearly seen by Descartes himself in the Second Meditation.

A distinction must therefore be drawn between the empirical self on the one hand and the thinking subject established by means of the *cogito* on the other. The nature of the empirical self is determined by the nature of its experiences, desires, thoughts, beliefs, acts, dispositions, habits, abilities, and so forth. Since these differ to some degree from person to person, the nature of the empirical self of one person also differs to some degree from that of another. It is only by empirical means of various sorts that one can discover empirical facts about the empirical selves of different persons, including oneself. No such facts can be discovered by anyone by means of the *cogito* alone. Instead, by means of the *cogito* one can establish only that one is thinking and therefore exists as a thinking subject. What one thinking subject can establish about himself by means of the *cogito* is therefore precisely the same as what any other thinking subject can establish about himself by means of it. For this reason the 'I' of the *cogito* is a purely abstract, universal, and empirically empty 'I', indicating only the thinking subject that knows that it is thinking and therefore exists. It is an abstract 'I' because it indicates only the thinking subject taken completely in abstraction from any consideration of the concrete nature of any empirical self. It is a universal 'I' because it can be used by anyone to indicate precisely the same kind of entity it indicates when used by anyone else. And it is an empirically empty 'I' because it has no empirical content, indicating as it does only an empirically undetermined thinking subject and not any particular empirical self as distinguished from any other.

As was mentioned above, Descartes saw clearly that the *cogito* by itself can provide no empirical knowledge at all of any empirical self in particular as distinguished from any other. He did not so clearly see, however, that neither does it provide much of what may be referred to as 'metaphysical' knowledge of the thinking subject other than that it thinks and therefore exists. Thus by means of the *cogito* alone it cannot be established that the 'I' of the *cogito* on two or more occasions of its use indicates the same or different subjects. This follows from the fact that it is an abstract, universal, empirically empty 'I'. If by means of the *cogito* I can know only that I think and therefore exist as a thinking subject, I cannot by it know who I am as an empirical self. I therefore cannot know whether the 'I' as I presently use it to indicate a thinking subject indicates the same or a different thinking subject indicated on some other occasion of its use. Since, that is, the 'I' of the *cogito* indicates only a thinking subject and nothing more, the *cogito* by itself provides no means of distinguishing one thinking subject from another. Such distinctions can be made only on empirical grounds not provided by the *cogito*. Since the latter by itself does not even so much as provide me with sufficient empirical knowledge to enable me to know who I am or even whether I have on some previous occasion used 'I' to indicate a thinking subject, I cannot by means of the *cogito* alone know whether 'I' as I use it now to indicate a thinking subject indicates the same or a different thinking subject which I might have used it to indicate on some previous occasion. In the absence, then, of empirical knowledge, which the *cogito* by itself cannot provide, I cannot know whether the 'I' of the *cogito* indicates on different occasions of its use the same or different thinking subjects. So far as can be determined from a consideration of the *cogito* alone, its 'I' might indicate the same thinking subject each time it is used or it might on each occasion of its use indicate a different subject. It is therefore a paralogism, as Kant saw, to argue from the fact that the *cogito* establishes the existence of a thinking subject to the conclusion that therefore there must exist a self-identical substantial self enduring throughout a span of time as the subject that has the various experiences constituting the content of the empirical self and distinguishing it empirically from other such selves.

It is also impossible by means of the *cogito* alone to determine what its thinking subject is other than a thinking subject. Descartes, of course, concludes that it is a thinking substance essentially different from any material substance. Such a conclusion, however, no more follows from the *cogito* than does the conclusion that its thinking subject is also a self-identical thinking substance persisting throughout a span of time. Descartes was on much sounder ground in the Second Meditation than later on in the *Meditations,* since in the Second Meditation he saw that from the *cogito* alone he could conclude only that he is a thinking subject regardless of whatever else he might be. Now it is true that from the *cogito* alone one can conclude only that one is a thinking subject, not that one is also in addition something else. From the fact, that is, that I am thinking it follows only that I am a thinking subject, not that I am in addition something else such as a body. Nothing follows one way or the other from the *cogito* taken by itself. This is the case even though I know with certainty and cannot doubt that I am thinking and therefore exist as a thinking subject but do not know with certainty and can doubt that I am also a body. In general, from the fact that I know with certainty and cannot doubt that *x* is *a* it does not follow that *x* is not also *b*, even though I do not know with certainty and can doubt that it is. If so, then the thinking subject the existence of which is established by means of the *cogito* might be identical with some body or with some part of some body such as its brain. Whether it is or not and, if it is not, what its relationship to the human body and brain is are further questions that cannot be answered on the basis of the *cogito* alone.

The significance of the *cogito*, then, does not consist in its establishing that the thinking subject the existence of which it does establish is identical with a self-identical substantial self persisting throughout the changing experiences of the empirical self as the subject that has these experiences. Neither does it consist in its establishing that this thinking subject is not identical with some body or some part of some body such as its brain. It consists rather in its establishing the following three propositions. The first is that there is at least one intentional object that is also an existent entity by virtue of its being an intentional object. The second is that this existent entity is a thinking subject, whatever else it might also be. The third is that if there are any intentional objects at all then there is at least one existent entity regardless of whether its intentional objects are also existent entities, since if there were no existent entities there could be no intentional objects. Even if none of these intentional objects were also existent entities, their objective reality as intentional objects entails the formal reality of an existent entity for whom they are intentional objects.

4. Intentions of Intentions

The use of the *cogito* to establish the existence of oneself as a thinking subject involves thinking of one's thinking or consciousness of one's consciousness. If, that is, by means of the *cogito* I am to establish my existence as a thinking or conscious subject, I must think of my thinking or be conscious of my consciousness. There is a sense of 'consciousness' according to which one can be conscious without being conscious of anything in particular. In this sense, to be conscious is more or less equivalent to being awake, as opposed to being asleep or unconscious, without thinking of anything in particular. There is, however, also another sense of 'consciousness' according to which to be conscious is to be conscious of something. In this sense, consciousness is essentially intentional and requires an object. In what follows we shall be concerned only with consciousness in this second sense. Since to think or to be conscious in the second sense of 'consciousness' is to think or to be conscious of something, thinking and consciousness require an object and are thus essentially intentional. If so, then the use of the *cogito* to establish the existence of a thinking or conscious subject involves an intention of an intention. The first intention consists of my thinking or being conscious of something, whatever it might be, which thereby becomes for me an intentional object. The second intention consists of my intending, thinking of, or being conscious of the first intention. In this section we shall consider the structure of intentions of intentions.

To some it might seem that the series of possible intentions of intentions is infinite or at least indefinite. This, however, would seem to be an illusion engendered perhaps by the fact that we have no difficulty conceiving any ordinal number as followed by its successor. An analysis of the structure of the intentions involved in such a series, however, reveals that after the third intention any possible succeeding intention would have the same structure as the third. The object of the first intention must be something that is not itself an intention. This is the case because in order to think we must think of something. Although we can think of our thinking, there would be no thinking to be thought of unless something other than our thinking were first thought of. Suppose, then, that I intend, think of, or am conscious of some object. Such an intention has a relatively simple structure: I am conscious of the object *O*. This first intention can become the object of a second, which has the following structure: I am conscious of my consciousness of O. Whereas the object of the first intention is O, that of the second is my consciousness of O. This second intention can become the object of a third, which has this structure: I am conscious of my consciousness of my consciousness of O. The object of the first intention is something that is not an intention, that of the second is my consciousness of something that is not an intention, that of the third my consciousness of my consciousness of something that is not an intention. These three intentions clearly have different structures: the object of the first is O, that of the second my consciousness of O, that of the third my consciousness of my consciousness of O. This means that the object of the first is something other than my consciousness, that of the second my consciousness of something other than my consciousness, that of the third my consciousness of my consciousness of something other than my consciousness. So far there is no repetition in the structure of any of these intentions.

If however, we add a fourth intention we do meet with such repetition, for its structure would be this: I am conscious of my consciousness of my consciousness of my consciousness of O. Whereas the object of consciousness of the first intention differs in nature from that of the second and that of the second from that of the third, that of the third does not differ in nature from that of the fourth. The object of the first intention is the object O, which is not itself an intention. The object of the second intention is my consciousness of the object O; its object is therefore an intention of something that is not an intention. The object of the third intention is my consciousness of my consciousness of the object O; its object is therefore an intention of something that is an intention. The objects of the first three intentions therefore differ in nature: that of the first is something that is not an intention, that of the second is an intention of something that is not an intention, and that of the third is an intention of something that is an intention. The fourth intention, however, has precisely the same kind of object as the third, since its object is also an intention of something that is an intention. The object of a fifth, sixth, or of any succeeding intention would also be an intention of something that is an intention.

Two intentions can differ in nature only if there is a difference in their objects, and there is no difference between the object of the third intention and what would be the object of the fourth if a fourth were possible. This can perhaps be seen more clearly if we recognize that only the objects of first intentions can differ in nature from one another. This means that first intentions alone can differ in nature from one another, since two intentions can differ in nature only by virtue of some difference in their objects. A consciousness of red, for example, can differ from a consciousness of blue only by virtue of some difference between red and blue or by virtue of some difference issuing from a difference between red and blue. Otherwise a consciousness of red and one of blue, considered simply as acts of consciousness and nothing more, do not differ. But since first intentions, considered simply as such completely in abstraction from their objects, do not differ from one another, neither can second intentions. Since, that is, intentions can differ in nature only by virtue of a difference in their objects, since first intentions considered simply as such in abstraction from their objects do not differ, and since first intentions are the objects of second intentions, no second intention, considered simply as such completely in abstraction from its object, can differ from any other so considered. Thus although my consciousness of red differs from my consciousness of blue by virtue of a difference between red and blue, my consciousness of my consciousness of red and my consciousness of my consciousness of blue, considered simply as second intentions the objects of which are first intentions taken in abstraction from their objects, do not differ in nature. This can be put by saying that second intentions, considered simply as intentions the objects of which are intentions the objects of which are not intentions, do not differ in nature from one another. Precisely similar considerations apply also to third intentions. Since second intentions, considered simply as such completely in abstraction from any consideration of the objects of first intentions, do not differ in nature from one another, and since second intentions are the objects of third intentions, neither do the latter differ in nature when taken in abstraction from any consideration of the objects of first intentions. Thus any third intention is the same in nature as any other insofar as each is considered simply as an intention of an intention that has an intention as its object.

But although no two intentions of the same level differ in nature when taken completely in abstraction from any consideration of the objects of first intentions, any intention of any of the first three levels necessarily differs in structure from any intention of either of the other two levels. As we have seen, the object of a first intention is something other than an intention, the object of a second intention is an intention of something other than an intention, and the object of a third intention is an intention of an intention. But since the object of a fourth intention, if such were possible, would also be an intention of an intention, there would be no difference in structure between third and fourth intentions. And since no fourth intention, taken completely in abstraction from any consideration of the objects of first intentions, would differ in nature from any other, no fourth intention would differ either in nature from any other fourth intention or in structure from any third intention. Moreover, although we do have phenomenological evidence for the occurrence of third intentions, we have no such evidence for the occurrence of fourth intentions. I can be conscious, that is, not only of the paper on which I am writing but also of my consciousness of my consciousness of the paper. Although one can increase indefinitely the number of tokens of the phrase "of my consciousness" and thereby construct increasingly long sentences, one would, so to speak, be only spinning one's wheels without moving, since after the third intention there is no phenomenological occurrence to be designated by such tokens. Even if there could be such an occurrence it would be idle, since the nature of its structure and object would not differ from that of the third intention.

It was contended above that the object of a first intention must be something that is not an intention. This, however, was an oversimplification. Stated more precisely, the contention is that the object of a first intention occurring within the same specious present as a second intention when both are intentions of the same conscious subject must be something other than some intention of the same subject occurring within the same specious present as the first and second intentions. What this means can be explained as follows. The object of my present first intention can be some intention I believe I had in the past. Thus in the present I can think that on a certain occasion in the past I thought of the Eiffel Tower. If so, the object of my present first intention is some first intention I believe I had in the past. Indeed, the object of my present first intention can even be some second or third intention I believe I had in the past. Thus in the present I can think that on some occasion in the past I was conscious of my thinking of the Eiffel Tower or that I was conscious of my consciousness of my thinking of the Eiffel Tower. In addition, the object of my present first intention can also be what I believe to be some past intention the object of which was what I believed at that time to be some earlier first, second, or third intention of mine. Thus the object of my present first intention can be what I believe to be my thinking on a certain past occasion of what I then believed to be my consciousness on some still earlier occasion of my consciousness of my consciousness of the Eiffel Tower. The object of my present first intention can also be what I believe to be another person's past or present first, second, or third intention. Thus I can think in the present of what I believe to be another person's present consciousness of his consciousness of his consciousness of the Eiffel Tower.

In all these cases, however, the object of my present first intention, whether it be what I believe to be some past first, second, or third intention of mine or some past or present first, second, or third intention of another person, can be a formal reality only if there is some past first intention of mine or some past or present first intention of another the object of which is something other than an intention. I can, of course, believe in the present that on some occasion in the past I was conscious of thinking of the Eiffel Tower when in fact I was not so conscious or that another person is presently conscious of his thinking of the Eiffel Tower when in fact he is not so conscious. If so, my belief is false, and my past intention or the other person's present intention, which constitutes the intentional object of my belief, is not a formal reality. But if my belief is true and I did in fact have the intention I believe I had or the other person does in fact have the intention I believe he has, such intentions are formal realities and as such are either first intentions or else presuppose first intentions. Moreover, even though the object of my present first intention be another intention, it cannot be some intention I have in the present. If it were, my present intention would not be a first but rather a second or a third intention. To be a first intention the object of which is another intention, its object must be either some past intention of mine or some past or present intention of another person or perhaps some possible future intention, either mine or another person's. Every intention therefore is either a first intention or else presupposes some first intention. This is to say that every intention either has something that is not an intention as its object or else presupposes such an intention, even though the object be only an intentional object and not also a formal reality.

No first intention, then, can have as its object another intention of the same person occurring within the same specious present. If its objects is an intention, the latter must be either some intention of another person or else some other intention of the same person occurring at a different time. This being the case, the object of a first intention, although necessarily an intentional object, might or might not also be a formal reality. If the object of a first intention is a formal reality, it can exist or occur simultaneously with the intention only if it is either an intention of another person or else something that is not an intention at all. If it is only an intentional object and not also a formal reality, it does not exist or occur at all and therefore cannot exist or occur simultaneously with the occurrence of the intention. Thus if the object of an intention is some other intention of the same person occurring within the same specious present, the intention is either a second or a third intention. It is a second intention if its object is a first intention, a third intention if its object is a second intention.

Since third intentions presuppose second intentions, which in turn presuppose first intentions, the intentional object of any third intention is some second intention, the intentional object of which is some first intention. This however, does not mean that every first intention is the intentional object of some second intention or that every second intention is the intentional object of some third intention. Thus I can think of the Eiffel Tower without thinking of my thinking of it, and I can think of my thinking of the Eiffel Tower without thinking of my thinking of my thinking of it. This means that a first intention can be a formal reality without being the intentional object of a second intention and that a second intention can be a formal reality without being the intentional object of a third intention. Whether, however, a first intention can be the intentional object of a second intention or a second intention the intentional object of a third intention without also being a formal reality depends upon whether a person can think that he is thinking of something when in fact he is not. We saw above that the intentional object of a first intention need not be a formal reality. I can think, for example, of a mermaid even though the intentional object of such a first intention is not also a formal reality. From the fact, however, that the intentional object of a first intention need not also be a formal reality it does not follow that second and third intentions can also have intentional objects that are not formal realities.

In attempting to answer this question it is important to remember that first, second, and third intentions are intentions of the same person occurring within the same specious present. As we saw above, if the intentional object of my present intention is what I believe to be some past intention of mine or some past or present intention of another person, my present intention is a first rather than a second or third intention, and its intentional object might or might not also be a formal reality. Although I might be convinced that on some previous occasion I had a certain intention or that in the past or the present another person had or has a certain intention, I might nonetheless be mistaken. It seems unlikely, however, that I can be mistaken as to whether I am presently thinking of the Eiffel Tower if I think that I am. I am mistaken if I think that I am not thinking of it when in fact I am, although this would be a mistake of a sort that not many people would be likely, if ever, to make. But if I think that I am thinking of it, the fact that I think I am thinking of it means that I am thinking of it, since I could not think that I am thinking of it without doing so. Indeed, one might well argue that I cannot even think that I am not thinking of it without thinking of it, since in thinking that I am not thinking of it I am thinking of it. Although the immediate object of a second intention is some first intention and that of a third some second intention, the object of the first intention, although it is the immediate object of the first intention alone, may perhaps be referred to as the mediate object or at least as part of the immediate object of the second and third intentions. Thus a second intention cannot be the object of a third and a first the object of a second unless the object of the first is at least indirectly intended in intending the first or the second intention. If, that is, I am conscious of my consciousness of the Eiffel Tower, I am thereby conscious not only of my consciousness of the Eiffel Tower but also of the Eiffel Tower. I cannot think of my thinking of the Eiffel Tower without also thereby thinking of the Eiffel Tower. Precisely similar considerations apply to third intentions. I cannot think of my thinking of my thinking of the Eiffel Tower without also thereby thinking of the Eiffel Tower. If so, then the immediate object of a first intention carries over, so to speak, as part of the object of second and third intentions.

From this, however, it does not follow that the immediate object of a second or a third intention must be a formal reality. Nor does the latter follow from the fact that I cannot think that I am thinking of some possible object of a first intention, such as the Eiffel Tower, without doing so. An intention, like any other formal reality, can have being as a formal reality only if it has such being independently of its being for anyone an intentional object. Thus a first intention, to have being as a formal reality, must have such being independently of its being the intentional object of a second intention, and a second intention, to have such being, must have it independently of its being the intentional object of a third intention. But from the fact that I cannot think that I am thinking of the Eiffel Tower without thereby thinking of it, it does not follow that within the specious present I am thinking of it independently of my thinking that I am thinking of it. If within the specious present I am not thinking of it independently of my thinking that I am thinking of it, then my thinking that I am thinking of it either is not a second intention at all or, if it is, it has as its intentional object a first intention that is not also a formal reality. If, in thinking that I am thinking of the Eiffel Tower, I think that within the specious present I am thinking of it independently of my thinking that I am when in fact I am not, then my present thought is a second intention the intentional object of which is not a formal reality. In that case the immediate intentional object of a second or a third intention is not necessarily also a formal reality.

The only way this conclusion could be escaped would consist in showing that if I think that within the specious present I am thinking of the Eiffel Tower when in fact I am not, my thinking that I am thinking of it is a first rather than a second intention. This, however, could be shown only if it could also be shown that in thinking that within the specious present I am thinking of the Eiffel Tower when in fact I am not I am thinking only of the Eiffel Tower. This, however, cannot be shown. It is true that in thinking that within the specious present I am thinking of the Eiffel Tower I am thinking of the latter, regardless of whether within the specious present I am thinking of it independently of my thinking that I am. As was indicated above, the immediate object of a first intention becomes also part of the object of a second intention, the immediate object of which is the first intention, when I think not only of the object of the first intention but also of the latter itself. From this, however, it does not follow that in the second intention I am thinking only of the object of the first intention, which would mean that the second intention in fact is a first rather than a second intention. And in point of fact if I think that within the specious present I am thinking of the Eiffel Tower, I am thinking not only of the Eiffel Tower but also that within the specious present I am thinking of it. I am thinking, that is, not only of the object of a first intention but also of a first intention. But just as from the fact that an object is the intentional object of a first intention it does not follow that it is also a formal reality, so also from the fact that a first intention is the object of a second intention it does not follow that it is also a formal reality.

If the preceding argument is sound, then from the fact that something is the object of an intention, whether it be a first, second, or third intention, it does not follow that it is also a formal reality. The only exceptions to this are those self-referential intentions connected with the *cogito*. If I think that I exist or that I am thinking, then necessarily I exist and am thinking, since I could think neither that I exist nor that I am thinking if I neither existed nor were thinking. Such self-referential intentions, however, are first rather than second or third intentions. The object of a second or third intention is always something other than itself, since the object of a second intention is always a first intention and the object of a third intention always a second. In thinking that I exist my intention is a first intention because its object is my existence, which is not an intention. And in thinking that I am thinking my intention is also a first intention, since its object is itself and not some other intention. Since it is an intention the object of which is itself, its intentional object necessarily is also a formal reality. Such self-referential intentions, however, are the only intentions the objects of which necessarily are formal realities because they are intentional objects. Although there might be some intentional object, such as God, the nature of which is such that necessarily it is a formal reality regardless of whether it is also an intentional object, it would be a formal reality because of its nature and not because it is an intentional object. We could know that it exists not through knowing that for us it is an intentional object but rather through knowing that its nature is such that it is impossible that it not exist. But I know by means of the *cogito* that I exist and am thinking not through knowing that my nature is such that it is impossible that I not exist or think but rather through knowing that my existence and thinking could not for me be intentional objects if they were not also formal realities.

The fact that the only intentions whose objects necessarily are formal realities because they are intentional objects are those self-referential first intentions connected with the *cogito* is somewhat anomalous in view of the fact that in general the objects of second and third intentions are much more likely also to be formal realities than are the objects of first intentions. Not only do we frequently think that various of the objects of our first intentions are formal realities when in fact they are not, but in addition we sometimes have as objects of our first intentions objects such as mermaids that we know are not formal realities. But rarely if indeed ever is the object of a second or third intention not also a formal reality. Yet even though the failure of such objects to be formal realities would rarely if ever occur, the considerations presented above, if acceptable, do mean that the fact that something is the object of a second or third intention does not mean that necessarily it is also a formal reality. Thus although almost always the objects of second and third intentions are formal realities as well as intentional objects, their being such realities is not necessary if they are to be the objects of such intentions. Although every intention is a formal reality regardless of whether it is also an intentional object, and although every intention, by virtue of its intentionality, necessarily has an intentional object, with the exceptions noted above no intentional object is necessarily also a formal reality because it is such an object. If it is such a reality it is for some reason other than its being an intentional object.

Notes

1. See Roderick M. Chisholm, *Perceiving: A Philosophical Study* (Ithaca: Cornell University Press, 1957), chapter 11.

2. For an incisive criticism of adverbial theories of consciousness, see Panayot Butchvarov, "Adverbial Theories of Consciousness," *Midwest Studies in Philosophy* 5 (1980): 261–80.

3. Stuart Hampshire, *The Age of Reason: The Seventeenth Century Philosophers*, selected, with introduction and interpretive commentary, by Stuart Hampshire (New York: George Braziller, 1957), p. 66.

6
Entities, States of Affairs, and Propositions

We return now to the question with which we ended Chapter Four. This question concerns the ontological status of the content of statements, judgments, and beliefs. As we saw, such contents are propositions, states of affairs, and the obtaining or the nonobtaining of the latter. We begin with states of affairs and what may be referred to as their constituents.

1. Possibilities and Impossibilities

As we have seen,[1] states of affairs are either necessary, contingent, or impossible. Necessary states of affairs necessarily obtain, impossible states of affairs necessarily do not obtain, and contingent states of affairs might or might not obtain. Since a state of affairs consists of something's being, having, or doing (or not being, not having, or not doing) something, each state of affairs involves some formal reality or some intentional object that is, has, or does (or is not, does not have, or is not doing) something. For the sake of simplicity, I shall refer to such formal realities or intentional objects as entities. So used, the term 'entity' will designate anything thinkable involved in some conceivable state of affairs. It will be helpful if we devote some attention to a consideration of entities before we turn to a consideration of states of affairs.

Entities might or might not be actual. Some are contingent, others impossible. Whether any are necessary is a disputed question into which we shall not enter here. Whether an entity is necessary, impossible, or contingent is dependent upon its nature. If an entity is necessary its nature is such that necessarily it exists; if an entity is impossible its nature is such that necessarily it never exists; and if an entity is contingent its nature is such that it might or might not exist. To some it might seem that nonexistent entities, whether contingent or impossible, are all intentional objects. This, however, would be a mistake. Whether an entity is

157

possible or impossible and, if contingent, whether existent or nonexistent, is independent of whether it is an intentional object. What makes an impossible entity impossible and a nonexistent contingent entity contingent is its nature, not its being an intentional object. A necessary and sufficient condition of something's being an intentional object is that it be intended in thought by someone. This, however, is neither a necessary nor a sufficient condition of something's being an impossible entity or a nonexistent contingent entity. Even if no conscious being ever existed square-circles would still be impossible. Similarly with nonexistent contingent entities such as mermaids. Even if no human beings ever existed it would still be possible that animals women from the waist up and fish from the waist down exist. The possibility of the existence of such animals depends only upon the self-consistency of their nature and in no way depends upon their being intentional objects.

The belief that impossible entities and nonexistent contingent entities must be intentional objects would seem to issue from either or both of the following suppositions. One is that to admit that impossible entities and nonexistent contingent entities need not be intentional objects is equivalent to maintaining that they do in fact exist. Such a supposition, however, ignores the fact that to say of something such as a square-circle that it is impossible or of something such as a mermaid that it is a nonexistent entity is to say that it does not exist. It is to say of the first that it cannot possibly exist and of the second that it does not in fact exist. A second supposition is that since the intended object of my thought if I think of a square-circle on the wall or of a mermaid on the couch is only an intentional object and not an existent entity, so also square-circles and mermaids are only intentional objects. This conclusion, however, does not follow. To think of a square-circle on the wall or of a mermaid on the couch is to have in each case a particular as the intended object of my thought. We can and do grant that particulars are either intentional objects or existent entities and that those particulars that are not existent entities are only intentional objects and nothing more. If no one thinks that a square-circle is on the wall or that a mermaid is on the couch, then what would be an intentional object if anyone had either of these thoughts has no being in any sense at all. This means that in the case of particulars to be is to be either an existent entity or an intentional object. Nothing can be a particular and also be neither an existent entity nor an intentional object.

The preceding means that impossible entities and contingent entities that are neither existent entities nor intentional objects are not particulars. Thus if no one ever thought of square-circles or mermaids such entities could still be entities only if they are not particulars. If, however, they are not particulars yet would still be either impossible entities or nonexistent contingent entities, a question arises as to what kind of entities they would be. The answer is that they are kinds. A square-circle is an impossible kind of entity, a mermaid a possible but nonexistent kind of entity. The kind of entity each is, is determined by the nature of the properties the combination of which is necessary and sufficient to constitute the kind. Being round and having four straight sides of equal length that form right angles is to be a square-circle, and being a woman from the waist up and a fish from the waist down is to be a mermaid. A kind is an impossible kind if the combination of properties constituting its nature cannot be exemplified. A kind is a nonexistent contingent kind if the combination of properties constituting its nature can be but in fact is not exemplified. Which combinations of properties can and which cannot be exemplified is determined by the nature of the properties. The combination of properties constituting the nature of an impossible kind is a combination of essentially incompatible properties. It is because of this that such a combination cannot be exemplified. But the combination of properties constituting the nature of a possible kind, since it is a combination of essentially compatible properties, can be exemplified even though in fact it never is.

Since a combination of essentially incompatible properties constitutes an impossible kind and a combination of essentially compatible properties a possible kind, which kinds are possible and which impossible is independent of any acts of thought on the part of anyone. Even if square-circles and mermaids were never for anyone intentional objects, a square-circle would still be an impossible kind of entity and a mermaid a possible kind. To say, however, of a kind of entity that it is an impossible kind is not to say that it cannot be an intentional object. Anyone who has concepts of properties that are essentially incompatible can think of impossible kinds constituted by the combination of such properties simply by thinking of the properties as combined. A kind is impossible, then, not because it cannot be an intentional object, but rather because the combination of properties constituting it is a combination of essentially incompatible properties. So also for possible kinds of nonexistent entities. Their possibility, since it issues from their nature regardless of whether they are ever intentional objects, in no way depends upon their ever being such objects.

Despite the preceding, some might still be reluctant to admit that impossible and possible but nonexistent kinds need not be intentional objects. If so, such reluctance might be diminished somewhat by the following considerations. First, such kinds are not particulars. As was indicated above, particulars are either intentional objects or existent entities, and any particular that is not an existent entity is an intentional object. The temptation to regard such kinds as particulars, albeit nonexistent particulars, can perhaps be overcome if we cease using the plural forms of the terms designating them. Thus instead of using the plural forms 'square-circles' and 'mermaids' it would perhaps be better to use the more pedantic Meinongian-like expressions 'the square-circle' and 'the mermaid'. This is especially appropriate in view of the fact that since there are no square-circles or mermaids there cannot be a plurality of them. Whereas the use of the plural forms might lead some to suppose that such use implies a belief in a plurality of such entities, the use of 'the square-circle' or 'the mermaid' more clearly suggests that a kind and not a plurality of particulars is being indicated. Second, kinds are not themselves existent entities but are rather possible combinations of properties. Thus the kinds square-circle and mermaid are not themselves existent entities. Instead, the first is the combination of the properties being round and having four sides, the second of the properties being a woman from the waist up and a fish from the waist down. The first combination is impossible in that it is not possible that any existent entity have both properties, the second possible in that it is possible that some existent entity have both properties. Both combinations are possible, however, in that both are possible intentional objects. But, as was indicated above, the impossibility of the exemplification of the first and the possibility of the exemplification of the second are independent of their being intentional objects and issues instead from the nature of the combined properties.

Kinds, then, rather than being existent entities, are instead possible combinations of properties. Combinations of essentially incompatible properties constitute impossible kinds. Since no existent entity can have essentially incompatible properties, no existent entity can be an entity of an impossible kind. But particular entities of an impossible kind can be intentional objects, as when one thinks of a particular square-circle as being on the wall to the right of the picture. Unlike particulars of possible kinds, they cannot be existent entities, so that if they are not intentional objects they have no being at all. Impossible kinds, however, unlike particulars of impossible kinds, are formal realities even though they cannot have instances. This is because their impossibility issues from the fact that they are combinations of essentially incompatible properties, taken in conjunction with the fact that which properties are essentially compatible and which essentially incompatible is determined by the nature of the properties themselves. Thus even if particular square-circles or the square-circle were never intentional objects for anyone, the square-circle would still be an impossible kind. As such, it has formal reality even though it never be an intentional object and even though it can never have instances.

The genus formal reality is therefore divisible into two species—one consisting of existent entities, the other of formal realities that are not existent entities. The latter species is divisible into two subspecies—one consisting of impossible kinds or impossibilities, the other of possible kinds or possibilities. Particular instances of impossible kinds can be intentional objects but not existent entities. Particular instances of possible kinds can be either intentional objects or existent entities. Particulars that are not existent entities have no being at all if they are not intentional objects.

There will doubtless be some who will object to the ascription to kinds of what to others will seem so attenuated a form of being as that of being formal realities without also being existent entities. Such an objection might be based on the assumption that there is only one kind of formal reality—that of being an existent entity. Those who make this assumption might admit that there are objective realities, i.e., intentional objects, as well as formal realities, yet insist that all formal realities are existent entities, so that the only alternative to being either an intentional object or an existent entity is to be nothing at all. Others might go even further and deny that there are any intentional objects that are not also existent entities, so that the only alternative to being an existent entity is to be nothing at all. Still others might deny even that there are any intentional objects, so that for them the only alternative to being an existent entity is to be nothing at all. Considerations I believe sufficient to establish the untenability of the latter two positions have already been advanced.[2] The third position could be sustained only if an adequate adverbial theory of thinking or consciousness could be developed in which all references to intentional objects are avoided. That such a theory can in fact be developed, however, is doubtful in the extreme, especially in view of the fact that the claim that there are intentional objects is at least as certain as is the claim that there are existent entities. The second position, on the other hand, can be sustained only if it can be established that every intentional object is also an existent entity. That this can be established, however, is also doubtful in the extreme, since the intentional object of my present thought is a mermaid on the couch, and this object is not an existent entity. Neither of these extreme positions, however, are presupposed by the claim that all formal realities are existent entities.

Those who advance this latter claim might do so for either of two reasons, one of which is realistic in character, the other nominalistic. Someone with realistic inclinations might maintain that all formal realities are existent entities for the following reasons. First, he might believe that if anything were a formal reality but not an existent entity it would have only an attenuated form of reality at best as contrasted with the reality of existent entities. It would be real but would not exist, and, he might believe, anything that is real but nonexistent is less real than something that exists. Second, he might also believe that if anything is likely to be a candidate for consignment to the category of nonexistent formal realities it is universals or kinds, not particulars. In order, then, to defend his view that universals or kinds are as real as particulars, he maintains that all formal realities are existent entities. Someone with nominalistic proclivities, on the other hand, might deny the distinction between formal realities and existent entities in order to establish that only particulars are real. Such a person might reason as follows. If all formal realities are existent entities, and if all existent entities are particulars, then, since no universals or kinds are existent entities, they are not formal realities either.

As I shall argue in more detail later, such forms of realism and nominalism are mistaken. The nominalist is correct in maintaining that universals or kinds are not existent entities but mistaken in denying that they are formal realities, the realist correct in maintaining that they are formal realities but mistaken in contending that they are also existent entities. The nominalist is correct in maintaining, and the realist mistaken in denying, that universals or kinds are not existent entities because existent entities are temporal whereas universals or kinds are not. This point is at least partly definitional. By definition, something is an existent entity only if it exists in time independently of its being an intentional object. If something has being only as an intentional object it is only an objective and not also a formal reality, and if something has being independently of being an intentional object but does not exist in time it is a formal reality but not an existent entity. Since universals or kinds have being independently of being intentional objects they are formal realities; and since they do not exist in time they are not existent entities. More needs to be said in defense of these claims.

It was maintained above that kinds are possible combinations of properties and that some kinds are possible, others impossible. It was maintained also that possible kinds are combinations of essentially compatible properties, impossible kinds combinations of essentially incompatible properties. It was further maintained that since the essential compatibility or incompatibility of properties in no way depends upon their being intentional objects, such compatiblities and incompatibilities are formal realities. If so, then which properties are essentially compatible and which essentially incompatible is independent of what anyone happens to think. It might, however, be objected that from this it does not follow that combinations of properties, whether the latter be compatible or incompatible, are also independent of what anyone might happen to think. On the contrary, such combinations presuppose acts of thought on the part of someone, since if no one ever combined in thought two properties there would be no combination of the two. Although one pair of properties might be essentially incompatible and another pair essentially compatible regardless of what anyone might happen to think, so that the essential compatibility of one pair and the essential incompatibility of the other are formal realities, the combination of the properties of each pair requires a mental act of combining them on the part of some person and can have being only as an intentional object for someone. And since kinds are nothing but such combinations of properties, kinds, rather than being formal realities, not only have being only as intentional objects, but in addition would not even have such objective reality were it not for the occurrence of a mental act on the part of someone by virtue of which they become kinds.

The reply to this objection is as follows. First, no property, considered by itself completely in abstraction from every other property, is either compatible or incompatible. Instead, compatibility and incompatibility are relational properties and as such presuppose at least two related properties. Thus being round, taken by itself completely in abstraction from every other property, is neither compatible nor incompatible, so that if there were no other properties there would be nothing with which it could be compatible or incompatible. But given another property, it either is or is not compatible with it. To speak, then, of a property as being compatible or incompatible is to suppose that it is taken in combination with some other property. It is combinations of properties, not single properties, that are compatible or incompatible, and which combinations are compatible and which incompatible depends completely upon the nature of the properties constituting the combination. If so, then to admit that certain combinations of properties are essentially compatible and others essentially incompatible independently of what anyone might think is inconsistent with maintaining that kinds come into being only as a consequence of the performance of mental acts of combining properties and have being only as intentional objects. To admit, that is, that the essential compatibility or incompatibility of two properties is a formal reality is inconsistent with denying that kinds also are formal realities, since kinds are nothing but combinations of properties presupposed by the latter's being compatible or incompatible. Without kinds, i.e., without combinations of properties, properties could be neither compatible nor incompatible. If, then, the compatibility or incompatibility of two properties is a formal reality, then so also is the kind consisting of the combination of the properties, since without the latter the properties would be neither compatible nor incompatible.

Second, any property is either compatible or incompatible with any other property. Some properties and combinations of properties are sometimes intentional objects, and for some we have names. Some, however, never become intentional objects, although it is, of course, impossible to instance any without their becoming intentional objects. Such properties and combinations, since they never become objects, have no names. Being round, for example, would still be a property and as such have formal reality even if it were never for anyone an intentional object and therefore even if for it we had no name. But if any property is either compatible or incompatible with any other property independently of their being intentional objects, then so are the combinations of such properties presupposed by their compatibility or incompatability. Such combinations are therefore formal realities that in no way depend upon mental acts of combining the related properties. Although the discovery of compatibilities and incompatibilities of properties requires our having the latter as intentional objects and relating them as such to one another, this is not required by the compatibility or incompatibility of the properties as formal realities. And whether the properties we think compatible or incompatible are in fact so depends upon their nature as formal realities. Were this not so we could create compatibilities and incompatibilities at will. This, however, we cannot do. Although we can in thought combine properties arbitrarily, whether the resulting combinations are combinations of compatible or incompatible properties depends completely upon the nature of the combined properties. Regardless of whether anyone in thought ever combines the properties of being round and being square or those of being a woman from the waist up and a fish from the waist down, the first is a combination of essentially incompatible properties, the second a combination of essentially compatible properties. The first combination is therefore an impossible kind, the second a possible kind, and as such each kind is a formal reality.

But although every kind, whether possible or impossible, is a formal reality, no kind is an existent entity. Kinds are therefore nonexistent formal realities. This, however, does not mean that they are nothing. To be nothing is not to be anything, and every kind is some combination of properties. Since each property is something, each combination of properties is also something. If properties were nothing, then no property could differ from any other, since nothing cannot differ from nothing. But properties do differ from one another. Indeed, properties necessarily or essentially differ from one another. Although it is possible that two numerically distinct particulars be qualitatively identical, provided that one has some spatial or temporal location the other does not have, it is not possible that two numerically distinct properties be qualitatively identical. There cannot, for example, be two numerically distinct but qualitatively identical properties, being round and being round. Properties therefore necessarily differ from one another essentially, so that the number of properties necessarily is identical with the number of essentially different properties.

Since properties differ essentially from one another, so also do combinations of properties. This means that the number of kinds necessarily is identical with the number of essentially different kinds. This number necessarily is larger than the number of single properties, since the number of possible combinations of single properties necessarily is larger than the number of single properties. The number of kinds therefore necessarily is larger than the number of single properties. In neither case, however, is the number a number of existent entities, since neither kinds nor single properties are existent entities. They are instead formally real possibilities or impossibilities.

Such formally real possibilities and impossibilities are absolute and nontemporal. They therefore differ from relative temporal possibilities and impossibilities. Absolute nontemporal possibilities and impossibilities are ontologically prior to existent entities, since nothing can exist unless its existence is possible. The situation is just the reverse in the case of relative temporal possibilities and impossibilities. Such possibilities and impossibilities require the existence of a world containing existent entities, since they are possibilities and impossibilities that can or cannot be actualized at a given time, given the nature and the configuration of the entities existing at that time. Since the nature and the configuration of entities existing at one time differs to some degree from that of those existing at another, the possibilities and impossibilities that can or cannot be actualized at one time will also differ to some degree from those that can or cannot be actualized at another time. Thus given the actual biological constitution of a fertile man and woman, their union can issue in the birth of a human being but not in the birth of a centaur or an alligator. Given their biological constitution, the birth of a human being is a possibility, the birth of a centaur or an alligator an impossibility. One of the aims of the natural sciences is the discovery of which events and states of affairs are possible and which impossible, given the nature, configuration, and action of various existent entities. Given the latter, such possibilities and impossibilities are formal realities, and any description of the nature of the actual world that does not include a description of them would be incomplete.

Relative temporal possibilities and impossibilities may be referred to as actual possibilities and impossibilities. Actual possibilities constitute a subclass of absolute nontemporal possibilities. This is the case because only that which is possible in an absolute nontemporal sense can be actual, taken in conjunction with the fact that which absolute nontemporal possibilities are also actual possibilities is determined by the nature, configuration, and action of existent entities. But although every actual possibility is an absolute possibility, not every absolute possibility is also an actual possibility. Thus whereas every absolute impossibility is also an actual impossibility, some actual impossibilities are absolute possibilities. It is absolutely possible but actually impossible that the union of a man and a woman issue in the birth of an alligator. Actual possibilities and impossibilities are of greater practical importance and concern. Thus whereas it is understandable that a young woman who finds herself with child have some concern as to whether the child to which she promises to give birth be normal and healthy, she would be silly if she worried about whether she will give birth to an alligator. Given her nature, it is an absolute but not an actual possibility that she give birth to an alligator. But although actual possibilities and impossibilities are of greater practical importance and concern, absolute possibilities and impossibilities are of fundamental metaphysical importance, since they constitute the limits of every absolutely possible world and therefore of the actual world.

2. Properties, Particulars, and States of Affairs

States of affairs, considered in abstraction from the question of whether they do or do not obtain, are formal necessities, possibilities, or impossibilities. The adjective *formal* is intended to indicate that states of affairs are formal realities regardless of whether they do or do not obtain. But since properties and combinations of properties are also formal realities, a question arises of how they differ from states of affairs. The answer is that states of affairs, unlike properties and combinations of properties, consist in something's being, having, or doing (or not being, not having, or not doing) something. Thus the necessary state of affairs consisting of blue's being more like green than red consists of something, blue, being more like green than red. Similarly, the impossible state of affairs consisting of a square-circle's being on the wall consists of something, a square-circle, having something, namely a location on the wall; and the contingent state of affairs consisting of the Eiffel Tower's being in Paris consists of something, the Eiffel Tower, having something, namely a location in Paris. By contrast, properties and combinations of properties do not consist in something's being, having, or doing something. Being round, being round and red, and being round and square, considered simply as properties completely in abstraction from any consideration of their exemplification or nonexemplification and of the relationships in which they do or do not stand to other properties and combinations of properties, do not consist in something's being, doing, or having something.

But although states of affairs on the one hand and properties and combinations of properties on the other differ in the way just indicated, there are necessary relationships between the two. First, states of affairs presuppose properties and would be impossible without them, since if there were no properties there could be no states of affairs. Second, just as any state of affairs presupposes some property, so also any property is ingredient in some state of affairs. This follows from the fact that any property is either exemplified or not exemplified and from the fact that any property stands in some relationship to any other property, even though the relationship be only one of essential difference. Given this, any property is ingredient in a number of states of affairs. Thus given any property, it is ingredient in the state of affairs consisting of its being exemplified, the state of affairs consisting of its not being exemplified, the state of affairs consisting of its standing (or of its not standing) in a given relation to some other property, and so on, some of which obtain and some of which do not. Thus just as states of affairs would be impossible without properties, so also properties would be impossible without states of affairs.

The presupposition of properties by states of affairs and the ingredience of the former in the latter hold regardless of whether the former are exemplified and of whether the latter obtain. Thus the property of being a mermaid, which is not exemplified, is ingredient in the state of affairs consisting of there being a mermaid on the couch, which does not obtain. Similarly, the property of being a square-circle, which cannot be exemplified, is ingredient in the state of affairs consisting of there being a square-circle on the wall, which cannot obtain. But properties that are not or cannot be exemplified are also ingredient in states of affairs that do obtain. Thus the property of being a mermaid is ingredient in the state of affairs consisting of there not being a mermaid on the couch, which does obtain; and the property of being a square-circle is ingredient in the state of affairs consisting of there not being a square-circle on the wall, which does obtain. Similarly, properties that are exemplified are ingredient both in states of affairs that do obtain and in states of affairs that do not. Thus the property of being green is ingredient in the state of affairs consisting of my desk blotter's being green, which does obtain, and also that consisting of my pencil's being green, which does not obtain. All this can be summarized by saying that for any property, regardless of whether it is exemplified, there is some state of affairs that obtains and also some state of affairs that does not obtain in which it is ingredient; and any state of affairs, regardless of whether it obtains, presupposes some property, regardless of whether the latter is exemplified.

Regardless of whether it does or does not obtain, any state of affairs that presupposes the exemplification of a given property by a given particular also involves the particular in question. Thus the state of affairs consisting of my desk blotter's being green, which does in fact obtain, not only presupposes the property of being green but also involves my desk blotter. Similarly, the state of affairs consisting of my pencil's being green, which does not obtain, presupposes the property of being green and involves my pencil. Moreover, just as any property is ingredient both in states of affairs that do obtain and also in states of affairs that do not, so also any particular is involved in states of affairs that do and in states of affairs that do not obtain. Thus my desk blotter is involved in the state of affairs consisting of its being green, which does obtain, and my pencil in the state of affairs consisting of its being green, which does not obtain. Just as to be a property is to be ingredient both in states of affairs that do and in states of affairs that do not obtain, so also to be a particular is to be involved both in states of affairs that do and in states of affairs that do not obtain. And since any particular necessarily exemplifies some property, any state of affairs involving a particular necessarily also presupposes some property exemplified by that particular, regardless of whether the state of affairs in question obtains. Thus the state of affairs consisting of my desk blotter's being brown, which does not obtain, presupposes the property of being a desk blotter.

States of affairs can also presuppose properties without involving particulars, regardless of whether the properties presupposed are exemplified. Thus the state of affairs consisting of blue's being more like green than red presupposes the properties in question, all of which are exemplified, but does not involve any particulars. Although any blue particular is more similar in color to any green particular than to any red particular, this is not because they are particulars but rather because being blue is more like being green than being red. The state of affairs consisting of blue's being more like green than red necessarily obtains regardless of whether any of these properties are ever exemplified. It is because of this that if any blue, green, and red particulars exist those that are blue necessarily are more similar in color to those that are green than to those that are red. We doubtless could not know that blue necessarily is more like green than red if we never saw blue, green, and red particulars. But our seeing such particulars is a necessary condition only of our coming to know that blue necessarily is more like green than red. It is not a necessary condition of blue's necessarily being more like green than red, and this state of affairs necessarily obtains regardless of whether we ever come to know it and of whether there are ever any blue, green, or red particulars.

The reason states of affairs can presuppose properties without involving particulars exemplifying them but cannot involve particulars without presupposing some property they exemplify is that properties are formal realities regardless of whether they are exemplified, whereas particulars cannot be formal realities without exemplifying properties. This means that properties are more fundamental metaphysically than particulars. Although properties exist only as exemplified by particulars, they would still have being as nonexistent formal realities even if there were never any particulars. Particulars, however, cannot exist without exemplifying properties. Thus whereas the being of properties as formal realities is a necessary condition of the existence of particulars, the existence of particulars is not a necessary condition of the formal reality of properties. Even nonexistent particulars having only objective reality as intentional objects can have such reality only through being intended in thought as what may be referred to as objective or intentional exemplifications of certain properties. To think of a mermaid as contrasted with thinking of a centaur is to think of the intended object of one's thought as exemplifying certain intended properties rather than others even though one believes that this object does not in fact exist. If one thinks of the object one intends as a man from the waist up and a horse from the waist down one is thinking of a centaur, not a mermaid.

Since properties are timeless formal realities, so also are states of affairs that presuppose them without involving particulars. Such states of affairs either necessarily obtain or necessarily do not obtain regardless of what happens in time. Those that obtain necessarily are necessary states of affairs. Those that necessarily do not obtain are impossible states of affairs. The necessity of the former and the impossibility of the latter constitute necessary limits determining what absolutely can and what absolutely cannot occur in time. They do not, however, determine which properties that can but need not be exemplified are in fact exemplified, nor do they determine which states of affairs that can but need not obtain do in fact obtain. Because of the nature of blue, green, and red, if any particulars exemplify these properties it is necessary that the blue ones be more similar in color to the green than to the red ones and thus impossible that they be more similar in color to the red ones than to the green. But that any of these properties be exemplified is not necessary.

Since states of affairs that presuppose properties without involving particulars are timeless, only those states of affairs that involve particulars are temporal. As we have seen, every particular is involved both in states of affairs that do obtain and in states of affairs that do not obtain. The Eiffel Tower, for example, is involved both in the state of affairs consisting of its being in Paris, which does obtain, and in the state of affairs consisting of its being in London, which does not obtain, as well as an indefinite number of other states of affairs, some of which obtain, some of which are possible but do not obtain, and some of which are impossible and therefore cannot obtain, such as its having a square-circle engraved on it. As a particular it exists throughout a span of time at some place, although not necessarily the same place, at each moment of this span of time. The state of affairs consisting of its existing in Paris throughout this span of time is temporal, as is also each of the indefinite number of states of affairs consisting of its existing in Paris at each of the moments included within this span of time. To say, however, of a state of affairs that it is temporal is not to say that it obtains. It is instead to say that if it does obtain it obtains at some time but not necessarily at all times. It is therefore to say that it is a possible rather than a necessary or impossible state of affairs. In order, however, for a temporal state of affairs to obtain, some particular involved in it must exist. Temporal states of affairs that obtain are therefore actual states of affairs, since they consist in some existent entity's being, having, or doing something.

Since, however, some temporal states of affairs do not obtain, not all are actual. Those that are not actual are divisible into those that do and those that do not involve existent particulars. Every existent particular is involved in a multitude of nonactual states of affairs, if for no other reason than that it is involved in each state of affairs the obtaining of which is incompatible with the obtaining of any actual state of affairs in which it is involved. Thus the Eiffel Tower, since it is involved in the actual state of affairs consisting of its being in Paris, is also involved in every nonactual state of affairs the obtaining of which is incompatible with its being in Paris, such as those consisting of its being in London, its being in Madrid, its being in Rome, and so on. In addition, each existent particular is involved not just in one but rather in a multitude of actual states of affairs, for each of which there is at least one nonactual state of affairs the obtaining of which is incompatible with it. This means that each existent particular is involved both in a multitude of actual states of affairs and in an even larger number of nonactual states of affairs, since for each actual state of affairs in which it is involved there is at least one nonactual state of affairs in which it is also involved. Each of the actual and nonactual states of affairs in which an existent particular is involved is abstract as contrasted with the concrete nature of the particular. Each of these states of affairs is, so to speak, only a partial expression of the full concrete determinate nature of the existent particular involved in them. So also is any combination of them less than the totality of all. Since no one can know the totality of the states of affairs in which any existent particular is involved, no one can know the full concrete determinate nature of any such particular. From this, however, it does not follow that no one can know anything at all about such particulars, nor does it follow that our knowledge of them cannot increase and thereby become increasingly adequate to their full concrete determinate nature.

Some states of affairs involving existent particulars also involve other particulars, whereas some do not. Thus the state of affairs consisting of the Eiffel Tower's being made of metal, taken completely in abstraction from all other states of affairs in which the Eiffel Tower is involved, involves no particular other than the Eiffel Tower. It involves the Eiffel Tower and presupposes the property of being made of metal. Thus as an absolute minimum every actual state of affairs involves at least one existent particular and presupposes some property that is or is not exemplified by that particular. If the state of affairs is positive, such as the Eiffel Tower's being made of metal, the particular exemplifies the presupposed property; if the state of affairs is negative, such as the Eiffel Tower's not being made of wood, the particular does not exemplify the presupposed property.

As was indicated above, a state of affairs involving an existent particular might also involve another particular. Thus the actual state of affairs consisting of the Eiffel Tower's being in Paris involves two particulars, the Eiffel Tower and Paris, each of which exists. And the actual state of affairs consisting of a centaur's not standing under the Eiffel Tower also involves two particulars, only one of which exists. If so, an actual state of affairs can involve a nonexistent as well as an existent particular. And if this is so, then any existent particular, which necessarily is involved in a multitude of states of affairs, some actual and others nonactual, necessarily is involved in a multitude of states of affairs, some actual and others nonactual, also involving nonexistent particulars. Thus the Eiffel Tower necessarily is involved in such actual states of affairs as those consisting of a centaur's not standing under it, a mermaid's not reclining under it, and a square-circle's not being engraved on it, and in such nonactual states of affairs as those consisting of the positive states of affairs corresponding to the negative states of affairs just indicated. But if actual states of affairs involving existent particulars can also involve nonexistent particulars, then it would seem that actual states of affairs can involve nonexistent particulars without also involving existent particulars. Thus the actual state of affairs consisting of a centaur's not talking to a mermaid involves only nonexistent particulars. Although actual states of affairs involving only nonexistent particulars would all seem to be negative, there are positive nonactual but possible states of affairs involving only nonexistent particulars, such as the state of affairs consisting of a centaur's talking to a mermaid or Laertes killing Hamlet. Although such states of affairs presuppose properties, they do not presuppose the exemplification of these properties and therefore do not involve existent particulars.

The admission as formal realities of states of affairs involving nonexistent particulars would increase enormously the number of formally real states of affairs admitted to a world already heavily populated not only with contingent states of affairs involving existent particulars but also with necessary and impossible states of affairs presupposing properties without involving particulars. The demands of parsimony therefore require that we avoid admitting the formal reality of such states of affairs if we can. This can be done if certain claims advanced previously are acceptable, since the admission of the formal reality of such states of affairs is incompatible with these claims.

One such claim is that nonexistent particulars are mere intentional objects. But if only formal realities can be presupposed by or involved in formal realities, then nonexistent particulars cannot be involved in formally real states of affairs. States of affairs that presuppose properties without involving particulars can be formal realities, since properties are formal realities; and states of affairs involving only existent particulars can also be formal realities, since existent particulars are formal realities. But states of affairs involving nonexistent particulars, even though they presuppose properties and might also involve existent particulars, cannot be formal realities because nonexistent particulars are not formal realities. Yet such states of affairs are not simply nothing, since they do differ one from another, and nothing cannot differ from nothing. The state of affairs consisting of a centaur's talking to a mermaid differs from that consisting of a centaur's talking to a unicorn. But if such states of affairs are neither formal realities nor nothing, the only other possibility is that they are mere intentional objects. If, that is, something is something and not nothing, then it is either a formal reality, an intentional object, or both. And since anything conceivable can be an intentional object regardless of whether it is or can be a formal reality, states of affairs involving nonexistent particulars not only can be but sometimes are intentional objects even though they cannot be formal realities. Thus a sufficient condition of a state of affairs' being a mere intentional object rather than a formal reality is its involving some nonexistent particular, even though it necessarily presupposes some property and might also involve some existent particular.

The treatment of states of affairs involving nonexistent particulars as mere intentional objects is also compatible with, if not indeed required by, certain other claims made earlier. One such claim is that the distinction between the denotation and the comprehension of a term is spurious.[3] If so, then the comprehension of a term with zero denotation is also zero. If, that is, terms such as 'centaur', 'mermaid', and 'unicorn' denote nothing, then neither do they comprehend anything. Such terms, rather than denoting or comprehending anything, name possible combinations of compatible properties, which is to say that they name possible kinds. Although such possible kinds are formal realities, it does not follow that there are possible but nonexistent formally real centaurs, mermaids, and unicorns. Instead, all that follows is that the terms naming these kinds have a connotation or intension but no denotation or comprehension. To say that nonexistent particulars are consistently thinkable is to say only that it is possible that the combination of properties constituting the corresponding kinds be exemplified. Such nonexistent particulars, as contrasted with the corresponding kinds, can have being only as intentional objects. Although kinds necessarily are formally real possibilities or impossibilities and exist only in the sense that particular instances of them exist, particulars are formal realities only if they exist. This means that kinds, like properties, are metaphysically more fundamental than particulars. Whereas any particular, whether it be an existent entity or only an intentional object, necessarily is a particular of some kind, every kind is a formal reality regardless of whether any particulars of that kind have being either as existent entities or as intentional objects. Kinds therefore are not reducible to particulars.

The treatment of states of affairs involving nonexistent particulars as mere intentional objects is compatible also with our earlier treatment of states of affairs, considered in abstraction from the question of whether they do or do not obtain, as objects of nominative as distinct from propositional acts.[4] So considered, states of affairs are nominated as possible objects of propositional acts by means of which they are judged to obtain or not to obtain. As objects of nominative acts states of affairs can be named. The state of affairs consisting of the Eiffel Tower's being in Paris is named by the complex name "the Eiffel Tower's being in Paris." Such an expression can be used to nominate the state of affairs in question as a possible object of a propositional act consisting of the judgment that it does or that it does not obtain. Every such propositional act presupposes some nominative act, since no state of affairs can be judged to obtain or not to obtain unless it is first nominated as the object of such a judgment. To use a name to nominate a state of affairs as a possible object of a propositional act is not to use it as a sentence, and no name so used is thereby being used as a sentence. Thus "the Eiffel Tower's being in Paris," which does not say that the Eiffel Tower is in Paris, is a name and not a sentence, whereas "the Eiffel Tower is in Paris," which does say that the Eiffel Tower is in Paris, is a sentence and not a name. Although it can function as a name, as when it is mentioned as a means of naming itself, it is a sentence rather than a name when it is used rather than mentioned. Sentences, since they can be used to say something about something, can be true or false; but names are neither, since as names they cannot be used to say anything about anything.

It was maintained earlier that every sentence, every word, and every properly formed expression is meaningful.[5] In order, however, for an expression naming a state of affairs to be meaningful, each of the words constituting the expression must have some dependent or independent meaning. Here we need only consider the categorematic words. Each categorematic word in an expression naming a state of affairs must have some independent meaning, and the meaning of the entire expression is determined in part by the meaning of each of its categorematic words. In order, however, that a categorematic term have a meaning it is not necessary that it denote anything. Instead, if it be a general term it is sufficient that it connote some property or combination of properties, and if it be a proper name or definite description it is sufficient that it indicate some intentional object. Similarly, in order that an expression naming a state of affairs be meaningful it is not necessary that the latter obtain; instead, it is sufficient that it be the intentional object of a nominative act. Thus just as it is not necessary that categorematic terms denote anything if they are to be meaningful, so also it is not necessary that the states of affairs nominated by the expressions naming them obtain if such expressions are to be meaningful. Such expressions are still meaningful by virtue of the fact that the states of affairs they nominate are intentional objects, just as categorematic terms that denote nothing are still meaningful by virtue of the fact that they either have a connotation or else indicate some intentional object.

The preceding means that there is a certain parallelism between categorematic terms on the one hand and expressions nominating states of affairs on the other. Just as categorematic terms are meaningful even though they denote nothing, so also expressions nominating states of affairs involving particulars are meaningful even though the nominated state of affairs is not a formal reality. This in turn means that just as one cannot argue from the fact that categorematic terms are meaningful to the conclusion that therefore they denote something, so also one cannot argue from the fact that expressions nominating states of affairs involving particulars are meaningful to the conclusion that therefore the nominated state of affairs is a formal reality. And just as categorematic terms can have a denotation only through denoting existent particulars, so also expressions nominating states of affairs involving particulars can nominate formal realities only if each term in the expression indicating a particular has a denotation. Thus the states of affairs nominated by "the Eiffel Tower's being in Paris" and "the Eiffel Tower's being in London" are both formal realities even though the first but not the second obtains because neither expression contains a term indicating a particular that fails to denote anything. But the states of affairs nominated by "a centaur's standing under the Eiffel Tower" and "a centaur's standing by a mermaid" are not formal realities because each expression contains at least one term indicating a particular that fails to denote anything.

3. Intentional States of Affairs

If the considerations advanced in the latter part of the preceding section are acceptable, then we must modify the claim made at the beginning of that section to the effect that states of affairs are formal realities regardless of whether they do or do not obtain. The modification required is that only those states of affairs that do not involve nonexistent particulars are formal realities. Those that involve such particulars are mere intentional objects. This last claim, however, is still not acceptable as it stands, since it applies only to what may be referred to as nonintentional states of affairs involving nonexistent particulars. Such states of affairs are those in which no particular involved in them or property presupposed by them is an intentional object of any other particular involved in them. By contrast, intentional states of affairs involving particulars are those in which some particular involved in them has as an intentional object either some particular involved in or some property presupposed by such states of affairs. The following are all intentional states of affairs: Plato's thinking of the property of being red, Plato's thinking of Aristotle, Plato's thinking of Pegasus, Hamlet's thinking of the property of being red, Hamlet's thinking of Aristotle, Hamlet's thinking of Ophelia. All intentional states of affairs necessarily involve particulars, since intentional objects necessarily are intended by some particular thinker. Such intentional objects, however, might or might not be formal realities. In the examples above, the property of being red and Aristotle are both intentional objects and formal realities, whereas Pegasus and Ophelia are intentional objects but not formal realities. Similarly, the particulars intending the intentional objects involved in intentional states of affairs might or might not themselves be formal realities. In the examples above, Plato is a formal reality but Hamlet is not. This means that in intentional states of affairs the particulars intending the intended objects involved in such states of affairs might or might not be formal realities regardless of whether the intended objects are formal realities or only intended objects.

Intentional states of affairs are themselves formal realities only if the particulars intending the intentional objects involved in such states of affairs are themselves formal realities. Such states of affairs are formal realities regardless of whether they do or do not obtain and regardless of whether the involved intentional objects are also formal realities. Thus in order that an intentional state of affairs be a formal reality it is not necessary that each particular involved in it be such a reality. Instead, some might be only intentional objects. It is necessary, however, that the particular intending the intended object be a formal reality. If it is not, the state of affairs in question is itself only an intentional object even though the intended object involved in it be a formal reality. Thus the states of affairs above involving Hamlet as the intending particular are only intentional objects rather than formal realities and would have no being at all were they not for someone intentional objects. They therefore do not obtain, since only those states of affairs that are formal realities can obtain. But the states of affairs involving Plato as the intending particular are formal realities, regardless of whether they did or did not ever obtain. Intentional states of affairs therefore differ from those that are nonintentional. A sufficient condition of the formal reality of an intentional state of affairs, regardless of whether it does or does not obtain, is that the intending particular involved in it be a formal reality, regardless of whether its intended object is also such a reality. But a necessary condition of the formal reality of a nonintentional state of affairs involving particulars, regardless of whether it does or does not obtain, is that each particular involved in it be a formal reality. Thus whereas nonintentional states of affairs involving particulars can be formal realities only if the expressions nominating them contain no categorematic terms that denote nothing, intentional states of affairs can be formal realities even though the expressions nominating them do contain categorematic terms that denote nothing, provided only that they contain some term that denotes a particular that intends some intentional object.

Nonintentional states of affairs involving particulars, then, are formal realities only if each involved particular is a formal reality. If any of the involved particulars do not exist, such states of affairs can have being only as intentional objects. If any of the particulars involved in them do not exist, and if such states of affairs are not for anyone intentional objects, then they have no being at all. Thus if they are to have any being at all some particular must exist. Each particular involved in them must exist if they are to be formal realities, and if they are not formal realities some particular must intend them if they are to have being as intentional objects. Otherwise they have no being at all. Similarly with intentional states of affairs. Such states of affairs are formal realities only if the intending particulars they involve are formal realities. If the intending particulars they involve do not exist, they can have being only as intentional objects. If the intending particulars involved in such states of affairs do not exist, and if the latter are not for anyone intentional objects, then they have no being at all. Thus if they are to have any being at all some particular must exist. Otherwise they have no being at all.

The preceding follows from the fact that particulars can have being only if they are either formal realities or objective realities. They are formal realities only if they exist, objective realities only if they are intentional objects for some existent particular. Thus particulars would have no being in any sense at all if no particular were ever to exist. The property of being a particular, like other properties, would have being as a nonexistent formal reality, but it could have no exemplification. But if no particulars at all existed, states of affairs involving particulars could have no being whatever. They could not be formal realities because there would then be no particulars to be involved in them, and they could not be intentional objects because there would then be no particulars for whom they could be such objects. But since properties are formal realities regardless of whether they are exemplified, states of affairs presupposing properties without involving particulars are formal realities regardless of whether particulars ever exist and therefore regardless of whether they are ever for anyone intentional objects.

The preceding attempt to eliminate states of affairs involving nonexistent particulars unless the latter are intended objects of existent particulars still might not satisfy some who have baroque sensibilities. If so, the following considerations might be helpful. It was argued earlier that the Meinongian-like expressions 'the mermaid' and 'the square-circle' are preferable to the plural forms 'mermaids' and 'square-circles', since such plural forms might lead one to suppose that there is a plurality of possible but nonexistent mermaids and a plurality of impossible and therefore nonexistent square-circles. The use of such plural forms might also lead one to suppose that a term expressing a self-consistent concept has a comprehension comprehending a plurality of entities, some of which might exist but others of which do not. Such plural forms might finally lead one to suppose that there is a plurality of possible and impossible formally real but nonexistent particulars that can be involved in states of affairs that are also formal realities. Since, it might be argued, there are formally real but nonexistent possible and impossible particulars, there are also formally real states of affairs in which they are involved. Once the formal reality of the former is admitted, the formal reality of the latter follows as a matter of course, given that every formally real particular necessarily is involved in some formally real state of affairs.

If, however, there are no formally real nonexistent particulars, then neither can there be any formally real states of affairs involving such particulars as formal realities. Instead, they could be involved in formally real states of affairs only as the intended objects of existent particulars also involved in them. It is true that nonexistent particulars could also be involved in states of affairs that have being only as intentional objects intended by some existent particular, since it is possible to think of states of affairs involving nonexistent particulars. Given, however, that the kinds of which such particulars would be instances if they existed are formal realities, there is no need to postulate the formal reality of such particulars. Since everything that could be accounted for by making such a postulation can be accounted for without making it, to make it would be to multiply entities beyond metaphysical necessity. That this is in fact the case can be shown as follows.

First, even those with the most extreme rococo sensibilities will grant that there are kinds or combinations or properties for which there are no instances or exemplifications. Some of these kinds, such as the mermaid, are possibilities, others, such as the square-circle, impossibilities. This is to say that it is possible that some, such as the mermaid, have instances, impossible that others, such as the square-circle, have instances. Such possibilities and impossibilities are necessary. Given, that is, that the properties the combination of which constitutes a possible kind are compatible, it follows necessarily that such a combination can be exemplified. Given also that the properties the combination of which constitutes an impossible kind are incompatible, it follows necessarily that such a combination cannot be exemplified. Thus whether a kind can or cannot have instances is determined necessarily by the compatibility or incompatibility of the properties constituting the kind. If they are compatible the kind can have instances; if they are not it cannot. To determine whether a kind can or cannot have instances it therefore is not necessary to postulate particulars, whether these be existent, possible but nonexistent, or impossible. It is the nature of the kind that determines completely whether it can or cannot have instances. If so, then for any possible or impossible kind there necessarily is some state of affairs that presupposes the kind regardless of whether it also involves particulars. For any possible kind, such as the mermaid, there necessarily is a state of affairs consisting of its possibly having instances; and for any impossible kind, such as the square-circle, there necessarily is a state of affairs consisting of its not having instances. For each possible and impossible kind, states of affairs of the sorts just indicated necessarily obtain. The obtaining of such states of affairs can be asserted by using such sentences as "The mermaid can have instances" and "The square-circle cannot have instances." Made about possible kinds they assert only that they can, not that they do, have instances; and made about impossible kinds they assert explicitly that they cannot have instances.

Second, although there are no formally real nonexistent particulars and no formally real nonintentional states of affairs involving such nonexistent particulars, such particulars and states of affairs can be intentional objects for existent particulars. Given this, and given the considerations of the previous paragraph, two consequences follow. One is that although there is no plurality of formally real nonexistent particulars of any kind, there is a plurality of intentional acts having such particulars as intentional objects. Thus the same person at different times and a plurality of persons at the same or at different times can have as intentional objects a plurality of mermaids, centaurs, or square-circles. One can think, for example, of ten mermaids in a swimming pool, ten centaurs in a pasture, and ten square-circles on a wall. This fact, taken in conjunction with the fact that most nouns have a plural form, might help to explain the widespread use of the plural forms of categorematic terms denoting nothing rather than the use of the corresponding forms prefixed by the definite article that indicate kinds that have no instances. From the fact, however, that there is a plurality of intentional acts having as objects nonexistent particulars it by no means follows that such intentional objects are also formal realities. The second consequence that follows is that if the formal reality of nonexistent particular intentional objects does not follow from the fact that such particulars are intentional objects, then neither does the formal reality of nonintentional states of affairs involving such particulars follow from the fact that such states of affairs are intentional objects. If such particulars are not formal realities, then neither are such states of affairs.

Perhaps the main reason that might incline some to suppose that there are formally real nonexistent particulars and nonintentional states of affairs involving them is that such particulars and states of affairs can be intentional objects. If it is possible to account for their being intentional objects without supposing that they are also formal realities, then we have no reason for making such a supposition. That such an account can be presented is established by the following considerations. Provided that he has sufficient imagination, anyone who has the concept of some impossible kind or of some possible kind that has no instances can think of such kinds as having instances involved in nonintentional states of affairs. All that is required for so thinking of them is that the person who does so have the concept of the relevant kind and have sufficient imagination to think of a possible instance of the kind as involved in some nonintentional state of affairs. Although it is necessary that the instance and the state of affairs involving it of which he thinks be for him intentional objects, it is not necessary that they be formal realities.

Given, however, that such nonexistent particulars and the states of affairs involving them are intentional objects, as such objects they necessarily are ingredient in and partly determine the nature of some formally real state of affairs involving some existent particular for whom they are intentional objects. This follows from the fact that if anything is to be an intentional object there must be some existent particular that does in fact intend it as such an object. This is not to deny that there can be intentional states of affairs involving nonexistent intending particulars, such as Hamlet's thinking of Ophelia. But any state of affairs involving a nonexistent intending particular, even though the object intended by this particular be an existent entity, such as Hamlet's thinking of Aristotle, can itself be only an intentional object, and as such must actually be intended by some existent particular. This can be put as follows.

An intentional state of affairs consists of some particular's intending something as an intentional object. The intending particular might or might not be an existent entity, and the intentional object might or might not be a formal reality. The intending particular, regardless of whether it be an existent entity, might or might not have some formal reality as its intentional object. Hamlet, who does not exist, thinks of Ophelia, who is not a formal reality, and also of Denmark, which is; and you and I, who do exist, can think also of Ophelia and Denmark and also of Hamlet. But intentional states of affairs involving nonexistent intending particulars, since they involve such particulars, cannnot be formal realities, regardless of whether the objects intended by such particulars are formally real. They are instead only intentional objects and therefore cannot obtain. But they can be intentional objects only if they are actually intended by some existent particular. Thus intentional states of affairs involving nonexistent intending particulars can have being only as intentional objects that presuppose intentional states of affairs involving existent particulars that in fact do obtain. The obtaining of such states of affairs consists of some existent particular's actually intending the intentional state of affairs involving the nonexistent intending particular.

The considerations just presented amount to an application to intentional states of affairs involving nonexistent intending particulars of considerations advanced earlier concerning nonintentional states of affairs involving nonintending nonexistent particulars. All such states of affairs are only intentional objects for existent particulars who intend them, and any nonexistent particular involved in them, whether it be an intending particular or the intended object of such a particular, can have being only as an intentional object for some existent particular that actually intends it. If a nonexistent particular be an intending particular, it is only an intended and not an actual intending particular; if it be the intended object of a nonexistent intending particular, it is only an intended and not an actual intended object. The act of intending either an intending nonexistent particular or the intended object of such an intended intention, however, must itself be a formal reality and not merely the object of an intention.

4. The Formal Reality of Propositions

We have distinguished between states of affairs of three types: those involving properties but not particulars, those involving existent but not nonexistent particulars, and those involving nonexistent particulars. Since properties are nontemporal formal realities, states of affairs of the first type are also such realities. As such, they either necessarily obtain or else necessarily do not obtain independently of any temporal occurrences and therefore independently of their being intentional objects for anyone. For each such state of affairs there is also a pair of propositions, one to the effect that it obtains, the other to the effect that it does not obtain. Those to the effect that a given state of affairs does obtain are true if it does, false if it does not; those to the effect that a given state of affairs does not obtain are true if it does not, false if it does. Such propositions are also nontemporal formal realities, since their truth or falsity is determined entirely by the obtaining or the nonobtaining of the states of affairs that constitute their content. Like the states of affairs constituting their content, such propositions can become intentional objects. But they are formal realities that are either true or false regardless of whether they are ever intentional objects for anyone and therefore regardless of whether by anyone they are ever asserted or denied.

From the fact, however, that such propositions are nontemporal formal realities it does not follow that so also is any proposition whose content is a state of affairs involving some particular, regardless of whether the latter be existent or nonexistent. For nonexistent particulars are not even formal realities, much less nontemporal formal realities; and existent particulars, though formal realities, are not nontemporal formal realities. Thus if propositions about particulars are nontemporal formal realities, their being so cannot depend upon particulars also being such realities. But can propositions about existent particulars be nontemporal, given that particulars are not? And can propositions about nonexistent particulars even be formal realities, given that such particulars are not? If, that is, existent particulars are temporal, must not propositions about them also be temporal? And if nonexistent particulars are only intentional objects, must not propositions about them also be only such objects rather than formal realities?

We begin with existent particulars. As we have seen, each such particular is involved in a vast multiplicity of temporal states of affairs, some of which obtain, some of which do not. But since the particulars they involve exist only at certain times and not at others, a question arises as to whether such states of affairs are formal realities at those times at which the particulars they involve do not exist and therefore are not formal realities. If, that is, such states of affairs are formal realities only because they involve formally real particulars, can they be formally real at those times at which the particulars they involve do not exist? And if they cannot be, then can propositions to the effect that they do or do not obtain be formal realities at the times at which the states of affairs constituting their content are not formal realities? If they cannot be, is there any sense in which they are nonetheless either timelessly true or timelessly false?

The question of whether a state of affairs involving an existent particular can be a formal reality at those times at which the particular it involves does not exist cannot be answered merely by pointing out that such states of affairs can be intentional objects before or after the involvement in them of the particulars they involve, since the fact that something is an intentional object does not mean that it is also a formal reality. A more promising approach is to appeal (1) to the distinction between states of affairs on the one hand and their obtaining or nonobtaining on the other and (2) to the fact that at any given time any state of affairs involving an existent particular either obtains or else does not obtain regardless of whether at any of these times the particular in question does or does not exist. The distinction between a state of affairs on the one hand and its obtaining or its nonobtaining on the other hand is a formally real distinction. If it were not, then there would be nothing to obtain or not to obtain, and it would also be impossible for anyone to think of a state of affairs, i.e., to have it as an intentional object, without also considering the question of whether it does or does not obtain. But one can have a state of affairs as an intentional object without considering this latter question. Any given state of affairs is therefore one thing, its obtaining or its nonobtaining another, even though every absolutely determinate state of affairs either obtains or else does not obtain. Moreover, for any given state of affairs there is also, as we have seen, a pair of propositions, one to the effect that it obtains, the other to the effect that it does not obtain. Just as one can have a state of affairs as an intentional object without considering the question of whether it does or does not obtain, so also one can have a proposition to the effect that a given state of affairs does (or does not) obtain as an intentional object without asserting or denying it.

As we have seen, states of affairs involving only properties either necessarily obtain or else necessarily do not obtain regardless of what, if anything, happens in time, so that propositions to the effect that such states of affairs obtain (or do not obtain) necessarily are either true or false regardless of what, if anything, happens in time. It is because of this that such states of affairs and propositions are nontemporal. By contrast, states of affairs involving existent particulars might or might not obtain, depending upon what happens in time, so that propositions to the effect that such states of affairs obtain (or do not obtain) also depend for their truth or falsity upon what happens in time. It is because of this that such states of affairs and propositions are temporal. Although such states of affairs obtain at certain times and do not obtain at others, at any given time any such state of affairs, provided that it be absolutely determinate, either obtains or else does not obtain. Thus the state of affairs consisting of the Eiffel Tower's being in Paris obtains (or obtained) in 1927 but does not obtain (or did not obtain) in 1827. Yet, as was argued earlier,[6] any proposition to the effect that a given state of affairs obtains (or does not obtain) at a given time is timelessly true or false. Although the truth or falsity of the proposition depends upon whether the state of affairs in question does or does not obtain at the time in question, its truth or falsity is nevertheless timeless in the sense that it cannot change. If true, it is true at any time it is asserted or denied, and if false, it is false at any time it is asserted or denied, regardless of whether the time at which it is asserted or denied is prior to, contemporaneous with, or subsequent to the time at which the state of affairs in question is asserted or denied to obtain (or not to obtain). Thus the proposition to the effect that the state of affairs consisting of the Eiffel Tower's being in Paris obtains in 1927 is true regardless of whether it be asserted in 1877, 1927, or 1977. And the proposition to the effect that the state of affairs consisting of the Eiffel Tower's being in Paris obtains in 1827 is false regardless of whether it be asserted in 1727, 1827, or 1927.

The truth or falsity, however, of a proposition to the effect that a given state of affairs obtains at a given time depends only upon whether that state of affairs does in fact obtain at that time. In no way does it depend upon its being entertained, asserted, or denied by anyone. Regardless of whether such propositions are ever for anyone intentional objects, and thus regardless of whether at any time they are ever by anyone asserted or denied, there is no time at which, if true, they are false, and no time at which, if false, they are true. If so, the truth or falsity of such propositions is a formal reality regardless of whether they are also ever for anyone intentional objects. But if their truth or falsity is a formal reality, then so also are they formal realities. This is the case because their truth or falsity is a property of them, and if an entity is not itself a formal reality, then neither can any of its properties, as properties of it, be such realities. Such propositions and their truth or falsity, then, for the reasons given and in the sense indicated, are timeless formal realities. But though timeless formal realities, such propositions nonetheless differ from propositions to the effect that states of affairs involving only properties do (or do not) obtain. Propositions of the latter kind, in addition to being timelessly true or false, are also nontemporal, since the states of affairs constituting their content are nontemporal. But propositions to the effect that some contingent state of affairs does (or does not) obtain at a given time are temporal even though they are timelessly true or false, since their truth or falsity depends upon the obtaining (or the nonobtaining) of the state of affairs in question at the time in question.

We turn now to nonexistent particulars. As was maintained in the last section, since nonexistent particulars are only intentional objects and not formal realities, states of affairs involving them are also only intentional objects. Thus in their case to be is to be for someone an intentional object. The being of nonexistent particulars and of the states of affairs involving them therefore requires the existence of particulars for whom they are intentional objects. They have no being at all if they are not actually intended by some existent particular. Given, however, that some nonexistent particular and some state of affairs involving it are actually intended by some existent particular, the latter is involved in the actual state of affairs consisting of his having them as intentional objects. This means that any nonexistent particular and any state of affairs involving it necessarily are involved in some actual state of affairs consisting of some existent particular's actually intending them. This, however, in no way means that they are formal realities, since they are involved in actual states of affairs only as the intentional objects of existent particulars. The fact that they are only intentional objects, however, means that a problem arises concerning the ontological status of propositions about them. Does the fact that they are only intentional objects mean that so also are propositions about them, or can such propositions be formal realities even though their content is not?

The most promising way of treating this question would seem to be to distinguish between (1) nonexistent particulars and the states of affairs involving them and (2) actual states of affairs consisting of some existent particular's intending such nonexistent particulars and the states of affairs involving them. Since states of affairs involving nonexistent particulars are only intentional objects and not formal realities because the nonexistent particulars they presuppose are only such objects, propositions to the effect that such states of affairs do (or do not) obtain are also only intentional objects. Since, that is, the states of affairs they presuppose are only such objects, so also are they. If so, then such propositions are not formal realities. They therefore have no being independently of their being intentional objects for someone. But actual states of affairs consisting of some existent particular's intending nonexistent particulars and states of affairs involving them, like actual states of affairs of any other kind, are formal realities. This is to say that actual intentional states of affairs, like actual nonintentional states of affairs, are formal realities. Since actual states of affairs of both kinds involve existent particulars, the considerations advanced earlier in this section concerning nonintentional states of affairs involving such particulars apply also to intentional states of affairs involving such particulars. For each such state of affairs there is a pair of propositions, one to the effect that it obtains, the other to the effect that it does not obtain. Thus for the actual state of affairs consisting of my thinking now of a mermaid, there is a proposition to the effect that it obtains and another to the effect that it does not obtain. Just as any proposition to the effect that a given nonintentional state of affairs does (or does not) obtain is a timelessly true or false formal reality, so also is any proposition to the effect that a given intentional state of affairs does (or does not) obtain. Thus just as the proposition to the effect that the state of affairs consisting of my sitting now obtains is a formal reality the truth of which is independent of anyone's ever entertaining, asserting, or denying it and of the time, if any, at which anyone entertains, asserts, or denies it, so also is the proposition to the effect that the state of affairs consisting of my thinking of a mermaid now obtains.

Notes

1. Chap. 4, sec. 4.
2. Chap. 5, sec. 1.
3. Chap. 3, sec. 5.
4. Chap. 4, sec. 5.
5. Chap. 3, sec. 3.
6. Chap. 4, sec. 2.

7
Properties, Essences, and Being

IN the last chapter it was maintained that any state of affairs involves or presupposes some property regardless of whether it also involves some particular. In this chapter we shall consider certain aspects of the relationship of properties and particulars to one another and to essences and being.

1. Essential and Nonessential Properties

It was contended in the last chapter that the distinction between a state of affairs on the one hand and its obtaining or nonobtaining on the other is a formally real distinction. This distinction is analogous to the distinction between a property on the one hand and its being or nonbeing on the other. If so, then the latter distinction is also a formally real distinction. That it is such a distinction can be shown as follows.

Everyone will agree that the property of being red is distinct from the property of being green. Either these properties are formal realities or they are not. Let us suppose that they are. In saying that they are we are saying precisely the same thing of each—we are saying of each that it has being independently of its being for anyone as intentional object. Neither therefore differs from the other insofar as each is considered as a formal reality taken completely in abstraction from any consideration of its difference from the other. But if there is no formally real distinction between either of these properties and its formal reality, then each property is identical with its formal reality. Since, however, neither differs from the other insofar as it is considered simply as a formal reality, and if each is identical with its formal reality, then there can be no distinction between the two. But being red is distinct from being green. Therefore each must be distinct from its formal reality. Let us now suppose that neither is a formal reality. In saying that they are not formal realities we are saying precisely the same thing of each—we are saying of

186

each that it has no being independently of its being for someone an intentional object. Neither therefore differs from the other insofar as neither is a formal reality. But if there is no formally real distinction between either of these properties and its not being a formal reality, then each property is identical with its not being a formal reality. If, however, neither differs from the other insofar as neither is a formal reality, and if each is identical with its not being a formal reality, then there can be no distinction between the two. But being red is distinct from being green. Therefore each must be distinct from its not being a formal reality. Regardless, then, of whether properties are formal realities, necessarily there is a formally real distinction between any property on the one hand and its being a formal reality or its not being a formal reality on the other.

The preceding can be put by saying that to predicate of a property such as being green either that it is or that it is not a formal reality is not to predicate of it either that it is or that it is not the property of being green. To say of the property of being green that it is the property of being green is to assert an identical proposition, and to say of the property of being green that it is not the property of being green is to assert a self-inconsistent proposition. But to say of the property of being green that it is a formal reality is not to assert an identical proposition even though the proposition asserted be necessarily true; and to say of the property of being green that it is not a formal reality is not to assert a self-inconsistent proposition even though the proposition asserted be necessarily false. This is to say that the concept of being green is a distinct concept from those of being and of not being a formal reality. But since, as we have seen, two concepts can differ only if their objects or contents differ, being green necessarily differs both from being a formal reality and from not being a formal reality.

Being green, being red, being a formal reality, and not being a formal reality are all properties, each of which is the object or content of the corresponding concept. Since being the objects of concepts is a property these properties have in common, they do not differ from one another by virtue of their having this property. Instead, they are identical in nature insofar as they are considered only as being objects of concepts. And since they are all properties, neither do they differ from one another by virtue of their being properties. They are instead identical in nature insofar as they are considered only as properties. Each differs from the other not by virtue of its being the object of a concept or by virtue of its being a property but rather only by virtue of its being the unique property it is. Being red, that is, differs from being green only because red or redness differs from green or greenness. This can be put in linguistic terms by saying that the expression 'being red' differs from the expression 'being green' only because 'red' occurs in the first expression and 'green' in the second. Since 'being' occurs in each expression, neither differs from the other by virtue of its including this term. The occurrence of 'being' in each indicates that each is the name of a property. But it does not indicate which property is being named. This is indicated only by the other term, 'red' or 'green'. The entire expression 'being red' names a property essentially different from that named by 'being green' only because 'red' names a different essence from that named by 'green'. Thus being red and being green are essentially different properties only because red and green (or redness and greenness) are different essences.

Such properties may be said to be essential properties, since their unique nature is determined by the corresponding essences that constitute their uniqueness. (This use of the expression 'essential property' differs from another, more established, use of this expression according to which an essential property of an individual is a property the individual has necessarily.) Without the essences red and green there could be no properties of being red or being green, and without these essences neither property could be the unique property it is. Not all properties, however, are essential properties, since some properties, such as being self-identical, being the object of a concept, and being (or not being) a formal reality are predicable of a multiplicity of essences and essential properties regardless of the essential differences between the latter. Thus being red, being green, red, green, or any other essential property or essence is identical with itself, can be the object of a concept, and is (or is not) a formal reality. Since such predications can be made of any essential property or essence, to make such predications of a given essential property or essence without saying anything else is to say nothing at all about the property or essence in question that would serve to distinguish it from any other property or essence. Such predications, taken by themselves, therefore cannot serve to distinguish any essence or essential property from any other.

Yet such nonessential properties, since they are predicable of any essence or essential property, are themselves properties. As predicable of essential properties they presuppose the latter in the sense that if there were no essential properties to serve as the subjects of such predications the latter could not be made. Moreover, the predicability of nonessential properties of essential properties presupposes the formal reality of the essences that constitute the uniqueness of essential properties. If, that is, there were no essences there could be no essential properties, and if there were no essential properties no nonessential properties could be predicable of them. In addition, there is a formally real distinction between any two nonessential properties, between any nonessential property and its own formal reality, and between any nonessential property and each of the essential properties of which it is predicable. The argument presented above to establish that there is a formally real distinction between any essential property and its formal reality suffices, with the obvious necessary changes, to establish that there is also a formally real distinction between any nonessential property and its formal reality. That there is a formally real distinction between nonessential properties follows from the fact that they are properties, taken in conjunction with the fact that no two properties can be identical. And that there is a formally real distinction between any nonessential property and any of the essential properties of which it is predicable follows also from these two facts and also from the fact that each nonessential property is predicable of a multiplicity of essential properties. Being self-identical, for example, is predicable not only of the property of being red but also of the property of being green.

But if essential and nonessential properties are formal realities formally distinct both from one another and from their formal reality, so also are essences. That this is the case can be seen by applying to essences, with the necessary changes, the argument used above to establish that essential properties are formally distinct from one another and from their formal reality. The formal reality of essences and their formal distinctness from one another and from their formal reality follows also from the fact that essential properties presuppose essences. If, that is, essential properties presuppose the corresponding essences in the sense that the former could not be formal realities unless the latter were, and if essential properties are formally distinct from one another and from their formal reality, then so also must essences be formally distinct from one another and from their formal reality. Thus if the property of being red and that of being green are formal realities formally distinct from one another and from their formal reality, then so also are red and green (or redness and greenness).

2. Kinds of Distinctions

Certain of the claims advanced in the previous section can be given additional clarification and support by considering in more detail the distinction between those distinctions that are formally real and those that are not. To say of a distinction that it is a formal distinction or a formally real distinction is to say that its being in no way depends upon its being an intentional object. A distinction can be the object of an intentional act without also being formally real. Although such distinctions have objective reality, they have no formal reality. The distinction intended here between those distinctions that are formally real and those that are only objectively real, despite a difference in terminology, is similar to but not identical with the well-known distinction John Duns Scotus makes and frequently uses between a real distinction and an objective formal distinction on the one hand and a purely mental distinction on the other. For Duns Scotus there is a real distinction between two things if and only if they are physically separable, at least by God; there is an objective formal distinction between two formalities, moments, or aspects of an object if they are objectively distinct but not physically separable; and there is a purely mental distinction when the intellect creates a distinction to which no real distinction or no objective formal distinction corresponds. There is thus a real distinction between a triangular and a rectangular figure, since each is physically separable from the other. There is an objective formal distinction between the triangularity and the three-sidedness of a triangular figure, since these, though not physically separable so long as the figure remains triangular, are formally distinct aspects of the figure. But there is only a purely mental distinction between being a triangular figure and being a three-sided closed plane rectilinear figure, since there is no formal distinction to which this distinction corresponds.

There are problems concerning precisely what the correct interpretation of Scotus's distinction between these three kinds of distinction is. Without, however, embarking on the long excursion that would be required in a serious attempt to resolve these problems, there seems clearly to be a difference between real, objective formal, and purely mental distinctions, given the brief characterization of them presented above. Moreover, regardless of what the correct interpretation of Scotus's position is, it would seem that his real distinction and his objective formal distinction are both species of what I have referred to as formally real distinctions and that his purely mental distinction is what I have referred to as an objectively but not formally real distinction. It would seem, that is, that Scotus's real distinctions and objective formal distinctions are formal realities and not mere intentional objects. If so, then real distinctions and objective formal distinctions are formal realities and as such have being independently of their being for anyone intentional objects, whereas purely mental distinctions are only objective realities that have being only as intentional objects.

The distinction between an essence or a property on the one hand and its formal reality on the other cannot be a Scotistic real distinction. As we have seen, a distinction of the latter kind holds between two objects if and only if they are physically separable, at least by God. But no essence or property can be physically separable from its formal reality. Nothing can be a formal reality unless it has some property other than that of being such a reality. If, that is, anything is to exemplify the property of being a formal reality it must also exemplify some other property. In the absence of its exemplifying some other property it would be nothing at all, and nothing at all cannot be a formal reality but is rather the complete absence of any formal reality at all. An essence such as red (or redness) must exemplify the property of being an essence if it is to be a formal reality, and a property such as being red must exemplify the property of being a property if it is to be a formal reality. But although nothing can be a formal reality unless it is also something other than simply a formal reality, such as the essence red or the property of being red, there is still a distinction between the essence red, the property of being red, and any other essence or property on the one hand and the property of being a formal reality on the other. As we have seen, insofar as each of these essences or properties is considered simply as a formal reality taken completely in abstraction from the unique nature of each, none differs from any of the others. But since the unique nature of each does in fact differ from that of each of the others, there is a distinction between each on the one hand and its formal reality on the other. Such a distinction, however, is not a Scotistic real distinction, since no formally real essence or property is physically separable from its formal reality.

Similar considerations apply to the distinction between the nature of an intentional object on the one hand and its objective reality on the other. Regardless of whether a given intentional object is also a formal reality, it must have some property other than that of being an intentional object if it is to be such an object. Even those intentional objects that are not also formal realities, such as mermaids, centaurs, and unicorns, must have some property other than that of being an intentional object. There is therefore a distinction between the objective reality of any intentional object on the one hand and its nature, by virtue of which it is the kind of intentional object it is, on the other. This distinction is not a purely mental distinction even though the intentional object itself be purely mental, i.e., be only an intentional object and not also a formal reality. Although an intentional object that is not also a formal reality would have no being at all if it were not such an object, this does not mean that the distinction between its nature and its objective reality is purely mental. If it were it would have no being at all unless it were for someone an intentional object. Instead, however, of this distinction's depending for its being upon its being for someone an object of thought, its formal reality is a necessary condition of the possibility of anyone's having anything as an intentional object. Although, then, the being of a mermaid depends entirely upon its being an intentional object, its being such an object depends upon its having a nature distinct from its objective reality as such as object. The distinction between the nature of an intentional object and its objective reality is therefore presupposed both by the object's being such an object and also by anyone's thinking of it, regardless of whether the distinction itself is also an intentional object.

But if the distinction between the nature of an intentional object and its objective reality is not purely mental, neither is it a Scotistic real distinction. The reasons given above to show that the distinction between an essence or property and its formal reality is not a real distinction suffice to show that neither is the distinction between the nature of an intentional object and its objective reality. Insofar as something is an intentional object, regardless of whether it is also a formal reality, its nature is not physically separable from its objective reality. And if something is only an intentional object and not also a formal reality it is, if anything, even more obvious that its nature is not physically separable from its objective reality, since it would have no being at all as a physical formal reality.

Everyone will doubtless agree that there are in fact Scotistic real distinctions between certain objects. A red apple, for example, is really distinct from a green avocado, since the two not only are physically separable but in fact are physically separate. Many, even if not everyone, will also agree that there are in fact Scotistic objective formal distinctions between the aspects, moments, or formalities of objects and between any aspect, moment, or formality of an object and the object itself. The redness of an apple, though not really distinct from the apple or its shape or sweetness in the sense of being physically separable from them, is formally distinct both from the apple and its shape and sweetness and also from its own formal reality and those of the apple and its shape and sweetness. The nature of these two kinds of distinction and their difference from one another seem fairly clear, as does the fact that distinctions of either kind are formal realities in the sense that their being in no way depends upon their being for anyone intentional objects. Initially the nature of purely mental distinctions and their differences from distinctions of the other two kinds might also seem fairly clear. Such distinctions are purely mental in the sense that no Scotistic real or objective formal distinctions correspond to them, so that they have no foundation in what Scotus terms objective reality. Or, to use the Cartesian language we have been using, such distinctions have no formal reality at all but instead have only the objective reality of intentional objects. Since, however, there are no Scotistic real or objective formal distinctions corresponding to such distinctions, a question arises as to how they are possible. How, that is, is it possible for anyone to distinguish between two intentional objects, regardless of whether they are also formal realities, if there is no formally real distinction between the two by virtue of which they can be distinguished?

This question is distinct from the question of how one of two concepts, proper names, or uniquely identifying descriptions can apply to some formal reality to which the other does not apply even though both nonetheless apply to the same existent entity. As we have seen,[1] the concept of the Evening Star differs from that of the Morning Star even though they both apply to the same existent entity to which the concept of the planet Venus also applies. The first is the concept of a body that has the property of appearing at a certain place in the heavens in the evening, the second the concept of a body that has the property of appearing at a certain place in the heavens in the morning, and these two properties are formally distinct even though only one existent entity, the planet Venus, has both. Since these two properties are formally distinct, the distinction between the Evening Star and the Morning Star is a formally real distinction rather than a purely mental distinction. Even though, that is, the same existent entity, the planet Venus, has both the properties in question, the fact that these properties are distinct formal realities means that the distinction between the Evening Star and the Morning Star has what Scotus would term an objective foundation and is therefore a formally real rather than a purely mental distinction. Whether it is a Scotistic real distinction or only an objective formal distinction we need not here inquire, since regardless of which of the two it is the fact that it is formally real means that it is not purely mental.

But if no distinction can be purely mental if there is some formally real distinction to which it corresponds and upon which it is based, our question as to how purely mental distinctions are possible still remains. One promising answer is that they are possible because there are different expressions that neither denote different objects nor connote different properties. Thus 'being a triangular figure' and 'being a three-sided closed plane rectilinear figure', though different expressions, do not connote different properties. If so, then the distinction between being a triangular figure and being a three-sided closed plane rectilinear figure, since it is a distinction neither between different objects nor between different properties, is a purely mental rather than a formally real distinction. Ignorance of the fact that these two expressions do not connote formally distinct properties might lead someone to believe that they indicate a formally real distinction when in fact the distinction in question is purely mental. Such distinctions, since they are only distinctions between expressions rather than between objects or properties, are mere verbal or linguistic distinctions for which there are no corresponding formally real distinctions. If so, then purely mental distinctions are only verbal or linguistic distinctions.

It will be remembered that in the last section a distinction was drawn between essential properties and their corresponding essences. A question now arises as to whether this distinction is formally real or only purely mental or linguistic. If, for example, neither of the expressions 'the essence red' and 'the property of being red' connotes some formal reality not connoted by the other, then the difference between these expressions signals only a purely mental or linguistic distinction to which no formally real distinction corresponds. Although the difference between the two expressions might lead one to believe that one connotes some formal reality not connoted by the other, this belief can be shown to be correct only if it can be shown that there is in fact some formal reality connoted by one but not the other. I shall argue that although the difference between these two expressions does not signal a formally real distinction between the essence red and the property of being red, they can be used in such a way that they connote a formally real distinction, albeit not a Scotistic real distinction, between the essence red on the one hand and the possibility of its exemplification by something else on the other.

The expression 'the essence red' can be used in such a way that it names only the essence red, considered strictly by itself completely in abstraction from any consideration of the possibility of its being exemplified by anything. The expression 'the property of being red', on the other hand, can be used in such a way that it indicates that the essence red is being taken, at least implicitly, as being possibly exemplified by something. So used, the expression 'the essence red' may be said to be an absolute expression, since it names only the essence red, which absolutely is what it is taken completely in abstraction from any consideration of its possible exemplification by something else. The expression 'the property of being red', on the other hand, may be said to be at least an implicitly relative expression, since it indicates that the essence red is being considered, at least implicitly, as possibly standing in a relation to something else that might exemplify it. If so, then the expressions 'the essence red' and 'the property of being red' do not indicate precisely the same thing. The first indicates the essence itself, the second the possibility of its exemplification by something. If this is so, then the difference between these two expressions does not indicate only a purely mental or verbal distinction but instead indicates a formally real distinction, although, again, not a Scotistic real distinction, between the essence on the one hand and the possibility of its exemplification on the other. This is the case because the essence is one thing, the possibility of its exemplification another. Even if every essence necessarily is such that it can possibly be exemplified by something, the essence itself is still one thing, the possibility of its exemplification by something another. This applies even to those essences, if any, that necessarily are exemplified by something. Even in their case the essence is one thing, its necessary exemplifications by something another. If so, then 'the essence red', used as an absolute expression, indicates only the essence red itself taken completely in abstraction from the possibility of its exemplification by something, whereas 'the property of being red', taken as a relative expression, indicates the possibility of the exemplification of the essence red by something else. So taken, these two expressions signal a formally real distinction between the essence red as it is in itself on the one hand and the possibility of its exemplification by something else on the other.

3. Forms of Being

We turn now to apply various of the considerations presented in the first two sections to the distinction between the property of being a formal reality on the one hand and formal reality on the other. Just as something has the property of being red only if it is red, so also something has the property of being a formal reality only if it is a formal reality. And just as the redness of an apple is formally but not really distinct from the apple, so also the formal reality of an apple is formally but not really distinct from the apple. Moreover, just as an apple, though red and thus a red thing, is not the essence red itself, so also an apple, though formally real and thus a formal reality, is not formal reality itself. Just as things other than the apple can be and are red, so also things other than the apple can be and are formally real. From the fact, however, that these analogies hold it does not follow that formal reality is itself an essence. And if formal reality is not itself an essence, the property of being a formal reality is not precisely the same kind of property as that of being red. Whereas properties of the latter kind are essential properties, the property of being a formal reality is a nonessential property if formal reality itself is not an essence.

Considerations have already been presented to show that essences, though formal realities, are not themselves formal reality itself. Even those who deny that essences are formal realities will doubtless agree not only that they are not formal reality itself but also that they would not be formal reality itself even if they were formal realities. To say of any existent entity that it is red or of any essence that it is the essence red is not equivalent to saying of it that it is a formal reality, since an existent entity or an essence can be a formal reality without being red or the essence red. At the same time, however, as we have seen, nothing can be a formal reality and nothing more. This is part of what is meant by saying that the distinction between an essence such as red and its formal reality, though formally real, is a Scotistic objective formal distinction and not a real distinction. Although the formal reality of an essence is not physically separable from it, the distinction between an essence and its formal reality is a formally real rather than a purely mental or mere linguistic distinction.

The distinction between essence and formal reality is more comprehensive and fundamental than that between essence and existence, since although all existent entities are formal realities, not all formal realities are existent entities. Something can be a formal reality without existing, but nothing can exist without being a formal reality. The distinction between essence and existence is therefore only a special case of and follows from the distinction between essence and formal reality. In addition to the distinction between essence and formal reality there is also, as we have seen, a distinction between essence and objective reality. This yields a distinction between essence on the one hand and existence, formal reality, and objective reality on the other. Anything conceivable is either an existent formal reality, a nonexistent formal reality, or an objective reality. Each existent formal reality has the property of existing or occurring in time independently of its being for anyone an intentional object; each nonexistent formal reality has the property of being (although not that of existing or occurring in time) independently of its being an intentional object; and each objective reality has the property of being an intentional object.

The first of these three properties is the property of existing or occurring, which may be referred to as the property of temporal formal being or reality; the second is the property of nontemporal formal being or reality; and the third is the property of objective being or reality. These three properties correspond to and presuppose three forms of being or reality—temporal formal being or reality, nontemporal formal being or reality, and objective being or reality. The distinction between these three properties and forms of being is not a purely mental or linguistic distinction to which nothing in reality corresponds but instead is a formally real distinction. This is the case (1) because nontemporal formal realities do not depend for their being upon the existence of temporal formal realities and (2) because formal realities, regardless of whether they be temporal or nontemporal, do not depend for their being upon their being intentional objects. Nor is the distinction only a distinction between three concepts. As we have seen, two or more concepts can differ only by virtue of a difference in their objects, so that if there were no difference between the three forms of being there could be no difference between the corresponding concepts.

Just as any of the three forms of being can be considered completely in abstraction from anything that has any of these forms of being, so also being itself can be considered in abstraction from each of its three forms. So considered, it is an absolute transcendental in the sense that anything, regardless of whatever it might be, has being or is a being. Its polar opposite is absolutely nothing (or absolute nothingness), or the complete absence of being and therefore of any of its three forms and of anything that has or is a being of any kind. The distinction between being and nothing can be expressed by saying that the term 'being' and the concept of being apply to anything conceivable, regardless of its nature, whereas the term 'nothing' and the concept of nothing apply to nothing, in the sense that they do not apply to anything at all. Neither being nor nothing, however, are identical with their concepts or the terms expressing the latter. The terms 'being' and 'nothing' and the concepts they express, like all other terms and concepts, have being. They therefore are not nothing. But although 'being' and the concept of being have being, they are not identical with being. And since 'nothing' and the concept of nothing have being, they cannot be identical with nothing.

The preceding can be put in the late medieval scholastic terminology used earlier.[2] Whereas 'being' has not only material and simple supposition but also personal supposition, 'nothing' can have only material and simple supposition but never personal supposition. Since 'being' applies to anything conceivable, it not only has material supposition when used to refer to itself and simple supposition when used to indicate the concept of being but also necessarily applies to something when used with personal supposition to indicate anything other than itself or the concept of being. The term 'nothing', on the other hand, although it can be used with material supposition to refer to itself and with simple supposition to refer to the concept of nothing, has no personal supposition, which is to say that it applies to nothing at all if used with personal rather than material or simple supposition. Since anything conceivable is something, 'being' applies to anything conceivable; and since nothing conceivable is nothing, 'nothing' applies to nothing conceivable if used with personal supposition. Being, in the sense of being something rather than nothing, is something that everything has in common. Being, having being, being a being, and being something, like being self-identical and being the possible object of a concept, are therefore absolute transcendental properties (or perhaps different forms of the same property) in the sense that anything conceivable is, has being, is a being, and is something in at least one of the three senses of 'being' distinguished above. And since they apply to anything conceivable, the term 'being' is an absolute transcendental term and the concept of being an absolute transcendental concept.

Nothing, however, can have being without also having some property other than that of having being. This can be put by saying that no absolute transcendental property can be possessed by anything unless it also possesses some nontranscendental property and that no absolute transcendental term or concept can apply to anything unless some non-transcendental term or concept also applies to it. Since every absolute transcendental property necessarily is possessed by anything conceivable, to know of something only that it has such properties is not to have knowledge of it sufficiently specific to distinguish it from anything else. Thus to say of something only that it possesses some absolute transcendental property, even though such a statement necessarily would be true, would be to say very little indeed about it. To say something about it that suffices to distinguish it from anything else it is necessary to predicate of it some nontranscendental property.

In addition to absolute transcendental properties, there are also what may be referred to as relative transcendental properties. The distinction intended between absolute and relative transcendental properties can be explained as follows. Any being, regardless of what kind of being it might happen to be, is either a formal or an objective reality. Although some beings are both formal and objective realities, and although some formal realities are not objective realities and vice versa, nothing can have being or be a being unless it is either a formal reality, an objective reality, or both. If so, then nothing can possess any absolute transcendental property unless it also possesses the property of being a formal reality, the property of being an objective reality, or both these properties. It is because anything that has or is a being necessarily possesses either or both of these properties that the latter may be referred to as relative transcendental properties. They are relative rather than absolute transcendental properties because although anything, to have or to be a being, must possess either, nothing need possess both.

Relative transcendental properties may therefore be said to be intermediate properties that are more specific than absolute transcendental properties and less specific than nontranscendental properties. Just as to say of something only that it has or is a being is to say very little indeed about it, so also to say of something only that it is a formal reality or that it is an objective reality is to say very little about it. Since anything of which anyone thinks has objective reality, and since anything conceivable can be an intentional object regardless of whether it is or can be a formal reality, to say of something only that it is an objective reality is to say nothing at all about it that could not also be said of any other intentional object. And since anything can be a formal reality provided only that it can be independently of its being an intentional object, to say of something only that it is or can be a formal reality is to say nothing at all about it that cannot also be said about anything else that is or can be such a reality.

Just as everything that has being is a formal or an objective reality, so also everything that is a formal reality is either an existent or a nonexistent formal reality. Thus nothing can possess the property of being a formal reality unless it also possesses either the property of being an existent formal reality or that of being a nonexistent formal reality. The latter two properties are therefore specific forms of the relative transcendental property of being a formal reality and may therefore be referred to as specific relative transcendental properties. Nothing can possess any specific relative transcendental property without also possessing some nontranscendental property. And since there are many existent and nonexistent formal realities, to say of anything only that it exists or that it is a nonexistent formal reality does not suffice to distinguish it in the first case from any other existent being and in the second from any other nonexistent formal reality. Nothing, therefore, can be a formal reality without possessing every absolute transcendental property, one of the two specific relative transcendental properties of formal realities, and some nontranscendental property. The possession of such properties, however, although necessary to the being of any formal reality, does not constitute its being, since in order that they be possessed it is necessary that there be some formal reality that possesses them.

4. Formal Realities and Their Properties

The claim with which the last section ended does not mean that essences and properties cannot themselves possess properties. On the contrary, any essence and any property possesses every absolute transcendental property, the relative transcendental property of being a formal reality, and the specific relative transcendental property of being a nonexistent formal reality. Thus any essence and any property possesses the absolute transcendental properties of being or having being, of being self-identical, and of being the possible object of a concept. In addition, any essence possesses the nontranscendental property of being an essence and any property the nontranscendental property of being a property. In order, however, that any essence or property possess any property it must itself have or be a being. Possession is a two-term relation, requiring both something to be possessed and something to possess it. That which is possessed is formally distinct from and therefore irreducible to that which possesses it, and that which possesses something is formally distinct from and therefore irreducible to that which is possessed. This is the case regardless of whether that which possesses something is itself an essence or property or a particular. If so, then no essence, property, or particular (with the possible exception of certain properties such as the property of being self-identical) can be identical with any property or set of properties it possesses. Since this claim is more disputable in the case of particulars than in the case of essences and properties, in view of the fact that it has sometimes been held that any particular is identical with the set of its properties, let us turn to consider briefly and somewhat provisionally and roughly the possession of properties by some particular such as an apple.

Let us suppose that our apple is red, round, solid, juicy, and sweet. Since many other material objects also have these properties, it does not differ from them by virtue of its possession of such properties. It also has a spatiotemporal location and history. But since all material objects have such a location and history, it cannot differ from any other by virtue of the fact that it does too. It might be qualitatively identical with some other apple, since some other apple might have precisely the same size and consistency it has and be red, round, solid, juicy, and sweet in precisely the same way it is. But no other apple and no other kind of material object can have precisely the same spatiotemporal location and history it has. Although it is possible that it should have had some other spatiotemporal location and history than the one it does in fact have and that some other material object should have had the same one it in fact has, given that it does in fact have the one it has, no other object can also have it. Given, that is, that it came into being at a certain time on a certain branch of a certain tree and continuously occupied certain places and traversed a certain path until its present location on my desk, no other object could have precisely the same spatiotemporal location and history it does in fact have. (The apple of our example, incidentally, does not exist and is only an intentional object. But let us nonetheless continue to assume that it does in fact exist.) Although two objects can be qualitatively identical provided that there be at least some difference between the spatiotemporal location and history of each, and although it is possible that some other qualitatively different object should have had precisely the same spatiotemporal location and history that a given object does in fact have, two material objects can be numerically distinct, i.e., be two objects rather than only one, only if they have different spatiotemporal locations and histories.

It might be thought that if the preceding claims are true, then the principle of individuation for any material object is its spatiotemporal location and history taken in conjunction with the set of properties it possesses. It is these that make it the individual object it is. Each material object, that is, is the unique individual it is because it possesses a certain set of properties and has a certain spatiotemporal location and history. Its possession of these properties and its having this spatiotemporal location and history constitute the source of its unique individuality. There might be some sense in which these claims are true. But if there is it does not follow that any material object is identical with or reducible to the conjunction of the set of properties it possesses and its spatiotemporal location and history. This is the case for two related reasons, both contained implicitly in what has already been said. The first concerns the possession of a set of properties by a material object, the second the having by a material object of a spatiotemporal location and history.

The preceding presupposes a distinction between the set of properties a material object possesses on the one hand and its spatiotemporal location and history on the other. To some this distinction might seem spurious, since the spatiotemporal location and history of a material object is one of its properties. There is, however, a difference between this property of a material object and those of its properties the possession of which is independent of its precise spatiotemporal location and history. Thus two apples can be red, round, solid, juicy, and sweet in precisely the same way even though necessarily there is some difference between their spatiotemporal locations and histories. If so, then their possession of properties of the former kind is independent of their spatiotemporal locations and histories. Although only those existent entities that have a spatiotemporal location and history can possess properties of the former type, such properties, since their possession is independent of the precise spatiotemporal location and history of the entity that possesses them, may be referred to, although perhaps somewhat misleadingly, as nonspatial nontemporal properties or, perhaps somewhat less misleadingly, as qualitative properties or simply as qualities. For the sake of simplicity, however, we shall continue in the present context to refer to them as the properties of a material object, as distinguished from the unique spatiotemporal location and history it has. These properties differ in kind from the property of having a unique spatiotemporal location and history.

As we have just seen, the set of properties possessed by a material object is distinct from its spatiotemporal location and history. Each of these in turn is distinct from the material object that possesses the former and has the latter. This gives us three distinct elements necessarily involved in the being of any material object—the object itself, the set of properties it possesses, and its spatiotemporal location and history. Each of these elements is itself a formal reality formally distinct from the other two. First, the set of properties is formally distinct from the material object that possesses it, both in the sense that it would still be a formal reality if it were not possessed by anything at all, and thus not by the material object that does in fact possess it, and also in the sense that it is possible that it be possessed by some other object rather than or in addition to the one that does in fact possess it. Second, the material object is formally distinct from the set of properties it does in fact possess. This is the case for two reasons. The first, as we have just seen, is that it is possible that precisely the same set of properties it possesses be possessed by some other object rather than or in addition to the one that does in fact possess it. The second is that it is possible that it possess some other set of properties rather than the one it does in fact possess. Although it could not be the unique individual object it is or the kind of object it is without possessing at least some of the properties it does in fact possess, it need not possess all the properties it does in fact possess, and thus need not possess the precise set of properties it does in fact possess, either to be the unique individual object it is or to be the kind of object it is. Third, it is possible that what is in fact the precise spatiotemporal location and history of a given material object either be the spatiotemporal location and history of some other material object possessing some other set of properties or else not be the precise spatiotemporal location and history of any material object at all. If each of these contentions is true, then any material object, the set of properties it possesses, and its spatiotemporal location and history are formal realities independently of the formal reality of either of the other two, and thus each is formally distinct from the others.

Although either the set of properties a material object possesses or the spatiotemporal location and history it has could be possessed or had by something other than it, it alone can both possess precisely the set of properties it does in fact possess and also have precisely the same spatiotemporal location and history it does in fact have. This, however, for reasons already given, does not mean that it is identical with or reducible to the conjunction of the set of properties it possesses and the spatiotemporal location and history it has. In addition, that the set of properties it possesses is in fact possessed by something and that the unique spatiotemporal location and history it has is in fact had by something presuppose that something exists that possesses the first and has the second. Thus although nothing other than it could in fact both possess the first and also have the second, this does not mean that its existence and its particularity or individuality consist in its possessing the first and having the second. Instead, its existence and its particularity or individuality are ultimate and fundamental, since if it did not exist as a particular or individual nothing could both possess precisely the set of properties it does in fact possess and also have the unique spatiotemporal location and history it does in fact have. It is true that a material object can be described partially only by specifying certain of its properties and/or certain phases of its spatiotemporal history and fully only by specifying all its properties and the entirety of its spatiotemporal history. This, however, is only to be expected and does not mean that it is identical with the conjunction of the set of its properties and its spatiotemporal location and history. On the contrary, such descriptions, since they are intended as descriptions of it, presuppose it as that to which they correctly apply. If so, then just as the possession of a set of properties and the having of a spatiotemporal location by a particular presuppose its existence, so also the description of a particular by specifying certain of its properties or its spatiotemporal location presupposes it as that which is so described. These considerations, if acceptable, mean that no particular can be identical with or reducible to the conjunction of the set of properties it possesses and the spatiotemporal location and history it has, even though no other particular can have precisely the same set of properties and the same spatiotemporal location and history.

This, however, does not mean that the principle of the identity of indiscernibles is true. Such a conclusion would be an oversimplification, since there are two versions of this principle, the truth of only one of which would follow from the truth of the preceding claims. The distinction between these two versions rests on the distinction between qualitative properties and spatiotemporal properties. As was indicated above, the spatiotemporal properties of a particular are tied to its spatiotemporal location, in the sense that it has them simply by virtue of its location in space and time. Since no two material objects can have precisely the same spatiotemporal location and history, each such object necessarily has some spatial or temporal property possessed by no other material object. If so, then the principle of the identity of indiscernibles is true, at least as applied to material objects, if it be interpreted as including the spatiotemporal as well as the qualitative properties of material objects. So interpreted, the principle states that no two material objects can have precisely the same set of spatiotemporal and qualitative properties.

There is, however, another version of the principle that is doubtful if not in fact false. This is that it is impossible that any two material objects have precisely the same set of qualitative properties. As was indicated above, qualitative properties differ from spatiotemporal properties in that a particular possesses properties of the latter but not of the former kind simply by virtue of its spatiotemporal location. Although the possession by an object of a property such as being red is impossible unless the object has some spatiotemporal location, its being red is not determined simply by its location in space and time. Two objects can be red regardless of whether they exist at different times at the same place or at the same time at different places, and the same object can be red at one time and green at another regardless of whether at the two times it exists at the same or at different places.

The first version of the principle of the identity of indiscernibles states only that no two material objects can have precisely the same set of spatiotemporal and qualitative properties. It does not state that no two objects can have precisely the same set of qualitative properties. This is what the second version states. From the fact that no two objects can have the same set of spatiotemporal and qualitative properties it does not follow that neither can they have the same set of qualitative properties. The truth of the first version of the principle therefore does not entail the truth of the second. The truth of the second version therefore cannot be established by appealing to the truth of the first. It can instead be established only by appealing to other considerations. This cannot be done by appealing to its self-evidence, since it is not self-evident. Nor can it be done by showing that its contradictory is self-inconsistent, since no contradiction is involved in claiming that two objects can possess precisely the same set of qualitative properties. Nor can its truth be established empirically. Even if empirical investigations were to fail ever to reveal any exceptions to the second version of the principle, it would not follow that it is impossible that there be any. Such investigations would also rest upon a misunderstanding of the principle, since it is a priori rather than empirical. Given this, and given also the fact that the contradictory of the principle is not self-inconsistent, the principle must be synthetic a priori. From this, however, as we saw in Chapter Two, it does not follow that it is true. In the absence of any reason for regarding the second version of the principle as true, we must conclude that it is at least doubtful, if not in fact false.

Notes

1. Chap. 5, sec. 1.
2. Chap. 3, sec. 4.

8
Resemblance and Identity

CERTAIN aspects of the relationship of particulars to their properties were discussed in the last chapter. One aspect of this relationship that was not discussed is the question of whether the properties or characteristics of particulars are singular or universal. In this chapter we begin our treatment of this question.

1. Resemblance and Identity Theories

Suppose that two red balls exist. Suppose also that the redness of each is identical with or exactly similar to that of the other. Whether the redness of each is identical with or exactly similar to that of the other depends upon whether the redness ingredient in each ball is itself universal or singular. If it is universal the redness of each is identical with that of the other; if it is singular the redness of each is exactly similar to but not identical with that of the other. Arguments can be and have been presented for each position.[1] We shall begin by considering in a summary way a few arguments in support of the resemblance theory, then a few in support of the identity theory.

One argument for the resemblance theory goes as follows. The first premise of the argument is that no universals are sensible. The second is that the redness ingredient in each ball is sensible. From these two premises it is concluded that the redness ingredient in each ball is not universal but rather is singular. The second premise seems true, since it is hard to see how we could ever know that any particular is red if we could never sense the redness of any. From this, however, it does not follow that the conclusion is also true, since its truth follows only from the truth of the first premise taken in conjunction with that of the second, not from the truth of the second alone. The truth of the first premise, however, is by no means evident and may therefore be regarded as question-begging by a supporter of the identity theory. An advocate of the latter theory can concede that no universal is sensible when taken completely in abstraction from its ingredience in some particular. From this, however, it does not follow that no universal is sensible as ingredient in some particular. The redness ingredient in each ball, as ingredient in each, can therefore be universal even though it is sensible. This response to the argument, although not sufficient by itself to establish that the redness ingredient in each ball is universal, does seem sufficient to show that the argument in question does not establish that the sensible properties ingredient in particulars are singular rather than universal. It might be possible to develop it in such a way that it would establish this, but it does not do so as it stands.

A second argument for the resemblance theory has a form similar to that of the first. The first premise is that no universals exist or have being in either space or time. The second is that the redness ingredient in each ball does have being in space and time. From these two premises it is concluded that the redness ingredient in each is not universal but rather is singular. As before, the second premise seems true, since the redness ingredient in each ball is located in space on the surface of each. If this were not the case it would be hard to see how each ball could be red or even to know what could be meant by saying that each is red. From this, however, it does not follow that the conclusion is true, since, as before, its truth follows only from the conjunction of the truth of the first premise and that of the second and not from the truth of the second alone. But again as before, the truth of the first premise is by no means evident and may therefore be regarded as question-begging by a supporter of the identity theory. An advocate of the latter theory can concede that no universal has being or exists in either space or time when taken completely in abstraction from its ingredience in some particular. From this, however, it does not follow that no universal exists or has being in space and time as ingredient in some particular. Thus some nonsensible dispositional property such as combustibility can be spatiotemporally present in each ball even though it never be sensibly manifested by their burning. As present in each it can be universal even though as present in each it is spatiotemporal. This response to the argument is not sufficient to establish that the combustibility present in each ball is universal. It does, however, seem sufficient to establish that the second argument does not demonstrate that the properties of particulars are singular rather than universal. Although it might be possible to develop it in such a way that it would establish this, it does not do so as it stands.

A third argument in support of the resemblance theory may be named "the inexact resemblance argument." This argument differs in form from the first two. This is because, unlike the first two, it denies not only that precisely the same universal can be ingredient in two or more particulars but also denies that any property of one particular can exactly resemble any property of any other particular. Whereas the first two arguments admit that there can be an exact resemblance between the redness of one particular and that of another, this argument maintains that there can be only an inexact resemblance between any property of one particular and any property of any other particular. It therefore makes a more extreme claim than either of the first two arguments. This claim, however, is false, since in point of fact some property of one particular can exactly resemble (or be identical with) some property of some other particular. The whiteness of one piece of chalk, for example, can be sensibly indistinguishable from the whiteness of another. This can be established through the performance of a number of obvious simple experiments. It might, however, be objected that the fact that some property of one particular is sensibly indistinguishable from some property of another does not establish that there is an exact resemblance (or identity) between the two. The basis of such an objection would presumably be that there might be some difference between the resembling properties that is not sensibly detectable. Such an argument, however, does not suffice to save the inexact resemblance argument. What the proponent of this argument must do is to show, not merely that there might be, but rather that it is impossible that there not be, some difference between the resembling properties that is not sensibly detectable. But that such an impossibility can in fact be established is very much to be doubted.

We turn now to consider in a summary way several arguments for the identity theory. One such argument is based on the principle of parsimony. According to this argument, to suppose that when two or more objects are exactly alike in some respect each possesses some singular property that exactly resembles some singular property possessed by the other is to multiply entities beyond necessity, since precisely the same situation can equally well be described by supposing that precisely the same property is possessed by each of the objects. If, that is, two objects are exactly alike in some respect, the resemblance theory supposes that four entities are involved, two objects and two singular properties, whereas the identity theory supposes that only three entities are involved, two objects and one universal property. From the standpoint of the principle of parsimony the situation becomes increasingly bad as the number of objects exactly alike in some respect increases. Thus if three particulars are exactly alike in some respect the resemblance theory supposes that six entities are involved, three particulars and three singular properties, whereas the identity theory supposes that only four entities are involved, three particulars and one universal property. But since such situations are described as adequately by the identity as by the resemblance theory, the latter theory multiplies entities beyond necessity. Since the identity theory, by postulating fewer entities, describes such situations as adequately as the resemblance theory, we have no reason to believe that the needless multiplicity of entities postulated by the resemblance theory do in fact exist or have being.

This argument is not entirely convincing. It is true that the resemblance theory is required to postulate a greater number of entities than the identity theory to describe the same situation. But the resemblance theory is nonetheless more economical than the identity theory in the sense that it postulates only entities of one type, singular or nonuniversal entities, whereas the identity theory postulates entities of two types, singular and universal. Although the identity theory is more parsimonious in that it requires a fewer number of entities regardless of the type of entity required, the resemblance theory is more parsimonious in that it requires a fewer number of types of entity. Moreover, from the fact that one theory is more parsimonious than another it does not follow that the entities postulated by the less parsimonious theory do not in fact exist or have being. Instead, all that follows is that such entities might not exist or have being, so that if we are to establish that they do we must present additional argument.

A second argument for the identity theory is that the proponents of the resemblance theory confuse the number of exemplifications of a property with the number of properties exemplified. If, that is, four particulars exemplify a given property, there are four exemplifications of that property. From this, however, it does not follow that four properties are exemplified, each by one and only one particular. The response to this argument is twofold. First, the argument is stated in a question-begging way. It assumes that a single universal property can be exemplified by a multiplicity of particulars. But since this is precisely the point at issue between the resemblance and identity theories, it cannot properly be assumed as a premise by advocates of the latter theory. Second, from the fact that proponents of the resemblance theory maintain that each exemplified property is singular rather than universal it does not follow that they are confusing the number of exemplifications of a property with the number of properties exemplified. It is true that if each exemplified property is singular it can be exemplified by one and only one particular, so that the number of exemplified properties will be identical with the number of exemplifications of properties. But there is nonetheless still a distinction between an exemplified property on the one hand and its exemplification on the other. The property exemplified is one thing, its exemplification another, since if there were no property to be exemplified there could be no exemplification of it.

A third argument for the identity theory is that there can be no unexemplified properties if all exemplified properties are singular. The reason for this is as follows. All self-consistent properties are exemplifiable regardless of whether they are in fact exemplified. A property, that is, is exemplifiable not because it is in fact exemplified but rather because it is self-consistent. But if a property is exemplifiable regardless of whether it is in fact exemplified, its being as an exemplifiable but unexemplified property cannot depend upon its being exemplified. Moreover, its identity as the property it is is independent of its exemplification or nonexemplification; it is what it is regardless of whether it is exemplified and regardless of the number of exemplifications of it. But if so, then the same property can be exemplified by a multiplicity of particulars, from which it follows that exemplified as well as unexemplified properties are universal. From this it follows that if all exemplified properties were singular there could be no exemplifiable but unexemplified properties. This in turn means that the resemblance theory can be true only if nominalism is true.

The response to this argument is as follows. First, it fails to distinguish between a property as exemplifiable and a property as exemplified. As exemplifiable it is universal; as exemplified it is singular. A property such as being red, for example, is exemplifiable regardless of whether it is in fact exemplified because it is self-consistent. As such it is universal and can be exemplified by a multiplicity of particulars regardless of whether it is in fact exemplified. Each particular that exemplifies it, however, does so not because it is a particular but rather because it is a red particular. Were it instead a green particular it would exemplify being green rather than being red. This point can be put more generally by saying that no particular exemplifies any properties at all simply by virtue of its being a particular, other than the property of being a particular and those properties entailed by its exemplification of this property. If a particular exemplifies any other property, it can do so only through the ingredience in it of some property not entailed by its being a particular. As ingredient in a particular, such properties are singular, and it is by virtue of the ingredience of such singular properties in particulars that the latter exemplify properties that are universal when taken completely in abstraction from any consideration of particulars and the singular properties ingredient in them. Although, then, properties are universal when taken completely in abstraction from particulars, as ingredient in particulars they are singular. Such ingredient singular properties may be said to be singular cases of universal properties. Since universal properties have being taken completely in abstraction from their singular cases and the particulars in which the latter are ingredient, the resemblance theory does not entail nominalism.

The preceding points can be supported by the following additional considerations. Let x, y, and z be three particulars. As such, each exemplifies the property of being a particular and any property entailed by their exemplification of this property. Each particular, in addition to the preceding properties, necessarily also exemplifies some other property or set of properties, although which property or set it does in fact exemplify is not entailed by its being a particular. Let us suppose that x is blue and round, y green and round, and z red and square. Since x, y, and z are each particulars yet differ in color, the color of each is neither entailed by nor identical with its particularity or its being a particular. Since each would still be a particular even if it had a different color, each as a particular is distinct from its color, and the color of each can be considered completely in abstraction from the particular of which it is the color. Similarly, since x and y are round and z square, the shape of each is neither entailed by nor identical with its particularity or its being a particular. Since each would still be a particular even if it had a different shape, each as a particular is distinct from its shape, and the shape of each can be considered completely in abstraction from any consideration of the particular of which it is the shape. Each particular is also distinct from its color and its shape because the color and the shape of each is just that—the color and the shape of each—and not the color of the color or the shape of the shape. This can be put by saying that the color and the shape of each is a property of each and not of itself, i.e., the color of each is not a property of the color of each, nor is the shape of each a property of the shape of each. Each particular is distinct from its color and its shape also because whereas they are properties of it, it is a property neither of itself nor of them. Since, then, each property of each particular is a property of it and not of itself, and since each particular is a property neither of itself nor of any of its properties, each particular is distinct from its properties.

At the same time, however, according to the resemblance theory, the color and the shape of each particular is singular and therefore unique to the particular of which it is the color and the shape. The color of each is located on the surface of each rather than on that of either of the other two and therefore has a different spatial location from that of either of the other two. Similarly with the shape of each. Its spatial location is that of the particular whose shape it is rather than that of either of the other two particulars. Each particular exemplifies the universal color and shape it does only because a singular case of that color and shape is ingredient in it. The particular x, for example, exemplifies the color blue because a singular case of that color is ingredient in it. Since there can be other singular cases of the color blue more or less resembling that of x, the universal blue exemplified by each particular in which these singular cases of blue are ingredient is not identical with any of its singular cases.

Each case of blue is singular with its own spatiotemporal location, whereas the universal blue has no location in space or time. And whereas each singular case of blue, like each blue particular, is sensible, the universal blue, like any other universal, is not. Although, then, the universal blue is exemplified by each blue particular, such exemplification is possible only by virtue of the fact that a singular case of blue is ingredient in each such particular with a spatiotemporal location tied to that of particular in which it is ingredient. Exemplification therefore involves entities of three distinct types, none of which is reducible to either of the others—a universal, a singular case of the universal, and a particular exemplifying the universal by virtue of the fact that a singular case of the universal is ingredient in it. In this way the proponent of the resemblance theory can sustain his essential contention without committing himself to nominalism.

Although such a version of the resemblance theory would escape nominalism, it does so only by postulating a greater number of types of entity than does either the identity theory or a nominalistic version of the resemblance theory. As we have just seen, it postulates entities of three distinct types—particulars, singular cases of universals, and universals exemplified by particulars by virtue of the ingredience in the latter of singular cases of the universals they exemplify. By contrast, as we have seen, the identity theory postulates entities of only two types—particulars and universals, which are universal not only in themselves taken completely in abstraction from their exemplification by particulars but also as exemplified by particulars. This version of the resemblance theory also postulates a greater number of types of entity than the nominalistic version does, since the latter version does not postulate universals in addition to particulars and singular properties. In addition, a state of affairs in which x and y are blue is described by the identity theory by postulating only three entities—two particulars and one universal—whereas the version of the resemblance theory presently being considered describes it by postulating five entities—two particulars, one universal, and two singular cases of this universal. In describing such a state of affairs this version of the resemblance theory also postulates a greater number of entities than does the nominalistic version, since the latter version postulates only four entities—two particulars and two singular properties. In its description of such a state of affairs the nominalistic version of the resemblance theory therefore postulates a greater number of entities than does the identity theory even though it postulates only one type of entity—singular or nonuniversal—whereas the identity theory postulates two types—particular and universal.

These considerations mean that in two respects what we may now refer to as the realistic version of the resemblance theory is less parsimonious than either the nominalistic version of this theory or the identity theory. In the first respect it postulates three types of entity, whereas the nominalistic version postulates only one and the identity theory only two. In the second respect it postulates a greater total number of entities, regardless of type, than does either of the other two theories in describing a state of affairs in which two or more particulars exemplify the same universal property or have exactly resembling singular properties. And while the identity theory is less parsimonious than the nominalistic version of the resemblance theory in the first respect, it is more parsimonious in the second respect. But, as we have seen, the fact that one theory is more parsimonious than another does not mean that it is also preferable. Instead, the less parsimonious theory is preferable if it accounts more adequately for the facts. I shall argue that of the three theories in question the realistic version of the resemblance theory is preferable, despite the fact that it is the least parsimonious of the three. The argument I shall present has two parts—one directed against the nominalistic version of the resemblance theory, the other against the identity theory. The major difficulty with nominalism is that it cannot account as adequately as realism, whether the realism be that of the resemblance theory or that of the identity theory, for the nature and status of universals taken completely in abstraction from their exemplification by particulars. The major difficulty with the identity theory is that it does not account as adequately as does the realistic version of the resemblance theory for the difference between unexemplified and exemplified universals, between universals in themselves taken completely in abstraction from their exemplification by particulars on the one hand and the exemplification of universals by particulars on the other.

2. Nominalism and Conceptualism

The major difficulty confronting nominalism can be explained more fully by appealing to considerations presented earlier.[2] Let us suppose, as before, that x is blue, y green, and z red. If so, then x is more similar in color to y than to z. This can be put by saying that the proposition that x is blue, y green, and z red entails the proposition that x is more similar in color to y than to z. The fact, however, that x is more similar in color to y than to z has nothing whatever to do with the nature of x, y, and z taken completely in abstraction from the color of each. Regardless of what the nature of each might be when taken in abstraction from the color of each, x necessarily is more similar in color to y than to z if x is blue, y green, and z red. In some other respect x might be more similar to z than to y. If y were red rather than green and z green rather than red, then, given that x is blue, x would be more similar to z than to y. Thus x is more similar in color to *y* than to *z* not because *x* is *x*, *y* is *y*, and *z* is *z* but rather because being blue is more similar to being green than to being red. And being blue is more similar to being green than to being red because blue is more similar to green than to red.

It is because blue is more similar to green than to red that it is true that for any *x*, any *y*, and any *z*, if *x* is blue, *y* green, and *z* red, then *x* is more similar in color to *y* than to *z*. But if so, then '*x*', '*y*', and '*z*' as variables taking particulars rather than colors as their values are dispensable in expressing the necessary truth that blue is more similar to green than to red. The nature of these colors is such that this necessary truth holds regardless of whether they are ever by anything exemplified and regardless of whether particulars of any kind ever exist. It therefore also holds regardless of whether blue, green, and red as exemplified by or ingredient in particulars are singular or universal. Although any blue particular necessarily is more similar in color to any green than to any red particular, this is the case not because of the nature of such particulars taken in abstraction from their colors but rather because of the nature of blue, green, and red taken in abstraction from any particulars that might or might not exemplify them.

We can agree with the nominalist that blue, green, red, and other essences or universals do not exist when taken completely in abstraction from their exemplification by particulars. From the fact, however, that essences or universals exist only as exemplified by particulars it does not follow that they have no formal reality at all in themselves regardless of whether they are ever exemplified. That they are formal realities regardless of whether they are exemplified follows from the fact that certain necessary relationships hold between them regardless of whether they are exemplified, since if they were not formal realities there would be nothing between which such relationships could hold. Thus although the nominalist is correct in denying that unexemplified essences or universals exist, he is mistaken in concluding that they therefore have no being at all. In addition, from the fact, if indeed it be a fact, that exemplified properties are singular rather than universal, it follows neither that there are no unexemplified properties nor that properties are singular when taken in abstraction from the question of whether they are exemplified. Since blue would still necessarily be more like green than red regardless of whether they are ever exemplified, and since this could not be the case if they had no formal reality regardless of whether they are exemplified, their formal reality in no way depends upon their being exemplified. And since properties can be singular only as exemplified, they cannot be singular when taken in abstraction from the question of whether they are exemplified. Since, that is, blue, green, and red can be singular only as ingredient in particulars, and since blue would still necessarily be more like green than red even if no particulars at all existed, such properties would still have being as nonsingular formal realities if no particulars at all existed.

If the preceding considerations are acceptable, then the nominalistic version of the resemblance theory must be rejected. An attempt might still be made, however, to avoid the realism of the realistic version of this theory and of the identity theory by developing an alternative that is neither nominalistic nor realistic. Such a theory would be conceptualistic. This gives us three versions of the resemblance theory—one nominalistic, one conceptualistic, and one realistic. The conceptualistic version is a version of the resemblance theory because it, like the other two versions, maintains that the properties of particulars are all singular. This distinguishes it from the identity theory. Whereas the identity theory holds that precisely the same property can be exemplified by a multiplicity of particulars and that such a property, as ingredient in a particular, is universal rather than singular, all three versions of the resemblance theory maintain that although there can be an exact resemblance between the properties of particulars, such properties are nonetheless singular. The conceptualistic version of the theory differs from the nominalistic in holding that there are not only universal names or terms but also universal concepts. It differs from the realistic version in denying that there are any universals as distinct from universal concepts. Thus as we pass from nominalism through conceptualism to realism there is an increase in the number of types of universal entity admitted by each. The nominalist admits only universal names or terms, the conceptualist universal concepts as well as universal terms, the realist formally real universals as well as universal terms and universal concepts. As versions of the resemblance theory, however, all three agree that the properties of particulars are singular rather than universal, and it is because of this that all three reject the identity theory.

The conceptualistic version of the resemblance theory is unacceptable for essentially the same reason as the nominalistic version. This is that it denies the formal reality of essences or universals taken in abstraction from their exemplification by particulars and therefore cannot account for the necessary relationships that hold between essences or universals regardless of whether they are exemplified. Such an account can no more be presented by substituting universal concepts for formally real universals than by substituting for the latter universal terms. Just as the term 'blue' is not more similar in color to the term 'green' than to the term 'red', so also the concept of blue is no more similar in color to the concept of green than to the concept of red. This is the case because only a color (or a colored particular) can be more similar in color to a second color (or colored particular) than to a third color (or colored particular), and neither terms nor concepts are colors or colored particulars. Although the color named by a given term can be more similar to the color named by a second term than to the color named by a third term, the terms naming the colors, if they be types or spoken tokens, are themselves neither colors nor colored particulars and therefore can be neither more nor less similar in color to one another. And although written token-words are themselves colored particulars, whether the color named by a given token is more similar to that named by a second token than to that named by a third depends entirely upon the nature of the colors named by such tokens and is completely independent of the color of the tokens. Given that 'blue', 'green', and 'red' are used with their ordinary sense, the color named by a red token of 'blue' is more similar to the color named by a blue token of 'green' than to that named by a green token of 'red' even though the green token of 'red' is more similar in color to the blue token of 'green' than to the red token of 'blue'.

But although written token color-words are themselves colored particulars, spoken token color-words, though particulars, are not colored particulars, and type color-words are not even particulars, much less colored particulars. Nor are words colors, whether they be taken as tokens or as types. Concepts too are neither colors nor colored particulars. Although we apply the concept of a given color such as red to a particular when we predicate being red of it, just as we might use the word 'red' in making such a predication, it is nonetheless the color red that we predicate of it and not the concept of red or the word 'red'. When we say of something that it is red we are saying of it that it is a color of a certain sort, not that it is a concept of a certain kind or a word of a certain type. Just as different color-words can name different colors only because of differences between the colors named, so also different color concepts can be concepts of different colors only because of differences between the colors of which they are concepts. Just as 'blue', 'green', and 'red' can name different colors only if blue, green, and red are in fact different colors, so also the concepts of blue, green, and red can be concepts of different colors only if blue, green and red are in fact different colors. Thus the concept of blue can be more similar to the concept of green than to the concept of red only in the sense that the object of the first concept is more similar to that of the second than to that of the third.

The fact, however, that concepts can differ only by virtue of a difference in their objects does not mean that concepts are identical with their objects. As we saw above, it is only the objects of concepts and not the concepts themselves that are predicable of particulars. Although the concept of red is applied to a particular when being red is predicated of it, it is the color red and not the concept of red that is predicated of it. If so, then the concept of red cannot be identical with the color red. Second, we have also seen that it is blue that is more similar to green than to red, not the concept of blue that is more similar to the concept of green than to the concept of red. Instead, the concept of blue can be more similar to the concept of green than to that of red only in the sense that the object of the first is more similar to that of the second than to that of the third. If so, then the object of each concept is different from the concept of which it is the object. Third, whereas concepts require subjects of consciousness, at least certain entities that can become the objects of concepts do not. If, that is, there were no thinking subjects there would be no concepts even though various entities that can become the objects of concepts would still be formal realities. Thus although there would be no concepts of blue, green, and red if there were no thinking subjects, blue would still necessarily be more similar to green than to red. Since this necessary relationship between these colors holds regardless of whether they are exemplified and regardless of whether there are concepts of which they are the objects, and since it could not hold unless the colors between which it holds are formal realities, the conceptualistic as well as the nominalistic version of the resemblance theory is unacceptable.

3. Realism and Resemblance

The fact, however, that the nominalistic and the conceptualistic versions of the resemblance theory are both unacceptable does not mean that the realistic version of this theory is also unacceptable. Instead, I shall argue, this version of the theory, all things considered, seems preferable to the identity theory despite the fact that in order to account for the same facts it postulates a greater number of nonuniversal or singular entities and of types of entity than does the identity theory. As we have seen, whereas the identity theory postulates only particulars and universals, the realistic version of the resemblance theory postulates not only particulars and universals but also singular cases of the universals exemplified by particulars. Thus if x and y are two red particulars exactly alike in color, the identity theory describes this situation by saying that the same universal, red, is exemplified by both x and y, whereas the realistic version of the resemblance theory describes it by saying that there is a singular case of the universal, red, ingredient in x and a distinct but exactly resembling singular case of it ingredient in y. Thus whereas the identity theory postulates only two particulars and one universal, the realistic version of the resemblance theory postulates in addition two singular cases of red. The question therefore arises of whether the latter theory multiplies entities beyond necessity. I shall argue that it does not.

Stated concisely, the argument is that since particulars both have and also exemplify properties but only exemplify and do not also have universals, the properties they have cannot be universals. Stated in more detail the argument is this. Suppose that *x* and *y* are both red. If so, each exemplifies but does not have the universal red. But each exemplifies and also has the property of being red. The universal red therefore cannot be identical with the property of being red, since, given the principle of the indiscernibility of identicals, two entities can be identical if and only if each has all and only those properties the other has. But since the universal red has the property of being exemplified by *x* and *y* but does not have the property of being possessed by *x* and *y*, whereas the property of being red has both these properties, the universal red is not identical with the property of being red. Although it could be identical with this property if each were only exemplified by *x* and *y*, it cannot be identical with it if the latter but not the former is possessed, as distinguished from being exemplified, by *x* and *y*. This can be put by saying that although the property of being red as exemplified by *x* and *y* can be identical with the universal red, since it too is exemplified by *x* and *y*, the property of being red as possessed by *x* and *y* cannot be identical with the universal red, since the latter is not possessed by *x* and *y*.

But if the property of being red as exemplified by *x* and *y* can be identical with the universal red whereas the property of being red as possessed by *x* and *y* cannot be identical with the universal red, the property of being red as exemplified by *x* and *y* cannot be identical with this property as possessed by *x* and *y*. If, that is, *a* can be identical with *b* but *c* cannot be identical with *b*, then *a* cannot be identical with *c*. We must therefore distinguish between the property of being red as exemplified by *x* and *y* and this property as possessed by *x* and *y*. But since only universals can be exemplified, the property of being red as exemplified by *x* and *y* is itself a universal. It necessarily is exemplified by all and only those particulars that exemplify the universal red and is in fact identical with this universal. In general, the property of being such-and-such, as exemplifiable by a multiplicity of particulars, is identical with the universal such-and-such, whatever the such-and-such might happen to be. As was maintained earlier with respect to the distinction between essences and properties,[3] to refer to the universal red or the universal such-and-such as the property of being red or the property of being such-and-such is to emphasize its susceptibility to being exemplified by particulars, whereas to refer to it as the universal red or the universal such-and-such is to emphasize its status of being what it is independently of any consideration of its susceptibility to being exemplified by anything at all. Despite, however, this difference of emphasis indicated by the two expressions, the universal red or the universal such-and-such is identical with the exemplifiable property of being red or being such-and-such.

Since properties as exemplifiable are identical with universals, since universals can be exemplified but not possessed by particulars, and since properties can be possessed by particulars, the properties that can be possessed by particulars cannot be identical with those exemplified by particulars. A distinction must therefore be drawn between properties as exemplified by particulars and properties as possessed by particulars. As exemplified they are universal; as possessed they are singular. Thus although the property of being red or the universal red is exemplified by both x and y, the property of being red possessed by x, although it exactly resembles the property of being red possessed by y, is nonetheless singular. This can be put by saying that just as each property exemplified by some particular is identical with some universal exemplified by that particular, so also each property possessed by some particular is identical with some singular case of some universal. Thus the redness possessed by x is a singular case of the universal red, and the redness possessed by y is a distinct but exactly resembling singular case of the universal red. It is because the redness possessed by x is a singular case of the universal red that x exemplifies the property of being red. Similarly, y exemplifies the property of being red by virtue of the fact that the color it possesses is a singular case of the universal red. Particulars, in short, exemplify the universal properties they do by virtue of the fact that they possess properties that are singular cases of the universals exemplified. Just as any property exemplified by any particular is identical with some universal it exemplifies, so also any property possessed by any particular is identical with some singular case of some universal it exemplifies. Although some property possessed by x might exactly resemble some property possessed by y, and although these properties are cases of some universal exemplified by the two particulars, each property, since it is a singular case of the exemplified universal, is uniquely possessed by the particular that possesses it.

It might, however, be objected that if any property possessed by a particular is identical with a singular case of some universal, then the particular must also possess that singular case of the universal in question. But although we frequently speak of particulars as possessing properties, we rarely if ever speak of them as possessing cases of some universal. Yet if the properties possessed by particulars are identical with cases of universals, it ought to be as natural to speak of them as possessing such cases as it is to speak of them as possessing properties. If, that is, it is natural to speak of x as possessing the property of being red, it ought also to be natural to speak of it as possessing a case of the universal red. To this objection there are two replies. One is that we do sometimes speak of particulars as possessing cases of something, as when we say of someone that he has a case of measles. The second reply is that we also sometimes explicitly speak of some particular's possession of some property as being a case of something, as when we speak of Socrates' wisdom as being a case of wisdom. Here we rather explicitly identify some property possessed by Socrates, his wisdom, as being a singular case of something, wisdom, which might be exemplified by someone other than Socrates. That we think of his wisdom as being a property he possesses is indicated by the possessive case "Socrates' wisdom," and that we think of his wisdom as being a singular case of something, namely wisdom, is indicated by our prefacing "case of wisdom" with the indefinite article, as when we say "Socrates' wisdom is a case of wisdom."

This last can be seen further to be the case if we contrast "Socrates' wisdom is a case of wisdom" with "Plato's wisdom is a case of wisdom." These two expressions are precisely alike, with the exception that in the first the name of Socrates occurs, in the second the name of Plato. The second expression can be used to say the same thing about Plato's wisdom that the first can be used to say about Socrates' wisdom, namely that it is a case of wisdom. Yet that about which this is said by using the first expression, i.e., Socrates' wisdom, differs from that about which it is said by using the second, i.e., Plato's wisdom. This means that Socrates' wisdom is distinct from Plato's wisdom even though the wisdom of Socrates by exactly like the wisdom of Plato. Socrates' wisdom is possessed and manifested by Socrates, not Plato, even though the wisdom of each be exactly like the wisdom of the other. Thus the expression "Socrates' wisdom is Plato's wisdom" can be used to make a true statement only if it is used to say either that Socrates' wisdom is exactly (or almost exactly) like Plato's wisdom or else that one of the two acquired his wisdom from the other regardless of whether it be exactly (or almost exactly) like that of the other. It is used to make a false statement if it is used to say that the case of wisdom possessed and manifested by Socrates is identical with the case possessed and manifested by Plato. Socrates' wisdom is possessed uniquely by the individual of that name, not by Plato, and similarly with Plato's wisdom. Otherwise we could just as well refer to Socrates' wisdom by speaking instead of Plato's wisdom, since then the two would be identical rather than distinct cases of wisdom. But that they are distinct rather than identical is indicated by the fact that although Plato could have acquired his wisdom from Socrates he could not have acquired from Socrates the latter's wisdom, except in the sense that the wisdom Plato acquired from Socrates was exactly (or almost exactly) like Socrates' wisdom. Each individual's wisdom is uniquely his even though it be acquired from another or be exactly like that of another.

An attempt might, however, be made to eliminate singular cases of universals, as distinct from the particulars that possess them and the universals of which they are the cases, by arguing that cases of universals

can be identified only by identifying both the particulars that possess
them and the universals of which they are the cases. Thus Socrates'
wisdom can be identified only by identifying wisdom and Socrates.
Similarly with Plato's wisdom. To identify wisdom by distinguishing it
from other universals is not to identify Socrates's wisdom. Instead, his
wisdom can be identified only by identifying him, since otherwise the
wisdom identified might be that of someone else. Once, however, we
have distinguished wisdom from other universals and Socrates from
other individuals and seen that Socrates exemplifies wisdom, we can
predicate wisdom immediately of Socrates without postulating a singular
case of wisdom possessed by him by virtue of which he exemplifies
wisdom. It is Socrates, not his wisdom, that is wise, and he exemplifies
wisdom not by virtue of possessing a case of wisdom but rather by being
wise. The postulation of singular cases of universals possessed by particulars is therefore a case of multiplying entities beyond necessity.

The response to this objection is as follows. We can agree that neither
the identification of a universal by distinguishing it from other universals nor the identification of a particular by distinguishing it from other
particulars is sufficient by itself to identify a singular case of a universal.
Instead, to do the latter it is also necessary (1) to identify some particular,
at least as the particular I am now intending regardless of whatever other
properties I ascribe to it, and (2) to see, or at least to believe, that it
exemplifies some universal as opposed to others. To see the latter,
however, I must see that it possesses a singular case of the universal in
question. Thus to see that a round red ball exemplifies the universal red I
must see not only that it is a ball and that it is round but also that it is red.
Indeed, I need not even notice that it is a ball or that it is round in order
to see that it is red. Regardless, however, of whether I notice that it is a
ball or that it is round, I must see its redness if I am to see that it
exemplifies the universal red. It exemplifies this universal not because it
is a ball, since it could still be a ball even if it were blue, and not because it
is round, since it could still be round even if it were green, but rather
only because of its redness. Although I can identify its redness as distinct
from the redness of something else only by identifying it, at least as the
particular I am now intending, I must nonetheless also see its redness if I
am to identify it as a red particular. And although its redness might
resemble exactly the redness of some other particular, it is its redness
that I see and not that of some other particular. It is this redness located
on the surface of this ball that I see and not some other exactly resembling redness of some other particular located on its surface. Even
though, then, I can identify some singular case of a universal only by
identifying some particular, at least as the particular I am now intending,
that exemplifies the universal in question, the particular I identify ex-

emplifies this universal only by virtue of its possession of this singular case of it. A particular, in short, exemplifies a given universal not by virtue of its being a particular nor by virtue of its possessing a singular case of some other universal but instead only by virtue of its possessing a case of the universal in question.

That the singular case of a universal possessed by a particular is not identical with the universal of which it is a case is indicated also by the form of an expression such as "Socrates' wisdom is a case of wisdom." The fact that "case of wisdom" is prefaced by the indefinite article indicates that Socrates' wisdom, rather than being identical with the universal wisdom, is instead only one of an indefinite number of possible cases of wisdom. Each actual case of wisdom, rather than being identical with the universal wisdom, which is exemplified by each wise individual, is instead uniquely possessed by some individual and, as was said above, can be identified only by identifying the individual who possesses it. Thus if we substitute for the expression above the expression "Socrates' wisdom is wisdom," the latter expression can be used to make a true statement only if it is used with the same sense as the first expression explicitly has. This can perhaps be seen more clearly if we reverse the two expressions so as to obtain "A case of wisdom is Socrates' wisdom" and "Wisdom is Socrates' wisdom." Whereas a case of wisdom can be identical with Socrates' wisdom, the universal wisdom itself cannot be identical with Socrates' wisdom. Whereas one singular case of wisdom can be identical with Socrates' wisdom, the universal wisdom cannot be, since it can be exemplified by Plato and a host of other individuals as well as by Socrates. Moreover, since Socrates' wisdom ceases to be actual when Socrates ceases to exist or to be wise, the universal wisdom, if it were identical with Socrates' wisdom rather than exemplified by Socrates, could not continue to be exemplified after the death of Socrates or the loss by him of his wisdom.

The form of the expression "Socrates' wisdom is a case of wisdom" also indicates that it is Socrates' wisdom, not Socrates, that is a case of wisdom. Whereas "Socrates' wisdom is a case of wisdom" necessarily is true, "Socrates is a case of wisdom," if used literally, necessarily is false. That Socrates is not identical with his wisdom is also indicated by the fact that whereas "Socrates is wise" is or can be true, "Socrates' wisdom is wise," if used literally, cannot be true. Since individuals alone and not cases of wisdom can be wise, Socrates cannot be identical with his wisdom. This can be put also by saying that since individuals alone and not cases of wisdom can exemplify wisdom, Socrates cannot be identical with his wisdom. Instead, individuals exemplify universals by virtue of their possession of singular cases of the universals they exemplify. If so, a distinction must be drawn between particulars, the universals they exemplify, and the singular cases of these universals they possess. And if this is so, then the realistic version of the resemblance theory seems preferable to the identity theory despite the fact that the latter theory is more parsimonious.

Notes

1. For an excellent detailed discussion of resemblance and identity theories of universals, see Panayot Butchvarov, *Resemblance and Identity: An Examination of the Problem of Universals* (Bloomington and London: Indiana University Press, 1966).
2. Chap. 6, sec. 1.
3. Chap. 7, sec. 2.

9
Predication and Predicables

IN the last section we made use of, without indicating that we were
doing so, a distinction between what late medieval scholastic philosophers referred to as predication *in quid* or quidditative predication
on the one hand and predication *in quale* or qualitative predication on
the other. In this chapter we shall discuss this distinction and also the
general topic of predication. Before doing so, however, it will be helpful
if we consider briefly two unacceptable views of predication.

1. Unacceptable Views of Predication

One unacceptable view of predication is the view that in making a
predication of a subject of predication we predicate a term of it. This
view has been held, for example, by Professor Wolterstorff, who, despite
the fact that he recognizes that we predicate properties of subjects of
predication, nonetheless also repeatedly states that we predicate terms or
words of them.[1] It cannot, however, be the case that in making a
predication of some subject of predication we are predicating a term of
it. If I say, for example, that an apple is red, I am not predicating the
word 'red' of the apple; I am not, that is, saying that the apple is the word
'red'. No one, not even those who espouse the view in question when
they are not explicitly espousing it, supposes that in predicating redness
of an apple they are saying that the apple is the word 'red'. Rather than
predicating words of subjects of predication, we use words to predicate
properties of them. At times, however, properties are predicated of
subjects without the use of any words at all, as when a person, regardless
of whether he possesses a language to enable him to use words to make a
predication, immediately sees or silently judges that something such as
an apple is red. Even when we make predications of words, as when we
say of 'red' that it is a predicate-term, we are not predicating words of

them but rather are saying that they have certain properties such as that of being a predicate-term.

Another unacceptable view of predication is that to make a predication of a given subject of predication is to judge or assert that it is a member of a certain class. Thus on this view to predicate of an apple that it is red is to judge or assert that it is a member of the class of red things. The unacceptability of this view issues essentially from the fact that classes presuppose properties, taken in conjunction with the fact that one can predicate a property of a subject without intending thereby to assert that the subject in question is a member of a certain class. Thus one can judge or assert that an apple is red without intending in the least to judge or assert that it is a member of the class of red things. Although nothing can in fact be red without being a member of the class of red things, so that its being a member of this class follows from its being red, nonetheless to judge or assert that something is red is not identical with judging or asserting that it is a member of the class of red things. Moreover, something is a member of the class of red things by virtue of the fact that it has the property of being red. Rather than something's being a member of the class of red things making it red, it is its being red that makes it a member of the class of red things. This can be put by saying that it is not because the class of red things has members that there are red things but rather because there are red things that the class of red things has members.

That the predication of a property of a subject is not identical with judging or asserting that the subject of predication is a member of a given class can also be seen by considering the fact that the necessary and sufficient conditions that must be satisfied if something is to be a member of a given class can be specified only by specifying the properties the possession of which by something is necessary and sufficient for its being a member of the class. It is true that a class can be constructed arbitrarily by randomly choosing for initial membership in it various items selected without any consideration of the properties they possess and that the membership of such a class can be increased arbitrarily by randomly selecting additional members without considering any similarities they might have to the original members. The predication of a property such as redness of something, however, is not identical with the arbitrary selection of it either as an original or as an additional member of such a class. Neither is the possession of a property such as redness by something sufficient for membership in such an arbitrarily constructed class. Instead, the possession of a given property by something can be sufficient for membership in a class only if the class is defined in such a way that possession by something of that property is sufficient for its membership in the class. Such classes, however, presuppose the properties in terms of which they are defined, so that if there were no properties there could be no definite as opposed to arbitrarily constructed classes. The fact, however, that nothing can possess any property the possession of which is sufficient for membership in some class defined in terms of that property without thereby being a member of that class does not mean that the predication of that property of something is identical with or reducible to judging or asserting that it is a member of that class. Instead, before one can justifiably judge or assert that something is a member of a class defined in terms of some property one must first see that the thing in question has the property in question. If so, then the predication of a property of something, rather than being identical with or reducible to judging or asserting that it is a member of the class defined in terms of that property, is instead presupposed by such judgments or assertions.

The preceding considerations, I believe, are sufficient to show that the predication of a property of something is not identical with or reducible to either (1) predicating of it the name of the property in question or (2) judging or asserting that the subject of predication is a member of some arbitrarily constructed class or of some class defined in terms of the property in question.

2. Quidditative and Qualitative Predication

We turn now to the distinction between predication *in quid* or quidditative predication on the one hand and predication *in quale* or qualitative predication on the other. To explain this distinction it will be helpful to distinguish between concrete general terms and the corresponding abstract singular terms. For many concrete general terms, however, such as 'ball', there are no corresponding abstract singular terms in ordinary use, so that if we want such terms we must coin them, perhaps by adding a suffix such as 'ness' or 'ity' to the concrete general term. Such a procedure would yield 'ballness' or 'ballity' as the abstract singular term corresponding to 'ball'. For any concrete general term 'x' we can also form a corresponding abstract singular expression 'being an x'. Such a procedure would yield 'being a ball' as an abstract singular expression corresponding to 'ball'. Concrete general terms denote particulars by virtue of the exemplification by the latter of the properties named by the corresponding abstract singular terms. Even if there is no corresponding abstract singular term in ordinary use for some concrete general term, there is nonetheless some property connoted by the latter that can be named by some abstract singular term or expression formed in either of the ways just indicated.

To explain the distinction between quidditative and qualitative predication it is also helpful to distinguish between concrete general substantive terms and concrete general property terms. Terms of the first type can be used to name particulars without connoting any properties other than those the exemplification of which by the particulars named is a necessary condition of the applicability to these particulars of the substantive terms applied to them. Since any concrete general term denotes a particular only by virtue of the exemplification by the latter of some property connoted by the term, any concrete general substantive term will connote some property exemplified by any particular to which the term can correctly be applied. Thus the concrete general substantive term 'man' connotes the property animality, since nothing can be a man without being an animal. It does not, however, connote the property of whiteness, since something can be a man without being white. Concrete general property terms, on the other hand, such as 'red' and 'round', can be used to name properties and singular cases of properties without also naming particulars exemplifying or possessing them. Even though some properties such as red and round can be exemplified only by particulars, to say of some particular only that it is red or that it is round is to name a property it exemplifies without also naming the particular.

We are now in a position to explain the distinction between quidditative and qualitative predication. A quidditative predication of a particular is made when some concrete general substantive term is applied to it, a qualitative predication when some concrete general property term is applied to it. If terms of both types are applied to it both a quidditative and a qualitative predication is made of it. Thus 'x is a ball' is a quidditative predication, 'x is red' a qualitative predication, and 'x is a red ball' both a quidditative and a qualitative predication. For any qualitative predication made of a particular there is some corresponding quidditative predication that can also be made of some property or aspect of the particular. Thus for the qualitative predications, 'x is red', 'x is round', and 'x is rubber', made of some particular, x, we have the corresponding quidditative predications 'the color of x is red', 'the shape of x is round', and 'the material of which x is made is rubber'. Such quidditative predications indicate what the color of x is, not what the color of x has, and similarly with the shape of x and the material of which x is made. Such quidditative predications also indicate more explicitly than do the corresponding qualitative predications that it is the color of x, not its shape or the material of which it is made, that is red; that it is the shape of x, not its color or the material of which it is made, that is round; and that it is the material of which x is made, not its color or its shape, that is rubber. They also indicate more explicitly than do the corresponding qualitative predications that it is because the color of x is red that x is red, because the shape of x is round that x is round, and because the material of which x is made is rubber that x is rubber. Were the color of x

some color other than red, x would be some color other than red, and similarly with respect to its shape and the material of which it is made. If so, then the qualitative predications 'x is red', x is round', and 'x is rubber', if true, can be true only by virtue of the truth of the corresponding quidditative predications, 'the color of x is red', 'the shape of x is round', and 'the material of which x is made is rubber'. Such quidditative predications are therefore also more fundamental than, as well as being more explicit than, the corresponding qualitative predications.

This, however, does not mean that a quidditative predication made of x, such as 'x is a ball', is equivalent or reducible to the set of qualitative predications that can correctly be made of it or to the corresponding set of quidditative predications that can correctly be made of its properties or aspects. Although nothing can be a ball unless it has some color and some shape and is made of some material, nothing, to be a ball, need be red, round, or made of rubber. Nor can any material object such as a ball be identical with or reducible to its properties or aspects, regardless of whether the latter be regarded as universal or singular. It is instead that which has these properties or aspects. It is this ball that is a ball, not its color, its shape, the material of which it is made, or the combination of these. And it is the color of this ball that is red, its shape that is round, and the material of which it is made that is rubber. This is part of what is meant by saying that to predicate being a ball of it is to make a quidditative predication of it, whereas to predicate being red, being round, or being made of rubber of it is to make a qualitative predication of it.

Since quidditative predications can be made of the properties or aspects of particulars as well as of particulars, it is not necessary that a concrete general substantive term or expression be applied to anything if a quidditative predication is to be made. Thus we can make quidditative predications of the color, the shape, or the material of which something is made by saying 'the color of this is red', 'the shape of this is round', and 'the material of which this is made is rubber'. In addition, a quidditative predication is made when an abstract singular term is applied to that which it names, as when, speaking of the universal of which one is thinking, one says 'the universal of which I am thinking is redness'. If instead the concrete general property term 'red' is used to predicate redness of some particular, as in 'x is red', we have an instance of qualitative predication. The essential difference between quidditative and qualitative predication is that in quidditative predication the essential nature of the subject of predication is indicated, whereas in qualitative predication some property or aspect of the subject of predication is indicated. To say of some particular that it is a ball, of the color of some particular that it is red, or of some universal that it is redness is to indicate what they are and is therefore to make quidditative predications of them, whereas to say of some particular that it is red is to indicate not what it is but rather that it has a property or aspect of a certain type and is therefore to make a qualitative predication.

Given the preceding, a distinction can be drawn between being something named by a concrete general substantive term, being something named by a concrete general property term, and being something named by an abstract singular term. To be a particular is to be nameable by a concrete general substantive term, to be a property or an aspect of a particular is to be nameable by a concrete general property term, and to be a universal is to be nameable by an abstract singular term. Thus 'ball' in 'x is a ball' names a particular and neither a property nor a universal, whereas 'being a ball' names a universal or universal property exemplified by any particular that is a ball. Second, 'red' in 'x is red' names a singular property possessed by the particular x that is also a case of the universal red exemplified by x. It is because of the exemplification of this universal by x that 'red' applies to but does not name x. Third, 'redness' or 'humanity', as in 'x is redness' or 'x is humanity', names a universal or universal property and neither a particular nor a singular case of a universal. No particular and no singular case of a universal is either redness or humanity. Although particulars can be red or human and singular cases of universals can be cases of redness or humanity, none can be either redness itself or humanity itself.

The preceding applies to terms only as they are used predicatively as opposed to nominatively. In 'x is a ball', 'x is red', and 'x is redness', 'ball', 'red', and 'redness' are all used predicatively rather than nominatively, since they are used to make a predication of something nominated by 'x' or whatever is substituted for 'x'. This, however, does not mean that concrete general terms, whether they be substantive or property terms, and abstract singular terms cannot also be used nominatively. As so used, concrete general substantive terms can be used to name genera or species rather than particulars, and concrete general property terms can be used to name universals rather than singular cases of universals. Thus 'man' in 'man is a species' names the species man rather than some particular man, even though from its truth it follows that any particular man is a member of the species man. Similarly, 'red' in 'red is a color' names the universal red rather than any particular or any singular case of this universal, even though from its truth it follows that any red particular exemplifies this universal and also that the redness of any particular is a singular case of it. The same applies to 'humanity' in 'humanity is a universal property'; it names the universal property humanity rather than any particular human being or any singular case of humanity.

Most concrete general substantive terms and all concrete general property terms and abstract singular terms, when used nominatively without being prefaced by the definite or indefinite article or an indexical expression, name genera, species, universals, or singular cases of universals rather than particulars. In general, if a concrete general substantive term is to be used nominatively to name a particular, it must be prefaced by the definite or indefinite article or some indexical expression, as in 'a man is walking', 'the man is fat', 'this man is tall', 'that man is short', and so on. Unless such terms are so prefaced when used nominatively, they name genera or species rather than some particular. But concrete general property terms and abstract singular terms, even when so prefaced when used nominatively, name universals or singular cases of universals rather than particulars. Thus 'this red' in 'this red is pleasing' and 'that redness' in 'that redness is not pleasing' name either some species of red or else some singular case of redness possessed by some particular rather than the particular itself. If they name some species of red, it is some specific shade of red that is said to be or not to be pleasing and not some singular case of this specific shade possessed by some particular. But if they name some singular case of red possessed by some particular, it is the singular case of red possessed by that particular that is said to be or not to be pleasing, not the particular that possesses it.

The preceding means that universals and singular cases of universals not only can be predicated of particulars but also can be named. They can not only be the objects of predicative acts in which they are predicated of some particular that is the object of a nominative act but can also be the objects of nominative acts in which some predication is made of them. As the objects of nominative acts universals can be intended without intending any particulars at all, as when blue is said to be more like green than red. Such a statement is about a relationship holding between the universals blue, green, and red regardless of whether they are ever by any particulars exemplified. As we have seen,[2] it is because this relationship necessarily obtains between these universals that blue particulars necessarily are more similar in color to green than to red particulars regardless of whether in other respects some blue particulars are more like some red than some green particulars. And since this relationship necessarily obtains regardless of whether blue, green, and red are ever exemplified and regardless of whether it is ever for anyone an intentional object, it is a formal reality regardless of whether any particulars ever exist. But if it is a formal reality, then so must the universals blue, green, and red be. Since they are the terms between which the relation holds, it cannot be a formal reality unless they too are such realities. And since, moreover, predications can be made of singular cases of universals that cannot be made of the particulars possessing these singular cases, they too are formal realities formally distinct from the particulars that possess them. Unlike, however, the universals of which they are the cases, they have formal reality only as ingredient in the particulars that possess them, since if there were no particulars there could be no singular cases of universals ingredient in them.

It was said above that the essential difference between quidditative and qualitative predication is that in quidditative predication the essential nature of the subject of predication is indicated, whereas in qualitative predication some property of the subject of predication is indicated. We have not, however, explained adequately the difference between indicating the essential nature of a subject of predication and indicating some property of it. We turn now to attempt to specify this difference more fully. Predications of both types can be made of universals and singular cases of universals as well as of particulars. Each of the following is an example of qualitative predication, the first of a particular, the second of a singular case of a universal, the third of a universal: (1) 'x is red', in which 'x' refers to some particular; (2) 'x is visible', in which 'x' refers to some singular case of a universal; (3) 'x is more like red than blue', in which 'x' refers to some universal. Each of the following, on the other hand, is an example of quidditative predication, the first of a particular, the second of a singular case of a universal, the third of a universal: (i) 'x is a particular'; (ii) 'x is a singular case of a universal'; (iii) 'x is a universal'. Certain of the essential differences between (1)–(3) and (i)–(iii) are as follows.

First, the predicate-terms in (1)–(3) name properties predicable of particulars, singular cases of universals, or universals, whereas the predicate-terms in (i)–(iii) name genera or species of which particulars, singular cases of universals, or universals are members. Particulars, singular cases of universals, and universals constitute distinct genera, no one of which is reducible to either of the others, and no member of any one of these genera can be a member of either of the others. No particular can be a universal or a singular case of a universal, no singular case of a universal can be a particular or a universal, and no universal can be a particular or a singular case of a universal. The predicate 'red' in (1) names a property predicable of particulars that exemplify the universal red and is therefore applicable to such particulars. But it does not name any particular. It is the name of a color, not of a particular, although it does apply to particulars that exemplify that color. It names a species or genus of color comprehending such subspecies as crimson, scarlet, and pink, not a species or genus comprehending particulars. Although the color red and its specific determinations are predicable of particulars, none is itself a particular and no particular is itself a color. It is because particulars are not colors although they can be colored that (1) is a qualitative rather than a quidditative predication. Similar considerations, with of course the necessary changes, apply to (2) and (3). In (2) 'visible' names a property predicable of various singular cases of universals and of various particulars; but it does not name any of the singular cases of universals or particulars of which it is predicable. Similarly, in (3) 'more like red than blue' names a property predicable of certain universals and singular cases of universals but does not name any of the universals or singular cases of universals of which it is predicable. The predications in (2) and (3), like that in (1), are therefore qualitative rather than quidditative.

Second, the predications in (1)–(3) could be transformed into predications that are both quidditative and qualitative as follows: (1) '*x* is a red particular'; (2) '*x* is a visible singular case of a universal'; (3) '*x* is a universal more like red than blue'. Each of these predications is quidditative because in each the subject of predication is placed within the genus comprehending it, and each is also qualitative because some property other than that of being a member of the genus comprehending it is predicated of the subject of predication. In (i)–(iii), on the other hand, we have quidditative predications that are not also qualitative, since the predicate-term of each is used to predicate of the subject of predication only membership in some genus without also predicating of it some property other than that of being a member of that genus. This can be put also by saying that in (i)–(iii) the only properties predicated of the subjects of predication are, respectively, that of being a particular, that of being a singular case of a universal, and that of being a universal. To exemplify any of these properties, however, is nothing other than to be a particular, to be a singular case of a universal, or to be a universal. It is for this reason that the predications in (i)–(iii) are quidditative rather than qualitative. And it is because no particular can be a red, no singular case of a universal can be a visible, and no universal can be a more like red than blue that the predications in (1)–(3) are qualitative rather than quidditative.

Third, the preceding can also be put in the following way. Whereas the predicate-terms of (i)–(iii) name genera comprehending particulars, singular cases of universals, or universals, those of (1)–(3) name properties, other than those of being a particular, a singular case of a universal, or a universal, that are exemplifiable by particulars, singular cases of universals, or universals. This can be put by saying that the exemplification of the properties connoted by the predicate-terms of (i)–(iii), that of being a particular, that of being a singular case of a universal, and that of being a universal, is entailed by the exemplification of more determinate forms of these properties, whereas the exemplification of the properties named by the predicate-terms of (1)–(3) is not. Thus '*x* is a ball' entails '*x* is a particular' but not '*x* is red'; '*x* is a singular case of sweetness' entails '*x* is a singular case of a universal' but not 'x is visible'; and 'x is the color green' entails 'x is a universal' but not 'x is more like red than blue'. To be a ball is necessarily to be a particular but is not necessarily to be red; something, that is, is a particular simply by virtue of its being a ball but is red not by virtue of its being a ball but only by virtue of its possessing the property of being red. Similarly, to be a singular case of sweetness is necessarily to be a singular case of a universal but is not necessarily to be visible and in fact is necessarily not to be visible. Finally, to be the color green is necessarily to be a universal but is not necessarily to be more like red than blue and in fact is necessarily to be more like blue than red.

The last two examples indicate that the propositions expressed by making quidditative predications of universals and singular cases of universals entail certain propositions that can be expressed by making certain qualitative predications of these universals and singular cases. Thus the proposition expressed by a quidditative predication of the form 'x is a singular case of sweetness' entails the propositions expressed by qualitative predications of the following forms: 'x is not visible' and 'x is tastable'. And the proposition expressed by a quidditative predication of the form 'x is the universal blue' entails the propositions expressed by qualitative predications of the following forms: 'x is more like green than red' and 'x is not more like red than green'. These entailments hold by virtue of the fact that universals and their singular cases stand in certain necessary relationships to one another. Being a singular case of sweetness, that is, entails both being tastable and also not being visible, and being green entails both being more like blue than red and also not being more like red than blue. At the same time, however, the property of being a singular case of sweetness and the properties it entails are not identical with any singular case of sweetness. The relationship to the universal green of the property of being green and of the properties this property entails is somewhat more complicated.

The property of being the universal green is a property exemplifiable only by the universal green. Whereas all green particulars exemplify the property of being green and all singular cases of the universal green exemplify the property of being a singular case of this universal, the universal green alone can exemplify the property of being the universal green. This can be generalized by saying that whereas the property of being a particular of the type x is exemplifiable by any particular of that type, and whereas the property of being a singular case of the universal x is exemplifiable by any singular case of x, the property of being the universal x is uniquely exemplifiable only by the universal x itself. But although in this respect universals differ from their singular cases and the particulars that exemplify them, the relationship of the universal x to the property of being the universal x is only a special case of the relationship in which anything stands to the property of being itself, regardless of whether the thing in question be a universal, a singular case of a universal, or a particular. Just as the universal green uniquely exemplifies the property of being the universal green, so also some singular case of the universal green uniquely exemplifies the property of being that singular case of the universal green and Socrates uniquely exemplifies the property of being Socrates.

3. Self-Identity and Self-Predication

From the preceding several consequences follow. The first is that a distinction must be drawn between a particular, a singular case of a universal, and a universal on the one hand and the property of being itself that each exemplifies on the other. Since Socrates is a particular whereas the property of being Socrates is not, even though it is ex-emplifiable only by Socrates, Socrates is not identical with the property of being Socrates. Instead, Socrates is strictly identical only with Socrates, and it is because Socrates and Socrates alone is strictly identical with Socrates that Socrates alone can exemplify the property of being Socrates. Similarly, since some singular case of the universal green is a singular case of that universal whereas the property of being that singular case of green is not, that singular case of green is not identical with the property of being that singular case of green. Instead, that singular case of green is strictly identical only with itself, and it is because it alone is strictly identical with itself that it alone can exemplify the property of being that singular case of green. Although it exemplifies the property of being that singular case of green, it is nonetheless it and not the property of being it that is that singular case of green. Finally, since the universal green is exemplifiable by a multiplicity of green particulars in each of which a singular case of that universal is ingredient, whereas the property of being the universal green is not so exemplifiable but instead is uniquely exemplified by the universal green, the latter cannot be identical with the property of being the universal green that it uniquely exemplifies. Instead, it uniquely exemplifies this property only by virtue of the fact that it and it alone is the universal green.

A particular such as Socrates, then, is strictly identical only with itself, not with the property of being Socrates, but instead uniquely exemplifies this property by virtue of its being Socrates. Similarly, some singular case of a universal, such as this singular case of green, is strictly identical only with itself, not with the property of being this singular case of green, but instead uniquely exemplifies this property by virtue of its being this singular case of green. And some universal, such as the universal green, also is strictly identical only with itself, not with the property of being the universal green, but instead uniquely exemplifies this property by virtue of its being the universal green. Socrates exemplifies the property of being Socrates not by being this property but by being Socrates; some singular case of green exemplifies the property of being that singular case of green not by being that property but by being that singular case of green; and the universal green exemplifies the property of being the universal green not by being that property but by being the universal green. If so, then no particular, no singular case of a universal, and no universal (with the possible exception, to be discussed later, of the property of being identical with itself), is identical with the property of being identical with itself but instead exemplifies this property by virtue of its being identical with itself.

If the preceding is correct, then a distinction must be drawn between any entity, whether it be a particular, a singular case of a universal, or a universal, and the property of being identical with itself that any entity exemplifies by virtue of being identical with itself. A distinction must also be drawn between (1) the universal property of being identical with itself that any entity exemplifies by virtue of its being identical with itself and (2) the singular cases of this universal property, each of which is uniquely possessed by one and only one entity by virtue of its being the entity it is and not another entity. Socrates, some singular case of green, and the universal green, by virtue of their being identical with themselves, all exemplify the property of being identical with themselves. Since they all exemplify this property, none is identical with it. But Socrates alone, by alone being Socrates, possesses the singular case of the universal property of being identical with itself that is the property of being identical with Socrates; some singular case of green alone, by alone being that singular case of green, possesses the singular case of the universal property of being identical with itself that is the property of being identical with that singular case of green; and the universal green, by alone being the universal green, alone possesses the singular case of the universal property of being identical with itself that is the property of being identical with the universal green.

It might be mentioned in passing that to some it might seem that sentences such as "Socrates is identical with Socrates," "this singular case of green is identical with this singular case of green," and "the universal green is identical with the universal green" do not express propositions or at least, if a distinction be drawn between genuine and nongenuine propositions, do not express genuine propositions. That they do, however, express propositions can perhaps be seen if one considers that their contradictories, such as "Socrates is not identical with Socrates," express self-inconsistent propositions that necessarily are false. It is hard to see how their contradictories can necessarily be false if they themselves are not necessarily true. It is also hard to see how they can be necessarily true if they do not express propositions. It is true that the propositions they express are identical propositions and that, as such, they are not informative. This, however, is true of all identical propositions, since only nonidentical propositions can be informative.

The relationship of the universal property of being identical with itself to singular cases of this property is a special case of the relationship of universals to their singular cases. Just as other universals such as blue, green, and red, once the concepts of them are acquired, can be identified and discussed independently of the identification and discussion of any of their singular cases and any of the particulars exemplifying them, so also the universal property of being identical with itself, once the concept of it is acquired, can be identified and discussed independently of the identification and discussion of any of its singular cases and of any of the particulars exemplifying it. Second, just as singular cases of other universals can be identified only by identifying the particulars in which these singular cases are ingredient, so also singular cases of the universal property of being identical with itself can be identified only by identifying some particular, some singular case of a universal, or some universal. Thus the property of being identical with Socrates that Socrates alone exemplifies can be identified only by identifying Socrates; the property of being identical with some singular case of green can be identified only by identifying that singular case of green, which can be done only by identifying the particular in which that singular case of green is ingredient; and the property of being identical with the universal green can be identified only by identifying the universal green. Third, just as particulars can exemplify universals only through possessing singular cases of the universals they exemplify, so also particulars, singular cases of universals, and universals can exemplify the universal property of being self-identical only through their possessing some singular case of this property. Fourth, just as no particular is identical with any singular case of any universal it possesses or with any universal it exemplifies, so also no particular, no singular case of a universal, and no universal (again with the possible exception of the property of being identical with itself) is identical with the universal property of being identical with itself.

Since no particular is itself a universal or a singular case of a universal, no particular, even though each particular is identical with itself, can be identical either with the universal property of being identical with itself or with any singular case of this property that consists of some particular's being identical with itself. Similarly, since any singular case of this universal property is distinct both from any other singular case of it and also from this universal property itself, no singular case of it can be identical with it. Each particular exemplifies and therefore is not identical with this universal property, and each singular case of it is a distinct singular case of it and therefore cannot be identical with it. Instead, each singular case of it, like each particular, exemplifies it. The only thing that can be identical with the universal property of being self-identical is that property itself. It therefore also exemplifies itself. Since, that is, it is identical with itself, it exemplifies the universal property of being identical with itself, which is to say that it exemplifies itself. Moreover, since no two universals can be exactly alike in every respect, two distinct universals can have being only if each differs in some respect from the other. But there is no respect in which the universal property of being identical with itself differs from itself. There therefore cannot be two such properties, one of which exemplifies the other. But if not, then the universal property of being identical with itself, since it is identical with itself, exemplifies itself. In being identical with itself it exemplifies itself.

There would seem to be only two alternatives to admitting that it exemplifies itself, neither of which is acceptable. The first consists in maintaining that it cannot exemplify itself because it is not identical with itself. Since, however, it is identical with itself, this alternative is unacceptable. The second alternative consists in maintaining that although it is identical with itself it does not exemplify itself but instead exemplifies some higher order property of being identical with itself. Either, however, this higher order property is identical with the property of being identical with itself or it is not. If it is, then it is not a property distinct from the property of being identical with itself and therefore is not a higher order property. If it is not, but instead is some property other than the property of being identical with itself, then the latter property can exemplify it only by virtue of possessing some property other than that of being identical with itself, such as, for example, the property of being self-consistent. But although the properties of being self-consistent and of being identical with itself exemplify each other, each is nonetheless distinct from the other. This is the case (1) because properties other than that of being identical with itself are self-consistent and (2) because any property, regardless of whether it is self-consistent, exemplifies the property of being identical with itself. No property exemplifies the latter property by virtue of being self-consistent but rather by virtue of being identical with itself. Thus although the property of being identical with itself exemplifies the property of being self-consistent, it also exemplifies the property of being identical with itself, which is to say that it exemplifies itself.

If the preceding is correct, then there is no higher order property of being identical with itself. If there were such a higher order property, an infinite regress would ensue. Since, that is, this higher order property would itself be identical with itself, either it would exemplify itself or it would exemplify some still higher order property of being identical with itself. But there is no reason for admitting that it exemplifies itself that is not also a reason for admitting that the original property of being identical with itself exemplifies itself. And if it does not exemplify itself, then the same questions concerning it also arise concerning any succeeding higher order property of the same type. Since the series of succeeding higher order properties would be infinite, we would be confronted with an infinite regress. This regress, however, can be avoided simply by recognizing that there are no higher order properties of being identical with itself and that the one and only property of being identical with itself, since it is identical with itself, exemplifies itself. By being self-exemplifying it differs from most properties, since most are not self-predicable. In being self-predicable, however, it is not unique, since certain other properties, such as the property of being a property, also exemplify themselves. Since the property of being a property is exemplified not only by all other properties but also by itself, it is self-predicable.

Some self-predicable properties, such as that of being identical with itself, are predicable of particulars as well as properties. Others, such as the property of being a property, are predicable only of properties. But no property predicable only of particulars can be self-predicable. Although each particular has the general quidditative property of being a particular and the singular quidditative property of being the particular that it is, no particular is itself a property or any combination of properties but instead, as we have seen, is something that has quidditative and qualitative properties. And although the self-predicable property of being identical with itself is predicable of any particular, it is not predicated of itself when it is predicated of a particular but instead is predicated only of the particular of which it is predicated. This applies also to the predication of self-predicable properties of other properties. In predicating them of other properties they are predicated of the properties of which they are predicated and not of themselves.

4. The Ontological Status of Predicables

If the considerations advanced in the preceding two sections are acceptable, a distinction must be drawn between (1) universal properties predicable of both universals and particulars, such as the property of being self-identical; (2) universal properties predicable only of properties, such as the property of being a property; (3) universal properties predicable only of particulars, such as the property of being a particular; (4) singular properties, each predicable only of one universal, such as the property of being the universal green; and (5) singular properties, each predicable only of one particular, such as the property of being Socrates. The admission of properties of these distinct types, however, does not require the admission of the existence of properties in any sense other than that of their exemplification by or ingredience in existent particulars. This is in accordance with our earlier distinction between those formal realities that are also existent entities and those that are not. Since only those that have temporal being are existent entities, and since no properties unexemplified by particulars have temporal being, no such properties are existent entities. The only properties, moreover, that can have being as formal realities independently of their exemplification by particulars are those of the first four types indicated above. Singular properties, each predicable only of one particular, are formal realities only by virtue of their possession by the particulars of which they are predicable. Although such properties can have being as intentional objects regardless of whether they are possessed by existent particulars, they can have being as formal realities only if they are possessed by such particulars.

Some properties, such as (1) universal properties predicable only of universals or of properties and not also of particulars, such as the property of being a universal or the property of being a property, and (2) singular properties, each predicable of only one universal, such as the property of being the universal green, are exemplified by formal realities that are not also existent entities, at least not when taken completely in abstraction from any consideration of their exemplification by particulars. Such exemplification, however, is not sufficient to confer existence on such properties. Since, that is, properties and universals, taken in abstraction from their exemplification by particulars, are nonexistent formal realities, their exemplification of universals or properties is not sufficient to confer existence on the universals or properties they exemplify. Instead, singular properties, each predicable of only one universal, can be said to exist only if and only in the sense that the universals that uniquely exemplify them are themselves exemplified by existent entities. Thus the singular property of being the universal green can be said to exist only if and only in the sense that the universal green is itself exemplified by some existent particular. Similar considerations apply to universal properties predicable only of universals or of properties. They too can be said to exist only if and only in the sense that the universals or properties that exemplify them are themselves exemplified by existent particulars.

But although universal properties predicable only of universals or properties and singular properties, each predicable only of one universal, can be said to exist if the universals or properties that exemplify them are themselves exemplified by existent particulars, it is only the universals or properties that exemplify them that can be exemplified by particulars. The properties of being a universal, being a property, and being the universal green can be exemplified, respectively, only by some universal, some property, or the universal green. They cannot be exemplified by any particular, since no particular is a universal, a property, or the universal green. Only properties predicable of particulars can be exemplified by particulars. Such properties too exist only if and only in the sense that the particulars exemplifying them exist; it is their exemplification by existent particulars that confers existence on them. Such exemplification, however, does not confer formal reality on them, since they must first be formal realities if they are to be exemplified. In this respect such properties are like properties predicable only of universals or properties. The exemplification of properties of the latter type by universals or properties cannot confer formal reality on them, since they must first be such realities if they are to be exemplified. Thus whereas the exemplification of a property by existent entities confers existence on it as exemplified by those entities, since it would not exist at all if it were not by some existent entity exemplified, the exemplification of a property by formal realities that are not also existent entities confers neither existence nor formal reality on it. Such exemplification cannot confer existence on it because the nonexistent formal realities that exemplify it do not exist. And although the formal realities that exemplify it are formally real, their exemplification of it cannot confer formal reality on it, since it must first be a formal reality if it is to be exemplified by anything.

Although some properties, such as that of being a square-circle, cannot be exemplified, any property, regardless of whether it be self-consistent or self-inconsistent, necessarily exemplifies some property. Thus the property of being a ball exemplifies the property of being a self-consistent property, and the property of being a square-circle exemplifies the property of being a self-inconsistent property. This means that the property of being a self-inconsistent property is itself a self-consistent property, since if it were itself self-inconsistent it could not be exemplified by anything. Since, however, it is exemplified by any self-inconsistent property, it is itself a self-consistent property. In order, however, that any property exemplify the self-consistent property of being a self-inconsistent property, it must itself be a self-inconsistent property and, as such, cannot be exemplified by anything. Thus the property of being a self-inconsistent property is a property that can be exemplified only by properties that cannot themselves be exemplified by anything. But although some properties cannot be exemplified, any property, as was said above, necessarily exemplifies some property. As we have seen, even the property of being a property exemplifies some property, namely itself. It also exemplifies the property of being a formal reality and that of being a being, since it is a formal reality by virtue of its being a universal property and a being by virtue of its being a formal reality. The property of being a being is a property than which no more universal can be conceived, since anything, whether it be a formal reality or only an intentional object, exemplifies it. Yet even it exemplifies some property, namely itself, since it is a property and therefore a being. Since, however, it is a property, it, like any other property, exists only if and only in the sense that it is exemplified by existent entities.

Universal properties and singular properties, each predicable only of one universal, are formal realities regardless of whether they are exemplified by existent entities. But, as was maintained above, singular properties, each predicable only of one particular, are formal realities only if they are exemplified by particulars. Thus the property of being Socrates or being identical with Socrates has formal reality only by virtue of the existence of Socrates. Had Socrates never existed it would have no formal reality at all. Prior and subsequent to the existence of Socrates, it, like Socrates, could and can for someone be an intentional object; but it, like Socrates, has formal reality only throughout the time he exists. Similarly, the singular case of green ingredient in my desk blotter has formal reality only by virtue of the existence of the latter. Had my desk blotter never existed, the singular case of green ingredient in it would have no formal reality at all, and once it ceases to exist both it and the singular case of green ingredient in it can have being only as intentional objects for any who then happen to think of them. If so, then universal properties and singular properties, each predicable of only one universal, are formal realities regardless of whether they are exemplified by existent entities and of whether they are intentional objects, whereas singular properties, each predicable only of one particular, and singular cases of universals are not formal realities unless they are possessed by some existent entity. If they are not so possessed they can be only intentional objects, not formal realities.

The preceding applies to singular properties, each predicable only of one particular, and singular cases of universals never possessed by any existent entity as well as to those that at some time are possessed by some such entity. If I think of some particular that never exists as exemplifying some universal property, and if I believe that particulars cannot exemplify universal properties except through possessing singular cases of the latter, then I might think of the particular of which I am thinking as possessing a singular case of the universal property I think of it as exemplifying. Thus if I think of Hamlet as exemplifying the universal property of being white, and if I believe that he can exemplify this property only through possessing a singular case of it, I might think of him as possessing a singular case of whiteness. But if Hamlet is only an intentional object and never an existent entity, the singular case of whiteness I think of him as possessing can be only an intentional object even though the universal property of being white I think of him as exemplifying is a formal reality regardless of whether Hamlet ever exists and of whether I think of him as exemplifying it. This is the case regardless of whether it is in fact the case that particulars can exemplify universal properties only through possessing singular cases of such properties, and thus regardless of whether the realistic version of the resemblance theory, as opposed to the identity theory, is true.

If the identity theory is true, there are no formally real singular cases of universal properties. Instead, if it is true particulars exemplify universals directly without the mediation of their possession of singular cases of the universals they exemplify. But if singular cases of universals are not formal realities, they cannot have reality in any sense at all unless it be the objective reality of intentional objects. Since, however, the distinction between a universal and its singular cases is intelligible regardless of whether it is formally real, singular cases of universals can be intentional objects regardless of whether they are also formal realities. Moreover, in order that for someone they be such objects it is not necessary that he believe that they are formal realities. Instead, once a person has acquired the concept of a singular case of a universal, he can consider some particular and raise the question of whether some property he believes it exemplifies or possesses, as exemplified or possessed by that particular, is universal or a singular case of a universal. Without believing either that there are or that there are not singular cases of universals, he can consider reasons for regarding the property in question as universal and reasons for regarding it as a singular case of a universal. In the first case he might think of it as being universal without believing that it is, and in the second he might think of it as being a singular case of a universal without believing that it is.

If so, then in the second case the object of his nominative act is the property in question, whereas the object of his predicative or suppositional act is its being a singular case of a universal. Such a supposition might be expressed as follows: "This property is a singular case of a universal." Once this is done, he might go on to suppose, still without believing, that this singular case of a universal has some further property, such as that of being darker than some other singular case of the same universal. Here, to speak somewhat loosely, the object of the predicative or suppositional act of the first supposition becomes the object of the nominative act of a second supposition. If so, then a singular case of a universal can be the object of both a predicative or suppositional act on the one hand and a nominative act on the other, regardless of whether it is also a formal reality and also of whether the person who performs these acts believes that it is such a reality. In addition, someone who believes that singular cases of universals are not formal realities can nonetheless have as at least part of the object of some predicative act he performs some singular case of a universal. This would happen if such a person had as the object of a nominative act he performs some property exemplified by some particular and judged that it is not a singular case of a universal. If so, then singular cases of universals, even if they are not formal realities, can be intentional objects even for those who believe that they are not formal realities.

Regardless, however, of whether a person who believes that no formal realities are singular cases of universals can have the latter as intentional objects, someone who does believe that they are formal realities can have them as intentional objects regardless of whether in fact they are such realities. This follows from the fact that anyone who believes that entities of a given type are formal realities can have such entities as intentional objects regardless of whether they are in fact such realities. Thus even if the identity theory is true, so that there are no formally real singular cases of universals, someone who nonetheless believes that particulars can exemplify universal properties only through possessing singular cases of such properties can have as an intentional object something he believes to be a singular case of some property. Thus someone who believes that Socrates and Plato both exemplify the universal property of being wise only through their possessing distinct singular cases of this property can intend the wisdom of Socrates, as distinct from the wisdom of Plato, as a distinct singular case of wisdom. This could be done, for example, by his thinking that the distinct singular case of wisdom possessed by Socrates is a case of the universal wisdom. If so, the distinct singular case of wisdom possessed by Socrates is his intentional object. It is the object of a nominative act he performs regardless of whether it is also a formal reality, and of this object he predicates being a case of wisdom. He is thinking, that is, of a distinct singular case of wisdom, and of this intentional object he predicates being a case of the universal wisdom.

To this a proponent of the identity theory might object that in point of fact the intentional object of such a person's nominative act, rather than being a singular case of the universal wisdom possessed by Socrates, is instead the universal wisdom itself as exemplified by Socrates. Since, the objection continues, there is no formally real singular case of wisdom possessed by Socrates, and since the person in question is thinking of the wisdom of Socrates, he can only be thinking of the universal wisdom as exemplified by Socrates. His intentional object is the wisdom of Socrates, which he mistakenly identifies as or believes to be a singular case of wisdom. But since there are no formally real singular cases of universals, and since the wisdom of Socrates is identical with the universal wisdom as exemplified by Socrates, the intentional object of anyone who thinks of the wisdom of Socrates is the universal wisdom as exemplified by Socrates. Even though someone who thinks of the wisdom of Socrates might think that his intentional object is a singular case of wisdom possessed by Socrates, it is in fact the universal wisdom as exemplified by Socrates.

To this objection the following replies may be made. First, even if we agree that the intentional object of someone's thought is the wisdom of Socrates and that the latter is identical with the universal wisdom as exemplified by Socrates rather than with a singular case of this universal possessed by Socrates, it does not follow that the intentional object of that person's thought is the universal wisdom as exemplified by Socrates. Put more generally, from the fact that the intentional object of someone's thought is x, coupled with the fact that x is identical with a rather than b, it does not follow that the intentional object of that person's thought is a rather than b. Instead, he might not know or believe that x is identical with a and might instead believe that x is identical with b. Believing that x is identical with b, he might make the judgment that x is b, in which x is the object of a nominative act and, to oversimplify somewhat, b the object of a predicative act. Having made this judgment he might later make the judgment that b stands in some relation to something else, c, in which case, again to oversimplify somewhat, the object of the predicative act of the first judgment becomes the object of the nominative act of the second. In such a case the object of the nominative act of the second judgment is b, not a. It is b, not a, that is judged to stand in some relation to something else, c. Thus someone who believes that the wisdom of Socrates is a singular case of the universal wisdom might make the judgment "The wisdom of Socrates is a singular case of the universal wisdom." Having made this judgment, he might later make the judgment "The singular case of wisdom possessed by Socrates is exactly like the singular case of wisdom possessed by Plato." The object of the nominative act of this second judgment is the singular case of wisdom possessed by Socrates, not the universal wisdom as exemplified by Socrates, even though the object of the nominative act of the first judgment, the wisdom of Socrates, in fact be identical with the universal wisdom rather than with what is in fact the object of the nominative act of the second judgment.

Second, if the proponent of the identity theory is correct in maintaining that the wisdom of Socrates is identical with the universal wisdom as exemplified by Socrates rather than with a singular case of this universal possessed by Socrates, and if this entails that the latter cannot be an intentional object, then the following unacceptable consequences follow. (1) No one could believe that the wisdom of Socrates is a singular case of wisdom. This is the case because in making a judgment of the form a is b the object of the predicative act, b, as well as the object of the nominative act, a, must be an intentional object for the person who makes the judgment. Since, however, those who believe that the wisdom of Socrates is a singular case of wisdom can make the corresponding judgment, they can have a singular case of wisdom as an intentional object. (2) Neither could anyone believe that the singular case of wisdom possessed by Socrates is exactly like the singular case of wisdom possessed by Plato. This is the case because in making a judgment of the form a is exactly like b the object of the nominative act, a, must be an intentional object for the person who makes the judgment. Since, however, those who believe that the wisdom of Socrates is a singular case of wisdom can judge that the wisdom of Socrates is exactly like that of Plato, they can have a singular case of the universal wisdom as an intentional object.

The preceding arguments, if sound, establish the unacceptability of the identity theory if the truth of the latter entails that singular cases of universals cannot be intentional objects. If, that is, the claim that exemplified universals but not singular cases of universals are formal realities entails the claim that singular cases of universals cannot be intentional objects, then, since the latter claim is false, so also is the first. Since, however, the first claim does not in fact entail the second, the falsity of the second does not entail the falsity of the first. Since, that is, singular cases of universals can be intentional objects even if they are not also formal realities, the fact that they can be intentional objects does not mean that the proponent of the identity theory is mistaken in maintaining that exemplified universals but not singular cases of universals are formal realities.

A proponent of the identity theory might concede that the claim that singular cases of universals are not formal realities does not entail the claim that they cannot be intentional objects. He might still, however, present the following argument. From the fact that the wisdom of Socrates is in fact universal rather than a singular case of a universal, it follows that anyone who has the wisdom of Socrates as an intentional object thereby has a universal as such an object even though he might also have a singular case of a universal as such an object. The structure of such an argument is this. Suppose that x (the wisdom of Socrates) is in fact a (a universal). Suppose also that someone, s, thinks that x is b (a singular case of a universal), when in fact it is not. If so, s might judge that x is b, in which case the object of his predicative act is b, which is therefore for him an intentional object. Similarly, s might also judge that

b is exactly like c, in which case the object of his nominative act is b, which is therefore again for him an intentional object. But since x is in fact a rather than b, s, in judging that x is b is in fact judging also that a is b, and, in judging that b is exactly like c, is also judging that a is exactly like c. Thus although b is for s an intentional object in each of these judgments, so also is a.

There are two replies to this argument. One is that it leads to absurdity. First, suppose that s, in judging that the wisdom of Socrates is a singular case of wisdom, is also judging that a universal is a singular case of a universal, since the wisdom of Socrates is in fact a universal. If so, then s is contradicting himself, since his judgment that the wisdom of Socrates is a singular case of a universal can be true only if the wisdom of Socrates is not a universal, and the judgment that a universal is a singular case of a universal can be true only if a universal is not a universal. But although s, in judging that the wisdom of Socrates is a singular case of a universal, might be making a false judgment, he is not contradicting himself.

Second, even if x is in fact a rather than b, someone, s, who believes that x is b or that b stands in some relation to c, can judge that x is also a or that a also stands in that relation to c only if, in the first case, a is the object of a predicative act on his part and, in the second case, the object of a nominative act on his part. But a can be the object of a nominative or a predicative act on the part of s only if a is an intentional object for s. Yet a can be an intentional object for s only if s thinks of a; if, that is, s never thinks of a, then a is never for s an intentional object. Thus even if x is in fact a rather than b, s, in judging that x is b or that b stands in some relation to c, can also be judging that x is a or that a stands in that relation to c only if a is for s an intentional object. But s can judge that x is b or that b stands in some relation to c even though s has never thought of a and therefore even though a has never been an intentional object for s. If, then, s has never thought of or had a as an intentional object, s, in judging that x is b or that b stands in some relation to c, cannot be judging also that x is a or that a stands in that relation to c even though in fact x is a rather than b. If this is not already clear, the following example might help to make it so. Suppose that Socrates is in fact the husband of Xanthippe rather than of Ophelia, the daughter of Polonius. Suppose also that someone, x, who has never heard of Xanthippe, thinks that Socrates is the husband of Ophelia. If so, then even though Socrates is in fact the husband of Xanthippe rather than of Ophelia, s, in thinking that Socrates is the husband of Ophelia, cannot be thinking that the husband of Xanthippe is the husband of Ophelia. From the fact that Socrates is in fact the husband of Xanthippe rather than Ophelia, then, it does not follow that anyone who thinks that Socrates is the husband of Ophelia is also thinking that the husband of Xanthippe is the husband of Ophelia. Anyone who did think this would thereby also be thinking that Socrates is either a bigamist or a polygamist. But someone can think that Socrates is the husband of Ophelia without thinking that he is either.

These rather protracted considerations are sufficient, I believe, to show that singular properties, each predicable only of one particular, and singular cases of universals, each possessed only by one particular, can be intentional objects regardless of whether they are also formal realities. In addition, they can be such realities only if they are possessed by or ingredient in existent entities. In this they differ from universals, universal properties, and singular properties, each predicable only of one universal, which are formal realities regardless of whether they are ever exemplified by existent entities and of whether they ever become intentional objects for anyone.

Notes

1. Nicholas Wolterstorff, *On Universals: An Essay in Ontology* (Chicago and London: University of Chicago Press, 1970), pp. 3, 28, 29, 31, 35, 46, 63, 64, 85, 119.

2. Chap. 6, sec. 1 and Chap. 8, sec. 2.

10
Particulars and Universals

IN this chapter we shall use certain of the contentions and distinctions made in earlier chapters to consider more fully than we have yet done certain features of the nature of material particulars and their constituents and the relationship to species, genera, and universals of such particulars and their constituents.

1. Wholes and Parts

There is a possible misunderstanding of the claim that singular cases of universals are formal realities that might lead some to reject this claim. Although to show that this misunderstanding is in fact a misunderstanding is not to establish the truth of this claim, it might remove one possible impediment to its acceptance. The misunderstanding in question consists in supposing that singular cases of universals are particulars. Such a supposition might be natural for someone who believes that although there are particulars and exemplified universals there are no singular cases of universals. Part of the point, however, of maintaining that there are singular cases of universals is to distinguish them not only from exemplified universals but also from particulars. Such a supposition might also be natural for someone who believes that the parts of particulars are themselves particulars and that singular cases of universals, if there were any, would be parts of particulars. If, that is, the parts of particulars are themselves particulars, and if singular cases of universals are parts of particulars, then they too must be particulars. We can agree that singular cases of universals are parts of particulars. But the conclusion that they are therefore themselves particulars follows only if all parts of particulars are themselves particulars. That this last is not in fact the case can be seen if we consider briefly some distinctions made by Husserl in his discussion of wholes and parts in his *Logical Investigations*.[1]

For Husserl any material object is a whole possessing parts that stand in various relationships to one another. Some of its parts are independent parts, others nonindependent parts. His characterization of some parts as independent and others as nonindependent corresponds to his distinction, discussed above,[2] between independent parts of speech, such as categorematic terms, and nonindependent parts of speech, such as syncategorematic terms. Independent parts of wholes he terms 'pieces', nonindependent parts 'moments'. Pieces of particulars are themselves particulars, whereas moments are singular cases of universals rather than particulars. The following example illustrates this. Suppose that a four-legged table exists. If so, it is a particular whole, each of the legs of which and the top of which is a particular piece. If each of the legs were separated from the top, these five pieces would still exist separately. It is because they can exist separately that they are independent parts or pieces of the table rather than nonindependent parts or moments. Suppose also that the top of the table and each of its legs are a uniform shade of brown. The proponent of the identity theory would say that the table and each of its pieces exemplify precisely the same shade of brown, whereas the advocate of singular cases of universals would say that the table and each of its pieces each possess a singular case of that shade of brown, each of which exactly resembles each of the others. Regardless, however, of which of these positions one takes, neither the brownness of the whole nor that of any of its pieces is itself a piece of the whole. Whereas each of the pieces can exist as a distinct particular when separated from the whole and from one another, neither the brownness of the whole nor that of any of its pieces can exist except as exemplified or possessed by the whole or the piece that does in fact exemplify or possess it. Rather than being an independent part or piece of the whole or of any of its pieces, the brownness of each is instead a nonindependent part or moment of each.

This last, however, requires some modification. If the proponent of the identity theory accepts our distinction between formal reality and existence, he maintains that the brownness exemplified by the whole and by each of its pieces could exist even if it were not by them exemplified, but only if it were exemplified by some other particular. The advocate of singular cases of universals, on the other hand, maintains that the singular cases of brown, each uniquely possessed either by the whole or by one of its pieces, can be possessed by no particular other than the one that does in fact possess it, so that each singular case can exist only as possessed by the particular that does in fact possess it. Despite this difference, however, for each of these positions the brownness of the whole and of each of its pieces would still be a nonindependent part or moment of the whole and of each of its pieces rather than an independent part or piece of the whole or of any of its pieces. Thus although the advocate of singular cases of universals maintains that the whole and each of its pieces uniquely possess a singular case of the universal brown, he, no more than the proponent of the identity theory, would maintain that such singular cases of brown are themselves particulars. They are neither universals nor particulars but rather singular cases of universals and therefore nonindependent parts or moments of particulars rather than independent parts or pieces.

There are, however, difficulties confronting Husserl's doctrine of wholes and parts. One such difficulty confronts this doctrine regardless of whether it is conjoined with the identity theory or with the theory of singular cases of universals. This difficulty is that whereas some wholes, such as a table, have pieces, such as a top and legs, that can easily be demarcated in an obvious and rather natural way, such wholes and their pieces can also be divided into pieces in an indefinite number of ways. Thus the top and each of the legs of a table can themselves be considered as wholes that can be divided, at least in imagination, into an indefinite number of pieces that contain other pieces into which they are divisible. Moreover, any piece of a whole can be a piece of an indefinite number of other pieces into which the whole is divisible. Thus one-fourth of the leg of a table is a piece not only of the table and of the leg in question but also of one-half of the leg of which it is a piece, and that one-fourth of the leg will itself be divisible into pieces that are pieces not only of it but of the half of the leg of which it is a piece, of the leg of which that half is a piece, and of the table of which that leg is a piece. Each particular whole, then, is divisible, at least in imagination if not also in actual fact, into an indefinite number of successively smaller pieces, and each of these successively smaller pieces in turn is a piece of successively larger pieces and of the original divisible whole. In addition to the spatial divisibility of a material whole into pieces, the temporal duration of any enduring particular is divisible, at least in imagination, into an indefinite number of successively smaller parts, each of which is a part of successively larger parts and of the original duration of which each of these successively smaller and successively larger parts is a part.

The fact that material wholes are spatially divisible and their duration temporally divisible in the ways indicated does not mean that an atomistic and staccatolike view of the world, according to which wholes are composed of and reducible without remainder to space-time slabs, is acceptable. It is true that a four-legged table could not exist as such a table if its pieces that are its legs and its top did not exist and that these pieces could not exist if their pieces did not exist. It is also true that its pieces and their pieces could exist even though it did not exist. But none of its pieces and none of their pieces is itself a four-legged table, nor do all its pieces taken together constitute a four-legged table. Instead, such a table exists only if its pieces stand in a certain familiar spatial relationship to one another. Similar considerations apply to the duration of a human being throughout his childhood, adolescence, young adulthood, middle age, and old age. Although he is successively a child, an adolescent, a young man, a middle-aged man, and an old man, and is different in these respects at each of these stages of his existence from what he is at each of the others, and although he could not exist at any of the later stages without having passed through each of the earlier stages, his existence and duration as a human being does not consist of a succession of staccatolike occurrences or moments but is rather the existence and duration of the same human being throughout each of the successive stages of his duration.

But although a whole is divisible into a multiplicity of pieces and the duration of an enduring particular into a multiplicity of parts, no insuperable difficulty seems to arise for the Husserlian doctrine of wholes and parts so long as we confine our attention to those parts that are also pieces. For regardless of how many pieces a material whole is divisible into, each of these pieces is still a particular, and as such each has moments that are not themselves particulars. And regardless of how many parts the duration of a particular is divisible into, each of these parts is still a part of the duration of some particular and is therefore itself a duration. When, however, we consider those parts of wholes that are moments rather than pieces, a difficulty more serious than the one just considered arises for Husserl's doctrine of wholes and parts if this doctrine is conjoined with the theory of singular cases of universals, as Husserl himself does even though he does not refer to his position by that name. This difficulty can be explained as follows.

2. Parts and Singular Cases of Universals

Let us suppose, as before, that a certain four-legged table exists and that it is uniformly a certain shade of brown. Its top and each of its legs is that shade of brown, and each visible piece into which each of these five pieces is divisible is also that shade of brown. Such a situation presents no difficulty at all for the identity theory, since it describes it simply by saying that the table and each of its pieces all exemplify precisely the same shade of brown without the mediation of a multiplicity of singular cases of this shade of brown, each of which is uniquely possessed either by the table itself or by some one of its pieces. Since, however, the table and each of the pieces into which it is divisible is a particular, and since, according to the theory of singular cases of universals, a particular can exemplify a universal only through its possession of some singular case of that universal unique to it, the table and each of the pieces into which it is divisible must possess some distinct singular case of a shade of brown unique to it, even though in color each of these singular cases is exactly like any of the others. Instead, then, of a situation in which one single shade of brown is exemplified by the table and each of the pieces into which it is divisible, the theory of singular cases of universals requires in addition that for the table and each of the visible pieces into which it is divisible there be a distinct singular case of that shade of brown. It might be thought that if this does not amount to multiplying entities beyond necessity it is hard to see what would.

The preceding difficulty is compounded further by the following considerations. Any leg of the table is divisible, at least in imagination, into two pieces of equal length, each of which is also divisible into two pieces of equal length, and so on indefinitely. If, however, the leg is not in fact divided into pieces, the same singular case of brown covers the entire surface of the leg. But since the leg is divisible into pieces, each of which possesses uniquely its own singular case of brown, and since each of these pieces is divisible into pieces, each of which possesses uniquely its own singular case of brown, and so on indefinitely, we have the following situation. A piece of the leg consisting of one-fourth of the latter possesses uniquely its own singular case of brown. But since that piece of the leg is a piece of a one-half piece of the leg, which possesses uniquely its own singular case of brown, the one-fourth piece will also possess uniquely the singular case of brown possessed uniquely by the one-half piece of which it is a piece. And since the one-half piece is a piece of the entire leg, which possesses uniquely its own singular case of brown, the one-half piece will also possess uniquely the singular case of brown possessed uniquely by the entire leg of which it is a piece. More-over, the singular case of brown possessed uniquely by the entire leg will also be possessed uniquely not only by a one-half piece of it but also by a one-half piece of the first one-half piece, and so on indefinitely.

The preceding can be stated in more general terms as follows. Each piece of the leg will possess uniquely not only its own singular case of brown but also (1) the singular case of brown possessed uniquely by any larger piece of which it is a piece and (2) the singular case of brown possessed uniquely by the whole of which each of these pieces is a piece. Conversely, (1) the singular case of brown possessed uniquely by the whole will also be possessed uniquely by each successively smaller piece into which it is divisible, and (2) the singular case of brown possessed uniquely by any piece of the whole will also be possessed uniquely by each of the successively smaller pieces into which that piece is divisible.

The theory of singular cases of universals seems clearly to have run into difficulty. For if each singular case of a universal is possessed uniquely by the particular that does in fact possess it, then no two particulars can each possess the same singular case of a universal. Yet if the preceding argument is sound this is precisely what is required by the theory of singular cases of universals in the case of any universal exemplified by a particular and by any or all of its pieces. This theory cannot be saved by pointing out that particulars can also exemplify universals that are not exemplified by any of their pieces, as in the case of the universal property of being a table, which is exemplified by a table but not by any of its pieces such as its top or its legs or any of the pieces of these pieces. On the contrary, the difficulty in question also casts doubt upon the adequacy of the theory of singular cases of universals as applied to universals exemplified by wholes but not their pieces as well as upon it as applied to universals exemplified both by wholes and by any or all of their pieces. For if the difficulty in question can be escaped only by abandoning the theory of singular cases of universals as applied to those universals exemplified both by wholes and by any or all of their pieces, a question arises as to why this theory ought to continue to be adopted in the case of those universals exemplified by wholes but not by any of their pieces. If, that is, this theory cannot be applied to universals of the first type, what reason can there be for applying it to universals of the second type? If there cannot be singular cases of universals of the first type, what reason can there be for supposing that there are nonetheless singular cases of universals of the second type? Thus although the difficulty in question applies directly only to the theory of singular cases of universals as applied to universals of the first type, it nevertheless also casts doubt upon this theory as applied to universals of the second type. If this theory is to be saved it is therefore of some importance that the difficulty in question be escaped.

One possible avenue of escape is the following, which contains several steps. First, a distinction must be drawn between actual and possible pieces of a whole. It is difficult to present a complete and adequate account of this distinction. Fortunately, however, it is not necessary for our purposes that we do so; instead, it will suffice if we say enough about this distinction to enable us to escape the difficulty in question. This last does not seem especially hard to do in the case of manufactured particulars such as tables that are constructed by conjoining separately existing particulars in a certain way to form a single particular whole. Thus suppose that the top of our four-legged table is constructed by conjoining in a certain way four separately existing slabs of wood and that the construction of the table is completed by conjoining in a certain way to the top thus constructed four separately existing pieces of wood which, when conjoined to the top, become the legs of the table. Each of these slabs of wood conjoined to form the top, the top itself, and each of the four pieces of wood conjoined to the top to form the legs remain actual pieces of the table once the construction of the table is completed. To generalize, any two or more separately existing particulars conjoined in some way to form a single particular whole remain actual pieces of the whole so long as they continue to be conjoined in that way.

By contrast, any piece of a whole that did not exist separately as a distinct particular prior to the formation of the whole but that can be separated, at least in imagination, from the rest of the whole is a possible as distinct from an actual piece of the whole. Thus one-half of one of the legs of our table, and one-half of that one-half, are possible pieces. Any possible piece of a possible piece of a whole is also a possible piece of the whole. Thus the number of possible pieces contained in any possible piece of a whole and therefore in the whole itself is indefinitely large. No possible piece of a possible piece or of a whole, however, is an actual piece unless and until it is actually separated from the whole of which it is a possible piece. Once it is separated from the whole, and for so long as it remains separated, it is no longer a piece of the whole of which previously it was a possible piece. It can, however, become again an actual piece of the whole by being conjoined again with the remainder of the whole from which it was separated.

Second, possible pieces, as contrasted with actual pieces, are not themselves particulars. Each actual piece of a whole and the whole of which it is a piece is a particular. Thus the table, its top, each of the four slabs of wood composing the top, and each of its four legs is a particular. This can be put by saying that the table is a particular whole consisting of these nine actual pieces, each of which is itself a particular. But the two halves of any of the legs into which it is divisible, and the two halves into which each of these halves is divisible, and so on, since they are only possible rather than actual pieces of one of the legs and thus of the table, are not themselves particulars. Instead, they become particulars only when they are actually separated from the rest of the leg and from the table. Once they are actually separated they remain particulars even though later they become actual pieces of the leg and the table by being conjoined again with the latter.

Third, since possible pieces are not themselves particulars, they cannot possess singular cases of universals possessed by the particular actual pieces or wholes of which they are possible pieces. Since, that is, only particulars can possess singular cases of universals, and since possible pieces are not themselves particulars, possible pieces cannot possess singular cases of universals. Thus from the fact that any leg of our table is divisible into two halves, which in turn are also divisible into two halves, and so on, it does not follow that each of these possible pieces possesses a singular case of the universal brown possessed by the leg itself. So long as they are only possible rather than actual pieces they are not particulars, and so long as they are not particulars they cannot possess any singular cases of universals at all. Instead, the singular case of brown possessed by the leg of which they are possible pieces is possessed only by the leg and not by them. If, however, they become particulars by being actually separated from the leg, then each possesses uniquely a singular case of brown exactly like the singular case of brown possessed uniquely by any other actual piece of the leg and exactly like the singular case of brown possessed by the leg prior to its division. Since each is then a distinct particular with its own distinct spatiotemporal location, the brownness of each is a distinct singular case of brown located on the surface of each. Even though the brownness of each resemble exactly the brownness of each of the others and that of the leg, the division of which caused their existence as distinct particulars, the brownness of each is located on the surface of each rather than on the surface of any of the others and is therefore a distinct singular case of a certain shade of brown exemplified first by the leg itself and then by each of these distinct particulars into which it is divided.

The theory of singular cases of universals is not yet, however, completely free from difficulty, as the following considerations show. Suppose that our table has not yet been constructed but that each of the four slabs of wood to be used in the construction of its top and each of the four pieces of wood to be used as its legs do exist as distinct particulars. Suppose also that each of these distinct particulars possesses a singular case of a certain shade of brown exactly like that possessed by each of the others. Suppose finally that once they are conjoined to form our table the latter also possesses a singular case of that shade of brown exactly like those possessed by each of what are now its actual pieces. The question now confronting the theory of singular cases of universals is this. If a whole and each of its actual, as distinct from its possible, pieces exemplify precisely the same universal, does the whole and each of its actual pieces possess uniquely a singular case of this universal exactly like that possessed by each of the others? We may concede, at least for the sake of argument, that each actual piece of the whole possesses uniquely a singular case of the universal in question, since each is a particular distinct from each of the others, and none is an actual piece of any of the others. But each actual piece, though a particular distinct from the whole, is nonetheless an actual piece of the whole. Moreover, the whole, although it is distinct from any of its actual pieces and possesses certain properties that none of the pieces possess, such as that of being a table, is nevertheless constituted by its pieces standing in certain relationships to one another. In addition, it exemplifies certain universal properties, such as that of being brown, only by virtue of the fact that each of its pieces exemplifies this property. If any of them did not exemplify this property neither would it, at least not over the whole of its surface, and if all of them exemplify it so also does it. But if so, then how can it possess a singular case of this universal distinct from those possessed by its pieces?

The reply to this question is as follows. As was maintained above,[3] a singular case of a universal can be identified only if two conditions are satisfied. One is that the universal in question must in some way be identified. The other is that some particular exemplifying it must in some way be identified. It is only through the identification of a given universal and of some particular that exemplifies it that a singular case of it can be identified. Thus which singular case of a universal is identified is determined by which universal is identified and by which particular exemplifying it is identified. In the case of our example there is no problem concerning which universal is exemplified, since it is the specific shade of brown exemplified by the table and by each of its actual pieces. Nor need there be any problem concerning which particular is being identified, since it might be either the table itself, its top, any of the slabs of wood from which the top is constructed, or any of the legs of the table. Once that specific shade of brown is identified, and once one of these particulars is identified as exemplifying that specific shade of brown, a singular case of the universal brown is thereby also identified. Given that the specific shade of brown in question has been identified, which singular case of it is identified depends entirely upon which particular is identified. If the identified particular is the table itself, then the singular case of brown identified is that possessed by the table; but if one of its actual pieces is identified, then the singular case of brown identified is the case possessed by that actual piece.

Another difficulty would still confront the theory of singular cases of universals if a certain supposition were true. This is the supposition that singular cases of universals are such that if a universal is exemplified both by a whole and by any or all of its actual pieces, then the singular cases of that universal possessed by the pieces must themselves be pieces of the singular case possessed by the whole. Such a supposition, however, would rest upon a failure to distinguish adequately between pieces and moments. Singular cases of universals, whether possessed by wholes or by their pieces, are moments rather than pieces of the particulars that possess them, and from the fact that a piece is a piece of a whole it does not follow that a singular case of a universal possessed by some piece of a whole is also a piece of the singular case of that universal possessed by the whole. Since singular cases of universals are moments rather than pieces, no singular case of a universal can be a piece of any other singular case of that universal or of any other universal. And since singular cases of universals are not pieces, no singular case of a universal can be a piece of anything at all, whether of the particular that possesses it, of some piece of this particular, of some whole of which this particular is a piece, or of some singular case of a universal possessed by some whole of which the particular that possesses it is a piece. Moreover, since singular cases of universals are moments only of the particulars that possess them, no singular case of a universal possessed by some piece of a whole can be a moment of the whole, except in the sense that it is a moment of a piece of the whole, and no singular case of a universal possessed by a whole can be a moment of any piece of the whole. Thus the singular case of brown possessed by some piece of our table can be a moment of the table only in the sense that it is a moment of a piece of the table, and the singular case of brown possessed by the table can be a moment only of the table and not of any of its pieces.

Thus even though a necessary and sufficient condition of the ex-emplification of a given universal such as brown by some whole over the whole if its surface be that each of its pieces also exemplify this universal over the whole of at least their exposed surfaces, the singular case of that universal possessed by the whole necessarily is distinct from the singular cases of it possessed by the pieces of that whole. This follows from the fact that a singular case of a universal requires for its identification not only the identification of the universal of which it is a singular case but also the identification of the particular that possesses that singular case. Although our table can be a uniform shade of brown only if each of its pieces is also uniformly that shade of brown on its exposed surfaces, the singular case of that shade of brown possessed by the table, since the latter is distinct from any of its pieces, necessarily is numerically al-though not qualitatively distinct from any of the singular cases of that shade of brown possessed by any of its pieces. If each of its pieces were separated from one another so that the table no longer exists, each piece would cease to be a piece of the table. Each, however, would remain a particular, and each would, or at least could, continue to possess the same singular case of the shade of brown it possessed while a piece of the table. The table, however, since it would then no longer exist, would then no longer possess a singular case of that shade of brown. If its former pieces were reassembled so as to stand in precisely the same relations to one another in which they stood before, the table then would begin again to exist and to possess again a singular case of that shade of brown. The singular cases of that shade of brown are, or at least can be, possessed by its particular pieces regardless of whether the latter are in fact pieces of the table and therefore regardless of whether the table exists. But the singular case of that shade of brown possessed by the table can be possessed by the latter only if, and only so long as, its particular pieces are in fact conjoined to form it and therefore only if and only so long as it exists. Therefore the singular case of that shade of brown possessed by the table necessarily is numerically distinct from, even though qualitatively identical with, the singular cases of that shade possessed by its pieces.

3. Intermittent Existence and Exemplification

It was said above that our table would cease to exist if each of its pieces were separated from one another and then begin again to exist if its former pieces were reassembled so as to stand again in the same relations to one another. This assumes that it is possible that particulars of certain kinds exist, then cease to exist, and then exist again. Such an assumption accords with our ordinary ways of thinking and speaking, as when we think and say that a clock that has been taken apart with its pieces lying about on a table is the same clock after it is reassembled as it was before it was taken apart. Whether we adopt such ways of thinking and speaking, however, depends upon what criteria for the continued identity of particulars we adopt, and to a certain extent at least which criteria we adopt is a matter for arbitrary decision. So long as we think and speak with sufficient clarity so that those we address can understand what we are thinking and saying, it is a matter of indifference whether we think and say that the same or a different particular exists after some particular has been taken apart and later reassembled. The decision we make, however, has consequences for the theory of singular cases of universals, as the following considerations show.

It was maintained above that a singular case of a universal can be identified only through identifying both the universal of which it is a case and also some particular that possesses that case. Thus, to return to our table, if the same table that existed prior to its being taken apart comes into existence again after its pieces are reassembled, then the singular case of brown possessed by the table prior to its being taken apart can again be possessed by that table once it comes again into existence. If so, then a singular case of a universal can exist for some time, through being possessed for some time by some particular, then cease to exist for some time, through that particular's ceasing to exist for some time, and then exist again, through that particular's coming to exist again. But if we choose instead to say that a numerically distinct particular comes into existence once the pieces are reassembled, then, since a different particular now exists, a numerically distinct singular case of brown also exists. Since, that is, a singular case of a universal necessarily is possessed uniquely by the particular that possesses it, the singular case of brown possessed by the first table, though qualitatively identical with the singular case of brown possessed by the second, is nonetheless numerically distinct from that possessed by the second.

Similar considerations apply to the intermittent exemplification of a universal by a continuously existing particular. Thus suppose that our table is first brown, then painted white, then painted again so that it is precisely the same shade of brown as before. If so, then it exemplifies that shade of brown for some time, then ceases to exemplify it, and then exemplifies it again. Does this mean that consistency requires that the proponent of the theory of singular cases of universals maintain that two numerically distinct but qualitatively identical singular cases of brown are successively possessed by the same continuously existing particular? Given only what has been said so far, the answer would seem to be that it does not, since from the fact that a singular case of a universal can be identified only by identifying the universal of which it is a case and the particular that possesses that singular case it does not follow that the particular that possesses it must do so continuously and therefore cannot possess it intermittently. Instead, the intermittent exemplification of a universal by a continuously existing particular can consistently be regarded by the proponent of the theory of singular cases of universals either (1) as the intermittent possession by that particular of the same singular case of that universal or (2) as the possession by that particular of numerically distinct but qualitatively identical singular cases of that universal.

There seems to be no conclusive reason for accepting either alternative to the exclusion of the other. Those who maintain that numerically the same particular cannot intermittently exist might be inclined to contend that neither can a continuously existing particular intermittently possess a given singular case of a universal. Those, on the other hand, who maintain that numericaly the same particular can intermittently exist might be inclined to contend that a continuously existing particular can intermittently possess a given singular case of a universal. Regardless, however, of whether numerically the same particular can intermittently exist, nothing at all follows as to whether numerically the same singular case of a universal can be intermittently possessed by the same continuously existing particular. Those who maintain that numerically the same particular can intermittently exist can consistently deny that numerically the same singular case of a universal can be intermittently possessed by a continuously existing particular. Similarly, those who deny that numerically the same particular can intermittently exist can consistently maintain that numerically the same singular case of a universal can be intermittently possessed by a continuously existing particular.

If the preceding is correct, then the answer to the question of whether numerically the same particular can intermittently exist and the answer to the question of whether numerically the same singular case of a universal can be intermittently possessed by a continuously existing particular are independent of one another. It was maintained above that an answer to the first of these two questions can be given only by deciding whether to regard intermittently existing particulars as numerically the same or as numerically distinct. It seems also that the second question can also be answered only by deciding whether to regard the intermittent exemplification of a universal by a continuously existing particular as involving (1) the intermittent possession by such a particular of one singular case of the exemplified universal or (2) the possession by such a particular of two distinct singular cases of the exemplified universal.[4] There seems to be no reason for taking either of these positions rather than the other. It is true that considerations of parsimony provide a reason for taking the first position. From the fact, however, that the first position is more parsimonious it does not follow that it is true and the second false. And if the theory of singular cases of universals is true, one of these positions must be true and the other false even though it be impossible to discover conclusive reasons for regarding one as opposed to the other as true.

The second question arises only in connection with the theory of singular cases of universals. Since, that is, for the advocate of the identity theory there are no singular cases of universals, for him the question never arises of whether numerically the same or numerically different singular cases of a universal are possessed by a continuously existing particular that intermittently exemplifies the universal in question. Instead, he describes such a situation by saying simply that such a particular intermittently exemplifies numerically the same universal. It might be thought that the fact that this question does not arise for the identity theory provides those who like in metaphysics to avoid questions that can be answered only arbitrarily a reason for rejecting the theory of singular cases of universals. The fact, however, that one theory as opposed to another avoids such questions does not mean that it as opposed to the other is the correct theory. Thus from the fact that the identity theory avoids the question confronting the theory of singular cases of universals it does not follow that the former theory is the correct theory. Moreover, if one theory is preferable to another only because the first but not the second avoids questions that can be answered only arbitrarily, there seems to be something arbitrary about regarding the first theory as preferable. Given that we have no more reason for believing the first rather than the second to be correct, an acceptance of the first merely on the basis that it but not the second avoids such questions seems itself to be arbitrary. This is especially the case if our concern is to discover which of the two is the correct theory, since, as was said, the fact that one theory but not another avoids such questions does not mean that the first is correct. If our concern is to discover the truth, as in metaphysics it ought to be, the proper procedure to adopt in such a situation would seem to be to suspend judgment as to which of the two theories is correct until we have some reason to believe that one rather than the other is the correct theory.

4. Particulars, Moments, and Matter

The universals of which moments, according to the theory of singular cases of universals, are singular cases may be referred to as qualitative as opposed to substantive universals. The distinction intended here between qualitative and substantive universals is connected with our earlier distinction between qualitative and quidditative predication.[5] To say of our table that it is brown is to make a qualitative predication of it, whereas to say of it that it is a table is to make a quidditative predication of it. The qualitative predication is true of the table not by virtue of its being a table but rather by virtue of its being brown, whereas the quidditative predication is true of it not by virtue of its being brown but rather by virtue of its being a table. The property of being brown is a qualitative property, that of being a table a substantive property. The first property is predicable of the table only by virtue of a certain moment of it, its brownness; whereas the second is predicable of it only by virtue of its being a particular comprehended by a certain species of particular, namely the species table. In general, particulars exemplify qualitative universals, and the corresponding qualitative properties are predicable of them, only by virtue of their having moments that are singular cases of such universals; whereas they exemplify substantive universals, and the corresponding substantive properties are predicable of them, only by virtue of their being particulars comprehended by a certain species of particular. As we saw in our earlier discussion of quidditative and qualitative predication, quidditative predications can also be made of moments. Thus to say of the color of the table that it is brown is to make a quidditative predication of it. Moreover, just as qualitative predications can be made of any particular, so also they can be made of any moment. Thus to say of the color of the table that it is darker than the color of the couch is to make a qualitative predication of it.

In order that particulars exemplify substantive universals, and the corresponding substantive properties be predicable of them, it is necessary that they also exemplify certain qualitative universals and have the corresponding qualitative properties. This follows from the fact that there can be no particulars that do not have moments. As we saw above, their moments are not themselves particulars but instead are either universals, if the identity theory is true, or singular cases of universals, if the theory of singular cases of universals is true. But just as there can be no particulars that do not have moments, so also there can be no moments that are not moments of particulars. This means that neither particulars nor their moments are reducible to one another. Although earlier, following Husserl, we referred to pieces as independent parts of wholes and moments as nonindependent parts, this means only that moments can exist only as qualities or aspects of wholes or pieces, and as such are predicable of particulars, whereas particulars, whether they be wholes or pieces, are not predicable of anything at all. It is precisely because moments are predicable of particulars that they are either universals (on the identity theory) or singular cases of universals (on the theory of singular cases of universals). Similarly, it is precisely because particulars are predicable of nothing at all that they can be neither universals nor singular cases of universals. Nor can they be combinations of universals or singular cases of universals, since such combinations are themselves predicables and therefore cannot be particulars. Although combinations of universals can constitute kinds of particulars, they cannot themselves be particulars. Nor can any combination of singular cases of universals constitute a particular, since singular cases of universals are not themselves particulars and can be identified only by identifying not only the universals of which they are singular cases but also the particulars that possess these singular cases.

The preceding can also be put in the following way. Any combination of universals is itself a complex or compound universal, not a particular. If the combination is an impossible combination it is predicable of nothing at all, since at least part of what is meant by saying that it is an impossible combination is that it is impossible that anything exemplify it. If, however, the combination is a possible combination, then it is possible that it be predicable of something. Whether such a combination is in fact predicable of anything depends upon whether anything exemplifies that combination. Since, however, such a combination is itself a complex universal, no such combination can be identical with any particular that exemplifies it. It is not reducible to any particular that exemplifies it, and no particular that exemplifies it is reducible to it. Similar considerations apply to any combination of singular cases of universals possessed by any particular. Such combinations necessarily involve the exemplification of the universals, of which the combined singular cases are singular cases, by the particulars that possess such singular cases. This is to say that each combination of singular cases of universals possessed by some particular necessarily involves the exemplification by that particular of the corresponding combination of universals of which the combined singular cases are cases. No combination of singular cases of universals, however, is identical with the particular that possesses that combination. Instead, it stands in the relation to that particular of being possessed by it, and the particular stands in the converse relation to the combination of possessing it. Neither the combination nor the particular that possesses it is reducible to the other.

Just as a combination of qualitative universals or qualitative universal properties is only a complex universal or universal property that might or might not be exemplified by a multiplicity of particulars but cannot itself be a particular, so also a substantive universal or substantive universal property might or might not be exemplified by a multiplicity of particulars but cannot itself be a particular. Thus the substantive universal property of being a human being, although predicable of any human being, is not itself a human being or a particular of any other kind. It, like any other substantive universal or substantive universal property, can be exemplified only by particulars that are not themselves identical with or reducible to such universals or properties. Similarly, the abstract singular terms corresponding to concrete general substantive terms name abstract substantive universals or properties that can be exemplified only by particulars. Neither such universals or properties nor the particulars that exemplify them are reducible to one another. Thus 'humanity', the abstract singular term corresponding to the concrete general term 'human being', names an abstract substantive property exemplified only by human beings. This property is neither identical with nor reducible to any human being, and no human being is either identical with or reducible to it. This property would still be a formal reality if no human beings existed and thus even though it would not then be exemplified.

Similar considerations apply to singular cases of abstract substantive universals or properties. If the theory of singular cases of universals is correct, Socrates and Plato both exemplify the abstract substantive universal named 'humanity' only by virtue of the possession by each of a unique singular case of humanity that can be identified only by identifying the particular that does in fact uniquely possess that singular case. Thus the singular case of humanity possessed by Socrates can be identified only by identifying Socrates, and the singular case possessed by Plato can be identified only by identifying Plato. No particular, however, is identical with or reducible to any singular case of any abstract substantive universal or property it possesses, but instead is that which uniquely possesses such singular cases. Just as Socrates uniquely possesses but is neither identical with nor reducible to the singular case of humanity that is his humanity, so also Plato possesses but is neither identical with nor reducible to the singular case of humanity that is his humanity. Although neither the singular case of humanity possessed by Socrates nor that possessed by Plato could exist if neither Socrates nor Plato existed, and although no particular can exist without possessing a singular case of some abstract substantive property, each particular is nonetheless neither identical with nor reducible to such singular cases but, instead, is that which possesses them and without which such singular cases could not exist.

Just as no particular is identical with or reducible to any or all of the universals or properties it exemplifies or to any or all of the singular cases of these universals or properties it possesses, so also no particular is identical with or reducible to its spatiotemporal location, taken either by itself or in conjunction with the set of nonspatial nontemporal properties the particular possesses. The nonspatial nontemporal properties of a particular are independent of its spatiotemporal location, so that it could still have these properties even if its spatiotemporal location were different from what in fact it is. By contrast, the spatiotemporal properties of a particular are those properties it has simply by virtue of its spatiotemporal location, so that if its spatiotemporal location were different from what in fact it is it would thereby possess different spatiotemporal properties.

Any region of space or any span of time, taken completely in abstraction from what occupies it, is qualitatively identical with any other region of space or span of time. If so, then any region of space can be distinguished from any other only by distinguishing between some particular or some part of some particular that occupies one region but not the other. Similarly, one span of time can be distinguished from any other only by distinguishing between something that exists or occurs in one but not the other. But if spaces and times can be distinguished from one another only by distinguishing between the particulars and events that exist or occur at certain places and times as opposed to others, such particulars and events can be neither identical with nor reducible to the places and times at which they exist or occur. Even though space and time would, or at least might, still be formally real if no particulars at all existed and no events whatever occurred, and even though particulars and events can exist or occur only in space and/or time, neither particulars nor events can be identical with or reducible to the places and times at which they exist or occur.

Moreover, since any region of space and any span of time, taken completely in abstraction from what occupies them, is qualitatively identical with any other region of space or span of time, no particular can possess any of its nonspatial or nontemporal properties simply by virtue of its spatiotemporal location. Thus if processes occurring within material objects slow down as the speed with which such objects move approaches the speed of light, this cannot be due simply to the spatiotemporal location of such objects. Thus if during the amount of time it takes the hour hand of a stationary clock to make one revolution the hour hand of a clock moving at a speed approaching that of the speed of light makes, say, only half a revolution, the difference between the speed of the movement of the two hands cannot be due to a difference in the temporal location of the movement of one hand as distinguished from that of the other, since the two movements occur during precisely the same span of time. Nor can such a difference be due to the distinct spatial locations of the two clocks, since this difference would still obtain regardless of their spatial location. The only properties of particulars that are determined solely by their spatiotemporal location are their spatial and temporal properties. Not even these properties, however, could be possessed by particulars if the latter did not exist and if the places and times at which they would exist if they existed were alone formally real.

In addition to having moments such as some color or some shape, each material particular, whether it be a whole or a piece of a whole, also is made of some material. The concept of matter is analogous to the concepts of color and shape. Each of these concepts is the concept of a genus or determinable that comprehends various species or has various specific determinations. Just as the genus color comprehends the species blue, green, red, etc., and the genus shape comprehends the species circular, triangular, rectangular, etc., so also the genus matter comprehends the species metal, stone, wood, etc. To be colored is to be blue or green or red, etc.; to have a shape is to be circular, triangular, or rectangular, etc.; and to be material is to be made of metal or stone or wood, etc. Various species of color and of shape comprehend various subspecies, and various species of matter also comprehend various subspecies. Thus to be red is to be crimson or scarlet or pink; to be triangular is to be right-angled or isosceles or scalene; and to be wood is to be cherry or oak or pine, etc. Nothing can be colored without being some specific color, nothing can have a shape without having some specific shape, and nothing can be made of matter without being made of some specific form of matter. Conversely, nothing can be crimson without being red and thus without being colored, nothing can be isosceles without being triangular and thus without having a shape, and nothing can be made of cherry without being made of wood and thus without being made of matter.

If the preceding is correct, the concept of matter, like the concepts of color and shape, is the concept of a generic formal reality that comprehends various species or has various specific determinations. So also are the concepts of various species of color, shape, and matter. Such concepts, however, are not concepts of existent entities, since neither color, shape, nor matter, nor any of their species, exist when taken completely in abstraction from the existence of colored, shaped, material particulars or, in the case of matter, in abstraction from the existence of some particular quantity of some specific form of matter. Instead, they exist only in the sense that such particulars exist. Although they would still be formal realities if such particulars never existed, they would not exist in the absence of the existence of such particulars. Since, however, material particulars do exist, so also do their colors and shapes and the material of which they are made.

The preceding concept of matter, taken in abstraction from the concepts of its various specific determinations, has certain affinities with the Aristotelian concept of prime matter. Indeed, not too great an injustice might be done the latter concept if it be construed as the concept of that which has metal, stone, wood, etc., as its specific determinations—as the concept of a genus that has these specific determinations as its species. Such a concept of matter also avoids certain difficulties various philosophers from Locke, Berkeley, and Hume to the present have had with the concepts of matter and material substance. Given such a concept of matter, the expression 'material substance' has two reasonably clear meanings. In one sense of this expression, any species or subspecies of matter—such as metal, stone, or wood; cherry, oak, or pine; chlorine, hydrogen, or oxygen—is a material substance. In another sense, any material particular, such as a chair, a table, or a tree, is a material substance in the sense that it is a particular made of some specific form of matter or of some combination of certain specific forms of matter. In this sense of the expression, to be a material substance is simply to be a material object. Thus in the second sense of 'material substance', a material substance is a particular made of some specific form of material substance in the first sense of this expression. In neither sense of the expression does it refer to some mysterious unknowable substratum of the sort that has mystified Locke, Berkeley, Hume, and various of their successors.

As was indicated in the previous chapter, quidditative and qualitative predications and predications that are both quidditative and qualitative can be made of particulars, of their moments, and of the material of which they are made. Given that "this" refers to a particular, "This is a ball" is a quidditative predication, "This is red" and "This is made of rubber" qualitative predications; "The color of this is red" and "The material of which this is made is rubber" are quidditative predications; and "This is a red rubber ball" is both a quidditative and a qualitative predication. Similarly, given that "this" refers to a color, "This is red" is a quidditative predication, "This is more like purple than green" a qualitative predication. Finally, given that "this" refers to some material, "This is

rubber" is a quidditative predication, "This is softer than wood" a qualitative predication. As was indicated in the previous chapter, such quidditative predications specify the quiddity or essence of the subject of
predication, whereas qualitative predications do not but instead predicate some property of the subject of predication. Predications that are at
once quidditative and qualitative do both.

5. Determinables and Their Determinations

All three forms of predication can be more or less determinate. Thus
to say of something that it is a baseball is to make a more determinate
quidditative predication of it than is made when it is said of it that it is a
ball, and to say of something that it is a ball is to make a more determinate quidditative predication than is made of it when it is said of it that it
is a material object. Similarly, to say of some particular that it is crimson is
to make a more determinate qualitative predication of it than is made
when it is said of it that it is red, and to say of some particular that it is
red is to make a more determinate qualitative predication of it than is
made when it is said of it that it is colored. Quidditative predications,
since they contain no qualitative element, can be more or less determinate only quidditatively; similarly, qualitative predications, since they
contain no quidditative element, can be more or less determinate only
qualitatively. Predications that are both quidditative and qualitative can
be more or less determinate both quidditatively and qualitatively. Moreover, one such predication can be more determinate quidditatively and
less determinate qualitatively than another. Thus "This is a red ball" is
more determinate quidditatively but less determinate qualitatively than
"This is a crimson material object."

Every determinable of any determination predicable of a particular is
also predicable of it. This means that any particular exemplifying a more
determinate or specific property or universal than some more indeterminate or general property or universal, of which the more determinate
or specific property or universal is a determination, also exemplifies
thereby the more indeterminate or general property or universal. Thus
if something possesses the property of being a baseball it also possesses
thereby the property of being a ball and the property of being a material
object, and if something possesses the property of being crimson it also
possesses thereby the property of being red and the property of being
colored. Moreover, any particular that possesses some general or indeterminate property thereby possesses also some more specific or determinate form of that property. Thus nothing can be a material object
without being some specific kind of material object, and nothing can be a
ball without being some specific kind of ball. Similarly, nothing can be

colored without being some specific color such as red, and nothing can be red without being some still more specific color such as crimson.

This last, however, applies only to existent entities. Intentional objects, regardless of whether they are also existent entities, need not be completely determinate as intentional objects. Thus whereas existent human beings have some completely determinate height and weight, one can think of some human being without also knowing what his determinate height and weight are and also without having any belief as to what they are. Indeed, our ideas of or beliefs about existent entities are always more or less indeterminate. Even though all such entities be absolutely determinate, in the sense that if they exemplify some property or universal they thereby exemplify some absolutely determinate form of that property or universal, any such entity of which we can think either possesses some property we neither know nor believe it possesses or else possesses some determinate form of some property we neither know nor believe it possesses even though we know or believe that it possesses the property of which that form is a determinate form. There is always some question that can be raised about any existent entity of which we might think that we cannot answer, and because of this our ideas of any existent entity of which we might think are relatively indeterminate.

Whether, however, each existent entity necessarily is absolutely determinate in every respect is a further question. To be absolutely determinate in every respect, such an entity must possess some absolutely determinate form of any relatively indeterminate property it possesses. A property or universal is relatively indeterminate if and only if there are determinations of it to which it stands in the relation of determinable to determination. On the other hand, a property or universal is absolutely determinate if and only if there are no determinations of it to which it stands in the relation of determinable to determination. An absolutely determinate property or universal is therefore an *infima species*. Although it can be exemplified by a multiplicity of particulars and is therefore universal, there are no universals to which it stands in the relation of determinable to determination. Thus whereas red is a determination of the determinable color and crimson a determination of the determinable red, and whereas the absolutely determinate shades of crimson are determinations of the determinable crimson, such absolutely determinate shades of crimson, by virtue of their being absolutely determinate, are not themselves determinables and therefore have no specific determinations. Each is instead an *infima species*.[6]

Infimae species frequently, perhaps usually, have no names that apply only to them as distinguished from other *infimae species* that are determinations of the same lowest determinable. The expression 'lowest determinable' refers to any determinable that stands in the relation of determinable to determination only to absolute determinations or *infimae species*. Lowest determinables therefore never stand in the relation of determinable to determination to other determinables; instead, their determinations are always absolute determinations. Although any *infima species* is named by the name of any determinable of which it is an absolute determination, various *infimae species* of the lowest determinable of which they are the absolute determinations frequently have no names that apply to them alone as distinguished from other *infimae species* of the same lowest determinable. Thus whereas 'color', 'red', and 'crimson' are names that apply to any *infima species* of the same lowest determinable, crimson, there seem to be no names that apply only to any of the *infimae species* of the lowest determinable, crimson, as distinguished from any of the other *infimae species* of this lowest determinable. From the fact, however, that *infimae species* frequently have no names that apply only to them it does not follow that they cannot be given such names. Just as 'red', 'blue', and 'green' are names of determinations of the determinable color, and just as 'crimson', 'scarlet', and 'pink' are names of determinations of the determinable red, so also names can be given to various of the *infimae species* that are the absolute determinations of the lowest determinable named 'crimson'.

Even if nameless *infimae species* could not be given names, nothing at all would follow so far as the question of whether existent entities necessarily are absolutely determinate in every respect is concerned. This question, again, is that of whether an existent entity can exemplify a determinable universal or property without also exemplifying some absolutely determinate form of that universal or property. This question arises regardless of whether one accepts the identity theory or the theory of singular cases of universals. This is the case because singular cases of universals as well as the universals of which they are singular cases are either determinable or else absolutely determinate.

6. The Determinateness of Particulars

If existent entities are absolutely determinate in the sense in question, then the relative indeterminateness of our knowledge of them is due to some defect in our knowledge rather than to some formal indeterminateness of the entities in question. If, that is, any crimson particular necessarily is some absolutely determinte shade of crimson, then my knowing that it is crimson without also knowing what absolutely determinate shade of crimson it is is due to some defect in my knowledge rather than to some formal indeterminateness of the particular in question. If, however, existent entities are not necessarily absolutely determinate in the sense in question, then the indeterminateness of our knowledge of

them can be due to some formal indeterminateness of the entities themselves rather than to some defect in our knowledge of them. Thus
suppose that some crimson particular is crimson without being some
absolutely determinate shade of crimson. Suppose also that I know that it
is colored without also knowing that it is red or that I know that it is red
without also knowing that it is crimson. If so, then the indeterminateness
of my knowledge is due to some defect in the latter rather than to some
formal indeterminateness of the particular, since I know only that it has
the determinable property of being colored or being red without also
knowing that it also has the more determinate property of being crimson. My knowledge of its color is more indeterminate than its color is
and is therefore relatively inadequate or incomplete. But if the particular in question is, as supposed, crimson without being some absolutely determinate shade of crimson, and if I know that it is crimson,
then the indeterminateness of my knowledge of its color, rather than
being due to some defect in my knowledge, is instead due to a formal
indeterminateness of the particular itself. Since the latter is crimson
without being some absolutely determinate shade of crimson, my knowledge of its color, though indeterminate, is not inadequate or incomplete
but rather is as determinate as is the color of the particular. If one's
knowledge of some property of an entity is as objectively determinate as
the property is formally determinate, one's knowledge of that property
of the entity in question is as complete and as adequate to the latter as it
can be. If the property is itself formally indeterminate, one's knowledge
of it is as complete and as adequate to the latter as it can be, provided that
the degree of its objective determinateness is not less than that of the
formal determinateness of the property itself. If one believed that the
color of the entity is some absolutely determinate shade of crimson when
in fact it is not, one's belief, though possessing a greater degree of
objective determinateness than the degree of formal determinateness
possessed by the color itself, would be false and therefore would not
constitute knowledge.

From the fact, then, that I believe that some existent entity possesses
some relatively indeterminate property without also believing that it
possesses some absolutely determinate form of that property, it does not
follow immediately, without further argument, that my belief about that
entity is in that respect incomplete or inadequate. Moreover, from the
fact that no one can determine whether existent entities of a certain sort
have absolutely determinate forms of some relatively indeterminate
property that entities of that type are known to possess, nothing at all
follows as to whether entities of that kind do in fact possess absolutely
determinate forms of the property in question. This is the case because
our inability to determine whether they do in fact possess such absolutely

determinate forms of the property in question might be due entirely to some irremediable impediment to our acquisitions of such knowledge, and from the existence of such an impediment nothing at all follows as to whether entities of that sort are formally indeterminate in the respect in question. From the fact, that is, that such an impediment exists it follows neither (1) that entities of that type are in fact formally indeterminate in that respect nor (2) that they are formally determinate in that and in every other respect despite the fact that we cannot discover certain of the absolutely determinate forms of certain of the relatively indeterminate properties they possess.

The belief that existent entities are formally indeterminate in those respects in which some irremediable impediment to knowledge prevents us from ever discovering whether in fact they are formally indeterminate might, but need not, be due to the acceptance of some form of verificationism according to which every meaningful question can in principle be answered. The acceptance of such a form of verificationism, however, rather than leading to an acceptance of the belief in question, ought instead to lead to its rejection. This is the case for two reasons. One is that if such a form of verificationism were correct, then the question of whether entities of certain types are in fact in certain respects formally indeterminate would be meaningless, since in principle it would be unanswerable if the impediment to our discovering the answer to it is in fact irremediable. The second reason is that if this question is in fact meaningless, then it cannot be the case that existent entities of the kind in question are in fact formally indeterminate in the respects in question. For the statement that such entities are in fact formally indeterminate in the respects in question would then in fact be the answer to the question of whether they are formally indeterminate in these respects. Such a statement would then be the answer to this question even if we could never know that it is, and to a meaningless question there can be no answer. Thus an acceptance of the form of verificationism in question, rather than requiring that one conclude that entities of certain sorts are in fact formally indeterminate in certain respects if certain irremediable impediments to knowledge prevent us from determining whether they are in fact indeterminate in these respects, requires us instead to conclude that the question of whether they are indeterminate in these respects is a meaningless question. This is the case even though the fact that this question is not meaningless means that such a form of verificationism is itself unacceptable.

On the other hand, the belief that existent entities possess no indeterminate properties without also possessing absolutely determinate forms of such properties, even though certain irremediable impediments to knowledge prevent us from ever discovering which absolutely determinate forms of certain indeterminate properties entities of certain sorts possess, might, but need not, be the result of an extrapolation from the fact that frequently we do succeed in discovering certain absolutely determinate forms of certain properties of certain entities. Since, it might be argued, we do frequently succeed in discovering certain absolutely determinate forms of certain properties of certain entities even though initially we have knowledge only of indeterminate forms of these properties, we are justified in believing that every existent entity that possesses any property possesses thereby an absolutely determinate form of that property even though certain irremediable impediments to knowledge prevent us from ever discovering certain of these absolutely determinate properties. The reply to this argument seems simply to be that from the fact that we do frequently discover absolutely determinate forms of properties possessed by existent entities it does not follow that any entity that possesses any property thereby possesses an absolutely determinate form of that property even though we can never discover precisely what certain of these absolutely determinate forms are.

Neither of the arguments we have just examined establishes either (1) that existent entities can possess properties without possessing absolutely determinate forms of these properties or (2) that any existent entity that possesses any given property thereby necessarily possesses an absolutely determinate form of that property. If, however, sensible appearances of existent entities are properties of such entities, then some such entities do possess certain indeterminate properties without possessing absolutely determinate forms of such properties. This is the case because some sensible appearances of existent entities are themselves indeterminate, as can be seen by considering the following example. Suppose that I see something in the distance but cannot determine whether it is a cat or a dog. The reason I cannot do so is that the sensible appearance of the entity I see is itself too indeterminate to enable me to make such a determination. As I approach the entity I see, however, something happens that can be described in either of two ways. One is that as I approach it the sensible appearance of it becomes sufficiently determinate to enable me to take it not merely as an animal but also as a dog. On this description, what happens is that the same sensible appearance becomes more determinate than it was at first. Whereas at first it was only an animal-like appearance, it becomes increasingly determinate until it is transformed into a doglike appearance. The second description of what happens is that as I approach the thing I see the initial sensible appearance of it is replaced by a series of increasingly determinate appearances until I am able to take what I see not merely as an animal but also as a dog. Whereas the initial sensible appearance was an animal-like appearance, the one that enables me to take what I see as a dog is a more determinate doglike appearance.

Regardless, however, of which of these two descriptions is accepted, certain sensible appearances are indeterminate. Regardless, that is, of whether the doglike appearance is (1) a more determinate form of the animal-like appearance or (2) a numerically distinct but more determinate appearance than the animal-like appearance, the latter appearance is indeterminate. So also is the doglike appearance, since it might be too indeterminate to enable me to determine the species, sex, size, color, age, and so forth, of the dog I see. Whereas it is sufficiently determinate to enable me to take what I see as a dog, and although I believe the dog I see possesses absolutely determinate forms of the properties just indicated, it is too indeterminate to enable me to determine precisely which absolutely determinate forms of these properties it does in fact possess. Since sensible appearances are frequently indeterminate, and since such indeterminate appearances are sometimes properties of existent entities, we must conclude that such entities can possess indeterminate properties without possessing absolutely determinate forms of these properties.

To this argument we may reply as follows. We can agree that sensible appearances of existent entities are frequently, perhaps usually or even almost always, indeterminate in the sense in question. From this, however, it does not follow that the existent entities of which they are appearances are also indeterminate in the sense in question. To be indeterminate in the sense in question they must possess some indeterminate formally real property without also possessing any absolutely determinate form of that property. The argument in question, however, has not established either (1) that sensible appearances of existent entities are properties of such entities or (2) that they are formally real properties of such entities. Yet it can succeed in showing that existent entities are formally indeterminate only if it can establish not only (1) but also (2). It must establish (1) because from the fact that sensible appearances of existent entities are sometimes indeterminate it does not follow that the entities of which they are appearances are also indeterminate unless such appearances are properties of such entities. If such appearances are themselves particulars rather than properties of existent entities, it is the appearances rather than the entities of which they are appearances that are indeterminate, and the entities as contrasted with their appearances might be absolutely determinate. And the argument in question must establish (2) as well as (1) because existent entities are formally indeterminate only if they possess some indeterminate formally real property without also possessing some absolutely determinate form of that property. Thus from the fact that sensible appearances are sometimes indeterminate it follows that the existent entities of which they are appearances are formally indeterminate only if such appearances are formally real properties of such entities.

One argument in support of the position that sensible appearances are themselves particulars rather than properties of existent entities is that such appearances can exist or occur even though the entities of which they are taken to be appearances do not in fact exist. If such entities do not in fact exist, then the appearances taken to be appearances of them cannot be formally real properties of them. Thus if on the basis of my visual sensing of a doglike appearance I believe that I see a dog in the distance when in fact there is no existent entity there, the sensible appearance in question cannot be a property of an existent entity. At least it cannot be a property of the dog I think I see, since that intended object does not in fact exist. Since such appearances are not properties of such nonexistent intended objects, and since there is no intrinsic difference between such appearances and those appearances sensed when one does in fact perceive an existent entity, appearances of the second sort must also be particulars if those of the first type are.

From the fact, however, if indeed it be a fact, that sensible appearances are themselves particulars rather than properties of existent entities, it does not follow that any existent entities are formally indeterminate. This is the case because sensible appearances, even if they are particulars, are not, or at least might not be, existent entities. Instead, they seem to have an intermediate ontological status that is neither that of an existent entity nor that of an intentional object. Like existent entities, they can become intentional objects, as sometimes happens in philosophical discussions of perception and when one assumes what is sometimes referred to as a 'phenomenological' as opposed to a 'natural' perceptual attitude or stance. But they can also exist or occur without becoming intentional objects for anyone. This happens when in natural or normal perceptual situations a percipient perceives an existent entity such as a material object of some sort by means of sensing various sensible appearances of it without attending to, perceiving, or intending such appearances. At the same time, however, such appearances are not existent entities, at least not in the full sense in which material objects are. For material objects exist regardless of whether they are ever perceived by or become intentional objects for anyone, whereas sensible appearances have being only as *sensibilia* sensed by sensitive subjects. Although such sensitive subjects need not attend to, perceive, or intend such appearances, and indeed might even in some cases be incapable of doing so, such appearances must nonetheless be sensed by sensitive subjects if they are to have any being at all. It is because their being as *sensibilia* does not depend upon their being intentional objects for anyone that sensible appearances can have being without being intentional objects. And it is because their being as *sensibilia* does depend upon their being sensed by some sensitive subject that sensible appearances are not full-fledged existent entities, since such entities are formal realities regardless of whether they are ever by any subject sensed or intended. For these reasons sensible appearances, if they are particulars, have an ontological status intermediate between that of mere intentional objects and that of existent entities.

But even if sensible appearances are not themselves particulars numerically distinct from the existent entities of which they are appearances, the fact that they are frequently indeterminate to some degree does not mean that the entities of which they are appearances are also indeterminate. This is the case for the following reasons. The most plausible alternative to regarding sensible appearances of existent entities as particulars numerically distinct from the entities of which they are appearances seems to be to regard them as appearings of such entities. On this alternative, the doglike appearance I sense when I see or think I see a dog in the distance, rather than being a particular numerically distinct from the existent entity I see or think I see, is instead an appearing of that entity. There are familiar problems confronting this alternative, occasioned by the fact that the entity I think I see might not in fact exist, since if it does not in fact exist it is hard, to say the least, to see how the sensible appearance I sense can be an appearing of it. This problem, however, regardless of whether ultimately it can be solved satisfactorily by the advocate of the alternative that treats sensible appearances as appearings of existent entities, is irrelevant so far as our present question is concerned. For this question is that of whether existent entities must themselves be indeterminate if indeterminate sensible appearances of such entities are appearings of them, and if certain sensible appearances are not appearings of existent entities the question indicated does not arise in connection with such appearances. Instead, it arises only in connection with those appearances that are appearings of existent entities.

The answer to this question seems to be essentially the same as the answer to the question of whether the fact that sensible appearances, regarded as particulars, are sometimes indeterminate means that the existent entities of which they are appearances are also indeterminate. For sensible appearances, regardless of whether they are regarded (1) as particulars numerically distinct from the existent entities of which they are appearances or (2) as appearings of such entities, have an ontological status intermediate between that of existent entities and that of mere intentional objects. This seems, if anything, to be even more clearly the case when they are regarded as appearings than when they are regarded as particulars. For if they are appearings they must be appearings to some sensitive subject regardless of whether they are also intentional objects for such subjects. They can be appearings only if they appear, and they can appear only if they appear to some sensitive subject. If so, then, unlike the existent entities of which they are appearings, they are not full-fledged formal realities. But if they are not themselves such realities, the fact that they are sometimes indeterminate does not mean that the existent entities of which they are appearings are formally indeterminate. This follows from the fact that an existent entity is inde-terminate in some respect if and only if it possesses some indeterminate formally real property without possessing an absolutely determinate form of that property.

The preceding can also be put in the following way. If appearings are properties of existent entities, they can be only relative as opposed to absolute properties of such entities. They can be, that is, only appearings of such entities to sensitive subjects. They therefore require for their being not only the formal reality of the existent entities of which they are appearings but also the formal reality of the sensitive subjects to whom they appear. This means that they would have no being at all if either the existent entities of which they are appearings or the sensitive subjects to whom they appear were not formal realities. Since they have being only if they appear to sensitive subjects, they are not themselves formal realities. In the absence of their appearing to sensitive subjects, the existent entities, of which they would be appearings to such subjects, still exist and possess whatever formally real properties they happen to possess. But since they would not then appear to sensitive subjects, the formally real properties they possess would not include such appearings. Thus the fact that such appearings are sometimes indeterminate does not mean that so also are existent entities. Since, that is, such appearings are not themselves formally real properties of existent entities, the fact that they are sometimes indeterminate does not mean that existent en-tities can possess indeterminate properties without also possessing abso-lutely determinate forms of these properties.

We have considered various arguments designed to show that existent entities are formally indeterminate in certain respects and have found them all wanting. The fact, however, that these arguments do not suc-ceed means neither that such entities always are in fact absolutely deter-minate in every respect nor that they must be. Nor does their absolute determinateness in every respect follow from the failure of any other argument designed to establish their formal indeterminateness in cer-tain respects. On the other hand, there does not seem to be any positive argument that can be used to establish that they always in fact are or must be absolutely determinate in every respect that would contain premises that seem more evident than the conclusion such arguments would be designed to establish. This is to say that the proposition that no existent entity can possess an indeterminate formally real property without also possessing some absolutely determinate form of that property seems as evident as any proposition that could be used as a premise in an argument designed to establish it as a conclusion. If in fact there is no proposition that seems more evident than the proposition in question that could be used in an argument designed to establish it as a conclusion, and if it is in fact evident, then there seems to be no point to attempting to establish its truth by appealing to still other propositions. And since it does in fact seem evident, there seems to be no point to attempting to establish it by means of argument.

Notes

1. Edmund Husserl, *Logical Investigations*, trans. J. N. Findlay (London: Routledge & Kegan Paul, 1970), Investigation III, vol. 2, pp. 435–89.

2. Chap. 3, sec. 3.

3. Chap. 8, secs. 1 and 3.

4. Those who take the second position would thereby be adopting a position somewhat similar to that taken by Professor Butchvarov in his distinction between quality-entities and quality-objects. Butchvarov's quality-entities are universals, his quality-objects at least roughly analogous to singular cases of universals as these would be conceived by those who take the second position. See Panayot Butchvarov, *Being Qua Being: A Theory of Identity, Existence, and Predication* (Bloomington and London: Indiana University Press, 1979), pp. 218–22.

5. Chap. 9, sec. 2.

6. For the classic treatment of determinables and their determinations, see W. E. Johnson, *Logic* (Cambridge: Cambridge University Press, 1921), part I, chap. 11.

Works Cited

Augustine, Saint. *On Free Choice of the Will.* Translated by Anna S. Benjamin and L. H. Hackstaff. Indianapolis: Library of Liberal Arts, 1964.

Butchvarov, Panayot. *Being Qua Being: A Theory of Identity, Existence, and Predication.* Bloomington and London: Indiana University Press, 1979.

———. *Resemblance and Identity: An Examination of the Problem of Universals.* Bloomington and London: Indiana University Press, 1966.

———. "Adverbial Theories of Consciousness." *Midwest Studies in Philosophy* 5 (1980): 261–80.

Chisholm, Roderick M. *Perceiving: A Philosophical Study.* Ithaca: Cornell University Press, 1957.

Descartes, René. *Discourse on Method* and *Meditations.* Translated, with an introduction, by Laurence J. Lafleur. Indianapolis: Library of Liberal Arts, 1960.

Green, Thomas Hill. *Prolegomena to Ethics.* Edited by A. C. Bradley. With an introduction by Ramon M. Lemos. New York: Thomas Y. Crowell, 1969.

Hampshire, Stuart. *The Age of Reason: The Seventeenth Century Philosophers.* New York: George Braziller, 1957.

Hegel, G. W. F. *Hegel's Philosophy of Right.* Translated with notes by T. M. Knox. Oxford: The Clarendon Press, 1952.

———. *Hegel's Science of Logic.* Translated by A. V. Miller. Foreword by J. N. Findlay. London: George Allen & Unwin, 1969.

———. *The Logic of Hegel.* Translated from *The Encyclopedia of the Philosophical Sciences* by William Wallace. Oxford: Oxford University Press, 1892.

———. *Phenomenology of Spirit.* Translated by A. V. Miller with Analysis of the Text and Foreword by J. N. Findlay. Oxford: Clarendon Press, 1977.

Husserl, Edmund. *Logical Investigations.* 2 vols. Translated by J. N. Findlay. London: Routledge & Kegan Paul, 1970.

Johnson, W. E. *Logic.* Part I. Cambridge: Cambridge University Press, 1921.

Kant, Immanuel. *Critique of Pure Reason.* Translated by Norman Kemp Smith. London: Macmillan, 1953.

————. *Prolegomena to Any Future Metaphysics.* Translated, with an introduction, by Lewis White Beck. Indianapolis: Library of Liberal Arts, 1950.

Körner, Stephan. *Conceptual Thinking: A Logical Inquiry.* New York: Dover Publications, 1959.

Lemos, Ramon M. *Experience, Mind, and Value: Philosophical Essays.* Leiden: E. J. Brill, 1969.

Lewis, Clarence Irving. *An Analysis of Knowledge and Valuation.* La Salle, Ill.: Open Court Publishing Co., 1946.

————. *Mind and the World-order.* New York: Dover Publications, 1956.

Moore, George Edward. *Philosophical Papers.* London: George Allen & Unwin, 1959.

Peirce, Charles Sanders. *The Philosophy of Peirce: Selected Writings.* Edited by Justus Buchler. London: Routledge & Kegan Paul, 1940.

Popper, Karl R. *The Poverty of Historicism.* London: Routledge & Kegan Paul, 1957.

Strawson, P. F. *Individuals: An Essay in Descriptive Metaphysics.* London: Methuen, 1959.

Waismann, F. *The Principles of Linguistic Philosophy.* Edited by R. Harré. New York: St. Martin's Press, 1965.

William of Ockham. *Philosophical Writings: A Selection.* Translated, with an introduction, by Philotheus Boehner, O.F.M. Indianapolis: Library of Liberals Arts, 1964.

Wolterstorff, Nicholas. *On Universals: An Essay in Ontology.* Chicago and London: University of Chicago Press, 1970.

Index

62, 168–84, 199–222, 225–40, 247–76; absolute determinateness of, 268–76; basic, 36; and combinations of universals, 261–62; and concrete general property terms, 226–27; and concrete general substantive terms, 226–28; criteria for the continued existence of, 257; description of, 202–3; divisibility of, 251–54; duration of, 249–50; and exemplified universals, 168–71, 206–12, 216–21, 247–76; as exemplifying qualitative universals, 260–62; as exemplifying substantive universals, 260–63; existence of, 202–3; existent, 181–84; formal indeterminateness of, 269–76; impossible, 177–78; individuality of, 200–204; and intentional objects, 158–61; intentional objects and nonexistent, 169, 172–80; intermittent existence of, 257–59; as involved in states of affairs, 175–84; and kinds, 159–60, 172–73; mental and extramental, 74, 80–81; and moments, 248–50, 255–56, 260–61, 264; and necessary truth, 213; nonexistent, 169–81, 184–85, 240; as not possessing universals, 217–21; numerical distinctness of, 200–204; particularity of, 200–204; parts of, 247–56; and pieces, 252–54, 261; pieces of, 248–56; as possessing properties, 217–21; as possessing singular cases of universals, 217–21, 251–59; possible, 177–78; and predication, 225–31; principle of individuation of, 200–204; and their properties, 199–204, 216–21, 225–27, 237, 260–76; propositions about, 181–84; qualitative identity of, 200–204; qualitative predication of, 225–31; and qualitative properties, 260–62; qualities of, 200–204; quidditative predication of, 225–31; and regions of space, 263; and self-identity, 233–36; and self-predicable properties, 237; and sensible appearances, 271–75; and singular cases of universals, 216–21, 229–32, 235, 238–40, 247–63; sin-

gular cases of universals and parts of, 248–57; and spatiotemporal location, 102; and their spatiotemporal location, 200–204, 263–64; and states of affairs, 168–80; states of affairs and existent, 170–72, 181–83; states of affairs and nonexistent, 170–72, 175–80; as subjects of predication, 225–32; and substantive properties, 260–63; uniqueness of, 200–204; and universals, 73–74, 79, 216–21, 229–32, 235, 238–40, 250–76; and wholes, 250–57, 261

Parts: independent and nonindependent, 248–50, 261; and wholes, 247–56

Peirce, C. S., 31, 34, 53, 55

Perception, 271–75

Phenomena, mental, 79

Philosophy: ancient Greek, 17–19; and common human experience and belief, 23–24, 26; and critical reflection, 23; and cultural and historical experience, 23–26; as existential or factual, 27; and factual knowledge, 27; historical definitions of, 15–16; late medieval scholastic, 18; linguistic, 16, 19–20; modern, 32–35; persuasive definitions of, 16; and phenomenology, 29; and science, 15–20, 23–24, 26–28; and special experience and knowledge, 23, 25–26

Phrases, nonsentential, 118–19

Pieces: actual, 252–55; conjunction of, 252–56; divisibility of, 249–54; and moments, 248–50, 255–56, 261; and particulars, 248–56; of pieces, 249–54; possible, 252–54; separated, 253–57; separate existence of, 248–49, 253–56; and singular cases of universals, 248–56; and universals, 250–56; and wholes, 248–57, 261; of wholes, 248–50

Plato, 18

Platonism, 50

Points of view, 69–71

Popper, Karl R., 25

Possession: and essences, 199; and particulars, 199–204; and proper-

DATE DUE